Ask
Graham

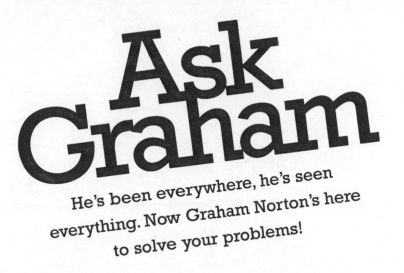

Ask Graham

He's been everywhere, he's seen everything. Now Graham Norton's here to solve your problems!

JOHN BLAKE

Published by John Blake Publishing Ltd,
3 Bramber Court, 2 Bramber Road,
London W14 9PB, England

www.johnblakepublishing.co.uk

First published in hardback in 2010

ISBN: 978 1 84358 297 7

British Library Cataloguing-in-Publication Data:

A catalogue record for this book is available from the British Library.

Design by www.envydesign.co.uk

Printed in the UK by CPI Mackays, Chatham, ME5 8TD

1 3 5 7 9 10 8 6 4 2

The Daily Telegraph

From a column in the *Weekend* section of The Saturday *Daily Telegraph*
devised and developed by Casilda Grigg.

Illustrations by Ned Joliffe

Papers used by John Blake Publishing are natural, recyclable products made from
wood grown in sustainable forests. The manufacturing processes conform to the
environmental regulations of the country of origin.

Introduction

If you are standing up while reading this, you might want to take a
seat because I have some rather shocking news: this book is not
about me! The stars of this handsome volume are the people who have
written to me asking for advice over the last four years. If you're not a
reader of the *Daily Telegraph* on a Saturday then perhaps I should
explain that the problems revealed here are universal: they involve
love, betrayal and social embarrassment. They do, however, feature
some words and phrases rather more than one might expect. Only a
posh estate agent has seen the words 'Aga', 'Cotswolds' and 'Waitrose'
as often as I have while I've been reading these cries for help. Don't be
fooled, though. Just because you'll find no mention of ASBOs, Lidl or
the etiquette of prison visits, it doesn't mean these people feel no pain.
These are genuine dilemmas written from the heart – with only the
occasional correspondent who just needs reminding of what a very
charmed life they lead.

Now on to the part that does concern me – the replies. When I went
back over the columns, I was shocked to find how very certain I seem.
I can assure you, this certainty is something I only manage to drum up
once every two weeks for a couple of hours as I tackle readers'
problems. In my own life, I am as paralysed by doubt and insecurities
as everyone else is.

The other thing that struck me was that, while I can dish it out, I don't appear to be able to take it. It seems that there is no reader's problem I can't solve – yet it's not a reader who isn't coping so well with being nearly 50, living alone, who has an unhealthy obsession with his two very badly behaved dogs and who consumes a vast amount of white wine. That would be me. If that's your problem, then don't ask Graham!

So what is this book for? Well, I hope it might make you smile a little, perhaps shed a tiny light on whatever issues you might have and, if nothing else, make you feel better about your own life. Remember the old adage – a problem shared is gossip!

Graham Norton

Dear Graham,
I am worried that I am falling for my secretary. We work for a large law firm and often have to stay late. There has always been an undeniable chemistry between us. Last night, we got carried away and kissed, and it was as sensational as I had imagined.
None of this would be a problem if I wasn't married. My colleagues would be suspicious if I sacked my secretary, as she is a brilliant worker. And there is no way I am going to leave my job because I have a promising future with the firm.
So how do we co-exist in such close proximity, knowing how we feel for each other? And what do I do about my marriage?
Henry W, Battersea

Dear Henry,
At first I felt very sorry for you. The situation you find yourself in isn't entirely your fault and it's very hard to know how to resolve it. However, when I re-read your letter, it struck me that all your concerns seem to relate to your job. It is only as you are signing off that you give your marriage a thought.

You are so focused on your career, I'm amazed that any awkward emotions managed to fight their way to the surface. In your strange corporate world, a passionate embrace becomes a misdemeanour. It seems you would have no problem with sacking this woman – it's only the worry about what others might think that prevents you. Are you guilty, confused, excited or merely inconvenienced?

Your one saving grace is that you aren't launching into an affair. This hints at some sort of decent human being.

Find out how your secretary is feeling. Explain that you want to protect your marriage. Perhaps you could help her find a new job? Colleagues will be less suspicious if she leaves of her own accord. If she is insistent she stays, or it becomes clear that her feelings are very strong, then you may have to confide in someone more senior at the firm and perhaps she could be moved.

Yes, people will talk, but better that they do it about something that didn't happen than wait until things go further. As for your marriage, maybe your new secretary could carve some time out of your diary for you to spend with your wife. All work and no play makes Henry a cheating bastard.

Ask Graham

Dear Graham,

I have a wonderful boyfriend I love very much, but he suffers from being too nice. A divorced colleague at his new job (she's 40, he's 26) recently asked him if he would like to accompany her and her 12-year-old son to a golfing range. Being the nice guy he is, he said yes.

He tells me he has no intention of going and felt that he couldn't say no, but I am furious that (a) he doesn't realise she probably sees this as a date and (b) he would rather hurt my feelings than those of a relative stranger.

Am I overreacting?

Abby L, Lincolnshire

Your boyfriend is weak and you shouldn't dress it up because you love him.

Ask Graham

Dear Abby,

It isn't so much that you are overreacting, it's more a case of having the wrong reaction. How has your boyfriend hurt your feelings? Was this the dream date you've always wanted to go on? Are you jealous that the 40-year-old divorcée didn't ask you out?

Whatever the colleague thinks, this is clearly not a date, so what on earth has it got to do with you? Consider for a moment that your boyfriend mentioned in the office that he liked golf. This woman thought how nice it would be for her son to have a game with a man because he doesn't get to see his dad so much any more. Now who's the monstrous cow?

What you should be upset about is that your boyfriend, whom you describe as 'too nice', is now saying he has no intention of going. Define 'too' nice. Backing out of plans with a friend is one thing, but when those plans involve a child I don't think the word 'nice' needs to be bandied about too much. Your boyfriend is weak and you shouldn't dress it up because you love him.

Force him to go on this non-date. A day involving a recently divorced woman, a child and golf must come pretty close to a working definition of hell. Maybe next time he'll grow a backbone, say no to unwelcome invitations and tell whining girlfriends who think the world revolves around them to shut up.

Dear Graham,

Can you give me some tips on flirting? I have recently become attracted to a man at work and would like to make him aware of the fact, but in a subtle way. I have never had a boyfriend (I am 26), but now I've met this lovely man I want to wow him with my latent animal magnetism. I tried flicking my hair once, but it got caught on his suit button and we became a bit tangled - leaving me beetroot-faced and him a little scared. Is there any advice you can give me?

Penny L, London

Dear Penny,

You are attempting to flirt with a man, so subtlety is not a quality you need. Wear lower tops and laugh at his jokes. My work here is done.

3

Ask Graham

Dear Graham,

I have a wonderful, clever, handsome husband who is also kind, affectionate and supportive. The only problem is that he has very little interest in sex. It is always me who instigates things, and most of the time he makes excuses. I have tried all the usual tricks - plunging necklines, high heels, expensive lingerie - to no avail. Despite the fact that we are both fit, healthy and in our early thirties, we have sex only about once a month (if I'm lucky).

My friends assure me that I'm attractive, but I struggle daily with my rising feelings of panic, misery and self-doubt. I've tried talking to him about the problem, but he gets cross and tells me I'm inventing difficulties that aren't there. He is so persuasive that sometimes I almost think that the problem is not his lack of ardour, but my high expectations.

Should I resign myself to sexual frustration, but feel thankful for all the other lovely things he brings? Or am I on a rollercoaster to self-delusion and heartbreak?

Minna R, London

Dear Minna,

Aren't relationships rubbish? They are never exactly the way we want them to be, and there must be many people reading your 'problem' who are dreaming of the day they can go to bed without the dread of grubby paws inching across a well-washed duvet.

Your description of your husband is so gushing and uncritical that it sounds to me as if you have been trying for some time to convince yourself that the situation isn't as dire as it actually is. He's a man in his thirties – something must be wrong. I wonder: was the sex ever that good? If it was, maybe you could try talking about specific times and attempt to remember how you were both feeling at that time.

At the risk of sounding like the scatological professor on *You Are What You Eat*, there could be clues in his diet. Is he eating lots of heavy red meat and drinking quite a bit? I've noticed that when I'm hungry, I'm really hungry, if you get my drift. My friend Stephan swears by raw ginger.

The trouble with working on your sexual relations is that it sounds as if it will only make matters worse for your husband. Maybe you should wait until you are on holiday, without your normal day-to-day stresses and see where an application of sun-tan oil might lead.

I have to admit, though, that at the end of the day a rather large, lazy part of me wants to suggest that you simply focus on what is working in the relationship and invest in battery-powered bliss. But be strong – we mustn't give in too easily.

Dear Graham,
A friend has recently snaffled an eligible young man. While I am happy for her, I am curious as to how the relationship is developing. When it comes to talking about men, however, she is a closed book, and will only reveal information under pain of death or buckets of wine. I feel it is my right to know the gory details as I introduced them. But short of giving her liver failure, I don't know how to go about it.
Should I employ a private detective, or stalk them myself? I can't understand her reticence. I happily divulge everything to my friends.

Jemima V, Primrose Hill

❝I would suggest that you are nuts. A loon. A *Sense and Sensibility* short of a complete set of Jane Austen novels.❞

Dear Jemima,
I'm not a trained counsellor – so I'm not sure if I'm using the correct vocabulary – but, as an interested amateur, I would suggest that you are nuts. A loon. A *Sense and Sensibility* short of a complete set of Jane Austen novels. Please re-read your letter. Do you understand how creepy it sounds? Why do your friends owe you graphic descriptions of their love lives just because you don't have one? The shock is that your friends are still speaking to you at all. Jemima, get a life! Your own!

Dear Graham,
A few months ago I met an amazing Californian at a dinner party. Things took off quickly and he now wants me to move to San Francisco. But the thought of giving up my job and being so far away from my family and friends is awful. San Fran isn't New York - it's much further away - and I'm scared I'll be lonely there.

My boyfriend doesn't want to live in England and is tied to San Francisco, where he works as an attorney. He's a typical bloke: work-oriented, independent and lazy about keeping up with friends. His parents live in Florida and he doesn't get on with his sisters, so I know I won't have much of a support network.

I am 35 and was single for years before I met him. I don't want to lose him, but the thought of moving lock, stock and barrel to the US terrifies me.

What should I do?

Nadine T, London
PS My mother, by the way, thinks he should ask me to marry him first.

❝ Transatlantic relationships always seem to end when the Atlantic is removed. ❞

Dear Nadine,
Being single for years does something to the mind and heart. I imagine that any man showing you, at 35, the least bit of affection would provoke a feeling not dissimilar to what the passengers on the *Titanic* felt as they rushed for the last lifeboat.

You need to calm down and ignore the huge looming iceberg of singledom. The issue of San Francisco being further away than New York shouldn't really be what you are focusing on. He doesn't get on with his family? So what? You only met this man a few months ago. If he lived on the other side of London, would you be moving in with him?

If you can truthfully answer 'yes' to that question, then I would encourage you to follow your heart and buy into a new life – now with added adventure! If you have any doubts, even the smallest degree of unease – and I'm sensing you do – then you must wait and see what happens to your long-distance love affair.

I've had transatlantic relationships and they always seem to end when the Atlantic is removed. There was an article in *Cosmopolitan* once called something like 'Living apart to stay together – how distance can bring you closer.'

Enjoy what you have and ignore your mother. Doesn't she know that you should never marry an attorney?

Dear Graham,

I am a 35-year-old single man, born and brought up in Birmingham. Both my parents emigrated from Goa in the 1960s, and ours is a very close and loving family. My three sisters are happily married to British Indians, whom they met through the wider Indian community here (their marriages were not, strictly speaking, 'arranged'). My parents, who are Catholic, are desperate for me to get married, and my mother is furious at my repeated refusals to follow up on all the lovely girls she regularly introduces me to. My unenthusiastic response to her latest candidate, a pretty and charming eye doctor, has particularly incensed her as she has glaucoma. The problem is: I am gay.

Rajiv, Birmingham

Dear Rajiv,

What a long and detailed letter for a dilemma that is very simple indeed. You claim that the problem is that you are gay. No it isn't. The problem is that your parents don't know that you're gay. Your choices are very clear. If you want the nagging to stop, you have to tell your mother that no woman will ever be good enough, or face the prospect of walking down the aisle with one of them. Coming out is never easy, no matter what culture you have grown up in, but you are 35 years old and live in an urban area. Everyone deserves to live with the truth: your parents, the poor women being paraded in front of you and, most of all, yourself. Good luck.

Dear Graham,
My girlfriend is about to move in with me and, although I love
her, the prospect fills me with dread. Living alone in my
bachelor pad (plasma TV, huge squashy sofas, state-of-the-art CD
player), I have become quite stuck in my ways. I know how hard
it is going to be for me to adjust to having a woman around.
    I am very particular about mess, and she has already
started leaving her clothes everywhere - not to mention leaving
the top off the toothpaste - when she stays over. To cap it all, she
now calls me 'darling' in front of my friends. How do I go
about mentally adjusting myself to this next big step?
                                    Mark P, Bath

> **Be a man, Mark. We all like to have things our own way, but videos in alphabetical order won't kiss you goodnight and make a pot of fresh coffee on a Sunday morning.**

Dear Mark,

Please read your letter again. Could you sound any more gay? A woman you claim to love is going to be snuggling up with you on your huge squashy sofa watching your plasma TV and looking into your eyes as Coldplay dribbles out of your CD player – that should be a good thing.

What isn't good is that you are taking this step with someone that you can't even discuss your toothpaste etiquette with.

Don't seethe in silence. No relationship will ever be exactly the way you want it, so the best way forward is to broker a deal. She will put the top back on the toothpaste, but you'll let her dump her clothes on the floor as long as she clears them up before she goes to work.

Tell her about your aversion to the word 'darling', and maybe, while you are at it, tell her you have started to use the word 'dread'. You owe it to your girlfriend, and your relationship, to let her know all your reservations before you make this big step.

On the plus side, presumably you will both be better off, so why not keep a track of those savings and use them for fun things you can do together outside the house – nice dinners, or even weekend breaks or holidays?

Be a man, Mark. We all like to have things our own way, but videos in alphabetical order won't kiss you goodnight and make a pot of fresh coffee on a Sunday morning.

Dear Graham,
Despite being happily married with two small children and living in the countryside, I have an insatiable urge to maintain the party lifestyle I led in my London days. My husband's urge, on the other hand, is to stay at home and watch Newsnight with a cup of cocoa. This leads to me hotfooting it on the train to Paddington - large G and T in hand - sans cocoa-lover, to paint the town red. While I have a fantastic time, I would, of course, prefer him to come with me. How do I resolve the situation?
Louisa T, Wiltshire

Dear Louisa,
Life, it seems to me, is about choices. You chose to get married, move to the country and have two children. While this doesn't necessarily preclude the odd trip up to the Big Smoke, it does mean that a weekly whirl of dinner parties and charity galas is no longer a realistic part of the equation. You can't have your cake and eat it because you ordered a thick slice of organic wholemeal bread.

You say you'd prefer your husband to come with you, but surely what you are really saying is that you'd like to be married to a man who enjoys parties. If your husband did accompany you on one of your London nights, you'd both have a miserable time.

Maybe you should accept that your life is different now, and moving on in different and fulfilling directions. Do you really envy your London friends and their party train to nowhere? Why not throw a party at home? Start living where your life is. You have so much to cherish – are you really going to choose a mirror ball and the queue for the coat check over a loving family?

Dear Graham,

When I was about 13, some friends and I raided my mother's wardrobe and fooled about putting on her clothes and make-up. To the others it was just a bit of fun, but over the years I found myself sneaking off on my own to try on my mother's and sister's clothes. Now 27, I work as a trader for a City bank, in a notoriously alpha-male environment. I have a girlfriend, who I met about three months ago, and on the surface life is good. The problem is that I cannot stop my secret cross-dressing habit. When I am at home on my own, I dig out my frocks, slap on make-up and dance around the sitting room to Gloria Gaynor.

My friends, colleagues and girlfriend have no idea. To them, I am a sports-mad man-about-town. But inside I am in turmoil. I want to be able to wear skirts and make-up in public and stop harbouring this guilty burden. I know I am not gay, I just want to be myself.

Mark F, Hoxton

Dear Mark,

Enjoy your secret! If it was truly acceptable, if you could casually wander into the pub wearing polka-dot pedal-pushers (very now, by the way), would you bother? Or would you just throw on a pair of jeans and a T-shirt? Remember Eddie Izzard? As soon as people stopped making a fuss of the fact that he wore women's clothes, he stopped doing it.

At some point, it might be good to tell your girlfriend about your secret. Three months into the relationship might be too soon, but certainly the woman needs to know before you get married or move in together, otherwise she'll think she's going mad when all her clothes seem to be stretched. Meanwhile, there is nothing better than a forbidden pleasure so revel in it.

PS: if you don't want people to think you are gay, them catching you in an off-the-shoulder peasant dress isn't a worry, but if anyone finds you dancing to Gloria Gaynor, I suggest you leave the country.

Dear Graham,
I noticed a strange thing the other day among my late 30-something peer group. Many of the people I know who have made a success of their lives seem to have had enormous quantities of psychotherapy. When they were going through it, I felt rather sorry for them - they left their jobs, remortgaged their homes and cut rather lonely, pitiful figures.

But now I realise that they were taking valuable time out to reassess things. They weren't pitiful at all; in fact, they were braver and more imaginative. When they changed direction, the results were often dramatic, whereas I feel as if I've been blindly rushing in the same direction all my life, with no plan.

Should I arrange to see a psychotherapist, even though I'm not sure what my problem is exactly, other than being less successful than most of my friends?

Patrick W, west London

Dear Patrick,

What's wrong with you? Nothing. What's your problem? Oh, you don't have one.

Seriously, Patrick, look at your life again. Why aren't you content? Some friends have been more successful than you. As we reach our late thirties, those sorts of disparities are bound to occur, with or without the help of therapy, and you must learn to live with the financial good fortune of your friends or get new friends or a better job. Those are the options.

I would never tell someone not to get therapy – I'm sure it can help all of us in some way – but, if you are worried about money, I can't see that shelling out cash on a shrink is a brilliant plan.

Surely there is a way to work through your jealousy. Instead of thinking, 'I don't have a swimming pool and John does,' think, 'Hurrah, my friend John has a pool so I can go and use it.'

Your friends must have ended up in pretty dark places in their lives to go through the dramatic changes they did. Be grateful that you have never reached the lows that drove them into therapy.

Ask Graham

Dear Graham,

This weekend I discovered my husband of 23 years has been talking to a woman on the telephone for three years. He met her through work and claims it is a platonic relationship. When I confronted him about it, he said that they never actually meet up, all they do is chat on the phone.

I have checked our telephone statements and they have certainly done a huge amount of chatting. When I asked my husband why he hadn't told me about his special 'friend', he said that there was no point telling me because I would react in a jealous way. I am devastated because we have been together since we were teenagers and I thought we had a good relationship. My husband insists I am overreacting.

Should I forgive and forget?

LL, Suffolk

Dear L,

This is a tricky one but I'm glad you've written to me because the worst thing you could do is to react in the heat of the moment. I can only imagine how you felt when you discovered these calls, but let's examine the evidence. Your husband is not pretending that he has been talking to this woman about work or that she shares the number with one of his male friends. Either he was too stupid to think of these easy excuses or he's telling you the truth.

If I were you, I would ask him what he is talking to her about that he can't discuss with you. And why, in three years, have they not started to meet? If your husband is being honest, then you have nothing to worry about, but I suspect he is blurring the truth a bit. It's hard to think that these conversations haven't veered into the sexual arena.

If they are just friends, why don't you ask her to come over to dinner and see how they both react? Whoever this woman is and whatever she is getting out of this odd arrangement, I think you should try to weather the storm. You've been with your husband for 23 years and he doesn't want to let you go. Don't hang up on him.

Dear Graham,
I'm a healthy male in my thirties from a strait-laced,
Presbyterian background (my father is a clergyman). I
recently 'came out' and am struggling to adapt to the casual,
no-strings culture of the gay scene. The problem is that I tend
to get heavy and serious too quickly and this puts a lot of men
off. Although I have no problem getting dates, I never seem to
be able to hang on to them, and this leaves me feeling used
and despondent. I have many (mainly heterosexual) friends,
but I long to have a proper partner for doing couply things
like walking the dog and going to Ikea. Do I give off the
wrong signals?

Luke D, Kent

> **“** Dogs and DIY are where relationships end
> up, not where they start. **”**

Dear Luke,

You have to run before you can walk. Dogs and DIY are where relationships end up, not where they start. For now, you're trapped on the dance floor working your way through a lot of frogs. It may take time to find your prince, but, if the worst that happens is a deal of casual sex before you and Rover tackle the flatpack coffee table, how bad is that?

Sex without love may not be ideal, but it is still sex. You might be doing it slightly later in life than most, but enjoy your own personal coming-out party. As I said to an earlier correspondent, you had better enjoy life with yourself before you can enjoy it with someone else.

Don't worry: one day you'll have your wedding list at Ikea and a reception with a DJ who talks too much. It might make me feel sick, but if that's what you want...

Dear Graham,
About six months ago, my 75-year-old mother-in-law came to
live with us, having declared that she was too frail to live on
her own. My Italian husband would not hear of putting her in
a nursing home or employing a carer. He works long hours and
expects me to be the dutiful daughter-in-law, attending to his
mother's every need.
    In front of my husband she acts fragile, but as soon as he
leaves she orders me around like a servant. I know the old
battle-axe is capable of looking after herself, but she plays me
off against my husband and he refuses to believe me. It has put
an incredible strain on our marriage, to the extent that I am
tempted to leave. Our children have all grown up so there is
nothing keeping me, except that deep down I still love my
husband and I am afraid of being on my own.
                                          Teresa C, Twickenham

Dear Teresa,

I pity you. Coming between an Italian man and his mother is only marginally less dangerous than finding yourself standing between John Prescott and a pie. In either case the advice is the same: show no fear and don't move. Remember that, despite the appearance of Mama, it's still your house. You are in charge, you are not a servant.

Explain this to your mother-in-law, making sure that she knows either things can get better, or they can get worse. Deep down she must be aware that, as bad as things may get between you and your husband, he is hardly likely to ask you to leave.

Difficult though it may be, spare a thought for the old lady, she is in a very difficult situation too and obviously isn't coping very well with handing over authority to a younger woman. Try to give her some independence or pretend to care about her opinion. What you have in common is that you both love her son. If, however, she is as possessive and manipulative as she sounds, it may be too late for any conciliatory gestures and time for war.

Perhaps you could feign an illness, so she is forced to look after herself, or your husband is forced to agree to the arrival of a carer. Another good ploy is to make your husband think that she is lying by hiding food in her room or hiding her belongings so she starts to look really gaga. It's mean, but at least it stops you being the victim. It also sounds like this new living arrangement is having no negative effect on your husband's life. That needs to change. Are there things he enjoys? Night outs? Golf trips? Make sure that somehow these are affected because you have to stay at home to look after his mother.

Whatever happens, Teresa, don't ask your husband to choose between you and his mother. Tragically, he is certain to choose her. Men are born babies and never really change.

Dear Graham,

My sister is perfect and can do no wrong. At least in the eyes of my parents. She is blonde and blue-eyed and has a glamorous career working for an investment bank in the City. Sporty and vivacious, she always has a string of men queuing up to take her out. I am her older sister, but sometimes I feel like her shadow. Referred to by my mother recently as 'a bit of a plodder', my career as a laboratory researcher does not make for stimulating dinner-party chat. I am constantly being told to 'be more like Susie', and often left out of family conversations altogether. I love my sister but I can't help feeling inadequate next to her.

Rosie P, Truro

Dear Rosie,
This isn't your problem. You have chosen your life and career – if it is 'plodding', then that is obviously a pace you are comfortable with. The people with a problem are your parents. Not to put too fine a point on it, their parenting skills are very poor indeed. Children should never feel they have to do something just to please their mum and dad. After they are long dead, you will still be living with the consequences.

Try to step outside your family unit and see it objectively. She may be prettier than you, I don't know, but don't ever think that a career as an investment banker is 'glamorous'. I for one would shed silent tears of boredom if I had to sit next to your sister at a dinner party. Just imagine how monumentally boring and objectionable all the people she works with must be. Pity your sister and see your parents for the inadequate people they are. Live your life for you. It's not a competition.

Dear Graham,
What exactly are men looking for in a woman? I am in my
mid-thirties and have been single for as long as I can
remember. With the exception of the odd drunken kiss, I barely
seem to so much as dangle a toe in the water. I have tried speed
dating, but find it shallow and contrived. Dating websites just
throw up dull men who work in IT. I am beginning to despair,
as all my friends are now married with children. Where am I
going wrong? Everyone tells me I am attractive and fun to be
with, so I don't understand.

Katie P, Lincolnshire

Dear Katie,

Live your life! Find happiness in the life you do have, rather than wait for the happiness that some fictional life of the future might bring. We have all come home and stared at our empty bed wondering why there is no one to share it with. But at other times we have all woken up wishing that the person whose head is on the other pillow wasn't there.

Your friends may be getting married, but look closely – how many of those relationships would you really like to be in? You turn down boring IT guys, but if you really needed someone else to validate your existence you would be reading *Computer Programming for Dummies* instead of writing to me.

There have to be things you like about your single life that mean you are not willing to 'settle'. Focus on these things. Indulge your every desire, fill your life with secret pleasures. Iron your sheets, light candles. Spend the night watching your favourite movies, snuggling up to Ben, Jerry and a spoon.

Boyfriends come and go, but the only person you are sure to spend the rest of your life with is yourself, so you had better enjoy her and treat her well. You are strong: people are envious of you. A shared life might seem like the perfect one right now, but experience tells us that it ends with a single heart ripped in two.

Dear Graham,

Why is the dating game so difficult? I'm an average bloke in my early thirties, but I find it hard to read the signals. I've never been good at body language and the women I come across make such an effort with their appearance that it's impossible to know if they're trying to impress me or just being themselves. On a date, should I break the ice with a joke? Some girls laugh at my one about the two nuns in a bath and others look down their noses.

The biggest dilemma is money. Should I accept if a girl offers to split the bill? I'm told they hate any hint of stinginess, but how can that be when most of them protest (albeit weakly) if I insist on picking up the tab? And in this politically correct age, isn't it better to go Dutch?

Will F, Bristol

❝ Feel free to be funny, but do it with stories and comments rather than punchlines that are older than Anne Robinson ❞

Dear Will,

I worry for you. Don't you have friends? Has no one talked you through this before? Women dress for dates because they want to look good for others and feel good about themselves. Lipstick doesn't automatically mean that a woman is a slag.

Now on to jokes. Nobody wants to hear a joke – no man, no woman, never. The ones who manage to fake a laugh are just moving their heads to try to see the nearest exit. Feel free to be funny, but do it with stories and comments rather than punchlines that are older than Anne Robinson.

Finally, money. Women only want to go Dutch so that they can go straight home and never see you again without feeling guilty. Will, I would despair, but the fact that women agree to go out with you at all suggests that you must have something going for you. Remember who that Will is and let women get to know him.

Dear Graham,
Can opposites really attract? As a dedicated vegan and eco-warrior, I find it abhorrent that people eat food that has caused suffering to animals. I am always finding ways to recycle and save the planet, from washing my clothes in the bath to using low-wattage light bulbs.

I recently met the most knee-tremblingly handsome man. We've enjoyed a couple of dates and when he walked me home last weekend and kissed me I saw stars. However, the awful truth is that this Adonis is a Tory-supporting blood-sports enthusiast who works for a bank and represents everything I detest. He guzzles steak, uses a tumble dryer and leaves his television on stand-by. I feel that, out of principle, I should never see him again. What would you do in my (non-leather) shoes?

Becky G, north London

❝ Climbing the stairs anticipating a romantic candlelit bath only to be confronted by your dungarees and pants soaking in a murky grey soup will dampen any man's ardour. ❞

Dear Becky,
If I were you, I'd take the clothes out of the bath, get in and slit my wrists, but happily I'm not you. Your problem provokes so many questions. How did you meet your Adonis? Do the Tories know they have an Adonis in their ranks and, if so, why isn't he the leader instead of the milky-breasted creature they have now? And the greatest mystery of all: why is a rat-haired tree-hugger like you reading the *Telegraph*?

Essentially, Becky, you don't have a problem because the ravishing right-winger will dump you very swiftly. True, taking a vegan out to dinner is fabulously cheap, but it's hard to really enjoy your bloody hunk of lamb if the person opposite you is eating something that looks like it has already been digested. Equally, climbing the stairs anticipating a romantic candlelit bath only to be confronted by your dungarees and pants soaking in a murky grey soup will dampen any man's ardour.

When Mr Right-wing realises that you are Ms Wrong, perhaps you could set your sights on David Cameron – he's been to India, you know. That's all I have to say, Becky, so please fold this paper neatly and take it straight to recycling.

Dear Graham,
I'm in my early forties and the tick-tock of my biological clock
has become thunderous. I've been with my boyfriend for a
couple of years and know he is open to the idea of having kids.
The problem is that I'm not in love with him any more. I'm fond
of him and believe he would probably make a decent father, but
the passion just isn't there. Would it be deceitful of me to go
ahead and try to have a child with him, given the ambivalence
of my feelings?

Nancy P, Aviemore

Dear Nancy,

I can't pretend to know what you're going through. To say goodbye to the possibility of having a baby must be heartbreaking; however, if you do decide to have a baby within a loveless marriage, surely you are being supremely selfish. Once you have a child, it stops being about you and becomes about the new person you have created.

I don't think the word 'deceitful' quite does justice to your plan. You are asking him to give up the possibility of having a full and loving life with someone who truly values him just so that your selfish needs can be met. Your biological clock is obviously ticking so loudly that you can't hear the voice of reason. Better that you are a bit unhappy than you make two other lives miserable.

Are you willing to raise a child by yourself? Sperm isn't hard to come by so the possibility of motherhood is still there. When I hear women of your age talking about wanting a baby, I often wonder, well, why don't they? Sometimes I hear myself telling people that I wish I could play the piano, but, if I really, truly wanted to play, wouldn't I have learned by now?

Ask Graham

Dear Graham,

I got divorced a couple of years ago and to my surprise have found it easy to meet attractive, unattached women. It seems that, thanks to a demographic blip, the pond is full to bursting with alluring female fish. What's changed since I got married fresh out of university is that women in my age group (35+) are all very experienced and tend to have a well-honed 'bag of tricks'. It makes everything rather intimidating and, frankly, not very romantic. Short of swinging from the chandeliers, things could hardly be more athletic.

It's so difficult to talk about sex. Even outwardly confident women go rather quiet and spaniel-eyed if you say anything that could be interpreted as even vaguely critical. How do you tell a girlfriend to be herself rather than try to score Olympic golds in the bedroom without hurting her feelings?

Simon S, Manchester

How do you tell a girl to be herself rather than try to score Olympic golds in the bedroom?

Dear Simon,
Bless you. All you want are romantic cuddles and cups of tea as the sun streams through the ivy-framed bedroom window. Or could it be that you are a selfish and lazy lover who doesn't like to feel pressured into making an effort?

I can't believe that, after the initial erotic flag-waving, things with a girlfriend don't settle down into a comforting pattern of passion and intimacy with no one feeling that their performance is part of a sweaty job application. Perhaps, beyond being a passive lump, you just don't enjoy sex that much. If this is the case, then it's unfair of you to be with women who quite frankly sound like they think *Footballers' Wives* is a documentary.

There must be ladies out there who will find it a relief that a brief spurt of the missionary position once a week will suffice. Hang around Blockbuster and any woman who checks out *Cold Mountain* or *The Notebook* will be happy to sit on a beach in winter drinking Cup-a-Soup.

Swinging on chandeliers and abseiling off wardrobes are all very well once in a while, but a bit like *Big Brother* – you don't want it every night of the week.

Dear Graham,
When I discovered my husband had been having an affair I was devastated. He has now ended it, but I find it very hard to forgive him. He is making a huge effort to be the wonderful man I married, but I've gone from feeling totally numb with shock to being resentful and angry. It's really hard for me to keep a lid on things and I hate myself when we fight in front of the children. There are days when I just want to do something vengeful. Go to a bar and pick someone up, for example.

Whenever we're in bed together, I find myself thinking about her. What did she look like? Was she more adventurous? I don't want my marriage to end but I'd so value your advice. I'm in my mid-thirties.

Jessica K, Reading

❝ Stay on the moral high ground – it's
much easier to swing a baseball bat
from there. **❞**

Dear Jessica,

This is one of the most difficult situations to deal with in any relationship. The thing to remember is that you can't turn the clock back and it sounds like that is what your husband is trying to do.

Things will never be the same again and your marriage must somehow learn how to incorporate the hurt, the guilt and the betrayal. It sounds simplistic, but I think the only thing that truly helps is time. When a wound becomes a scar, we still know a bad thing happened, but it somehow becomes part of our personal history and not an immediate source of pain.

If the two of you stay together, then, as the months slip by, you can begin to appreciate that your husband chose you over the affair. It doesn't matter if she was more exciting or had a bosom like two Pope's hats because he is in bed with you not her.

Forgiveness can't be given overnight and trust has to be earned but the memory of surviving this skirmish as part of your shared history may eventually make your marriage stronger. Of course, the downside, which cannot be ignored, is that maybe you married a philandering fool and would be wiser to go your separate ways.

If, after several months, you still find it impossible to move on, then seek professional help. Whatever you do, fight all the urges you have to pick up a stranger in a bar. Stay on the moral high ground – it's much easier to swing a baseball bat from there.

Dear Graham,

I own a romantic old farmhouse north of Perpignan. Every summer I am ambushed by friends who, for lack of other holiday plans, descend on me. It is always the same routine. They ring up, schmooze me energetically, then invite themselves.

None of these waifs and strays ever hires cars, all need collecting and dropping off at airports, and no one ever shows any inclination to either shop or cook.

I now get them to contribute to a kitty but it always seems to be empty.

I inevitably spend a large part of the summer feeling like an unpaid taxi service/caterer.

My husband blames Ryanair and easyJet and is overjoyed at the news that the no-frills airlines might be cutting back on some of their routes, even though it will, of course, affect our own travel plans.

I don't mind short visits but what I dread is guests who overstay their welcome. How can I (politely) get friends to move on?

Charlotte N, Perpignan/Kent

Dear Charlotte,

This isn't rocket science. Toughen up and tell a few lies.

It's great that you have friends who want to come and stay, but you need to limit their options. Tell people that you have other guests arriving soon and that you only have room for three days. Ask them if they are renting a car or if they would like the number of a cab company. Don't offer to drive unless you don't mind.

Because this sort of selfish behaviour is so simple to shut down, I wonder whether, over the years, there hasn't been a small part of you that has enjoyed playing the victim. Obviously, the thrill has now worn off and it's time to get tough.

What's the worst that will happen? They won't come. End of story.

In the future, think very carefully before you send postcards bearing the legend 'wish you were here'.

Dear Graham,

How do you break the news to a girl that you don't fancy her? I keep getting invited to dinners and parties by a girl I met on holiday, but, although I like her, I'm not interested in her romantically. We've been out a couple of times, but they haven't been 'dates' as far as I'm concerned, just casual evenings at the cinema with a quick pint afterwards. It only dawned on me that she might be keen when a male friend pointed it out. Now I realise that she does hang on my every word and seems to be a bit overdressed and over-attentive when I see her.

How do I go about letting her down gently?

Luke S, Cornwall

Dear Luke,

You don't because you can't. No one likes to be told they aren't attractive. If Ann Widdecombe told George Clooney she wasn't interested, he might not burst into tears but he'd still feel a little less fabulous.

You seem like a nice – if slightly dopey – guy, so accept that she will be hurt but construct a situation where she can hold on to her dignity. If she is just a friend, then treat her like a friend. Ask her if she has met any guys lately or comment on how some other woman is your type. Be clear that you think of other women in a sexual way, but not her. Eggy, I know, but she will get the message and should be able to hold it together until she gets home and sobs in front of one of those late-night ITV quizzes where she is sure that the missing word after door is knob.

Whatever happens, don't acknowledge her feelings for you and you might manage to be friends, rather than someone you bump into and then act like you owe them money. Do all of this quickly because any minute now she might crack and confess her feelings to you. Then you'll sleep with her so as not to hurt her feelings.

She'll never hear from you again, become distraught then angry, shave her head and become a nun or a lesbian, or a lesbian nun. Be very careful.

Ask Graham

Dear Graham,

My boyfriend has suddenly announced - completely out of the blue - that he's planning to cross the Andes on horseback over Christmas, before travelling up to the Atacama desert for New Year. He is taking three university friends with him. When I told him how upset I was, he said he'd been planning it for over a year (we've been going out for eight months) and it wasn't 'a girlfriendy sort of holiday' as no couples are going.

Two of his friends are female and unattached. While I trust him completely, I do mind that he's going off without me and never thought to discuss it with me first. I am now facing a bleak family Christmas in the Brecon Beacons, where I'll probably be the only single person for miles.

Whenever I bring up the subject (I try not to sound bitter), he accuses me of being 'possessive' and 'unreasonable'. Am I?

Gillian C, Lincs

Dear Gillian,
I feel as if you've missed what is really going on here. You're so fixated on how much better Christmas in the Atacama desert will be compared to Wales that you have failed to notice that your boyfriend is essentially dumping you.

Grab some Kleenex and let me explain. He started planning this trip a year ago. He started dating you eight months ago and failed to mention his plans. It doesn't take a genius to work out that he never imagined that he would still be dating you by the time the trip took place.

For some reason, he simply hasn't got around to splitting up with you, presumably because he was so busy planning a special holiday without you.

Given that you are this upset about not being included in his travel plans, I'm guessing he is simply avoiding the screaming hysteria that will follow the old heave-ho.

Sorry to be the bearer of such bad news, but, on the plus side, you have just got rid of a man who thinks it'll be fun spending New Year's Eve in the middle of a desert with some dreary people he went to university with.

Gillian, you can do better. Frankly, you could only do better.

Dear Graham,
I am being pursued by a man I don't fancy at all and never will. He bombards me with dinner invitations, sends me flirtatious texts and appears to be too thick-skinned to read my negative signals.

The first time I met him (at a family christening), I made the fatal mistake of agreeing to go out for dinner with him. We were supposed to meet in a restaurant but, at the last minute, he changed the venue to his house, saying he felt like cooking. The evening was a nightmare: he made lecherous overtures and I couldn't get away soon enough. The problem is that he's the older brother of my sister-in-law.

Any ideas on how to send him packing while preserving family harmony?

Ella C, Norfolk

> **" Like Jude Law's career, he will soon fade away. "**

Dear Ella,
Rest assured, you have done nothing wrong – apart from live in Norfolk, but let's not go down that road. The normal escape route from your situation, telling him that you are dating someone else, won't work here. Your lies will be found out because of the family connection.

Your brother may not want to find out that he is married to the sister of a man with all the charm and personality of wet wool, but he should be your first port of call. Explain the situation to him or, if you are close to your sister-in-law, describe your predicament to her. Don't be too harsh on the brother. Explain that you are flattered, of course, but that you are not in the right mindset at the moment – anything that doesn't make him sound like a man who steals panties from washing lines.

Be prepared for the reaction when his sister or brother-in-law has a quiet word with him. He will feel humiliated and will doubtless lash out and try to blame you. Don't overreact. Like Jude Law's career, he will soon fade away. You may never be great friends with this man, but do you really care?

Please learn an important lesson from this experience: don't accept dates at funerals, weddings or christenings. If someone finds you attractive in a hat, there is something wrong with them.

Dear Graham,

Having spent an enormous amount of money buying a new house, I have discovered that I appear to be living opposite a bordello.

On most evenings red fairy lights festoon the upper floors, taxis pull up and a succession of businessmen troop out, looking distinctly shifty.

I feel strongly that it lowers the tone of the neighbourhood. And as a man in his mid-forties, with neither a girlfriend nor a wife, I fear that in some way I might be implicated. How liberal should one be? I don't want to deprive the girls of their livelihood but, having lived most of my life in Godalming, I'm not used to this sort of thing.

Guy U, west London

Dear Guy,

Pull your curtains and get on with your life. Obsessing about every car that slows down will drive you insane.

I'm fairly sure your neighbours won't think you bought your house for the local amenities. I live next door to a pub but people accept that isn't the sole reason I purchased the house.

Have you discussed your fears with others on the street? Perhaps there's some other explanation – the house is populated by beauty therapists specialising in heavy-duty waxing? They run doggy day care? If you'd all like it shut down, presumably you can make that happen. People aren't allowed to just start running a business in a residential property.

Nothing unites a community quite like the disapproval of a neighbour. You'll probably make lots of friends and, before you know it, you'll be posting leaflets through doors demanding an end to the tyranny of wheelie bins.

One final tip – be very careful what Christmas decorations you put up. Use the wrong coloured lights and you may run out of mulled wine faster than you expect.

Dear Graham

I grew up on a farm on the west coast of Ireland and have just moved to London. My flatmates, whom I met through a website, are frighteningly trendy and party every night. My job in customer care is soul-destroying because people are always rude to me and I often come home in tears. I find the city scary, especially at night, and I am constantly getting lost.

Although I'm lonely and desperately homesick, I am loath to admit this to my parents and friends back home for fear of sounding pathetic, so I pretend that everything is OK and that I am forging a successful career in the bright lights. How can I learn to love London as all Londoners seem to? I don't want to return home a failure.

Niamh D, Ealing

Dear Niamh,

Hang on. Don't leave London defeated or it will haunt you for the rest of your life. You haven't been living in the capital long and it does take a while to crack. The trick is to find the London that's right for you. The place is so huge that when one first arrives it is easy to get sucked into a world of nightclubs, guest lists and designer shops, or at least start to believe such things are all-important.

In this respect I imagine your trendy flatmates are only making matters worse. Not enjoying those things doesn't mean you don't like London. There is a group or organisation for every taste and every interest. Even if it is as simple as wanting to meet others who are from rural Ireland, you'll find them in London if you look hard enough.

Go on walking tours, sit on that open-top bus, get to know the capital. Don't sneak glances at it from behind corners, embrace it.

Also try to remember why you wanted to leave where you grew up. Could it be that because you are feeling low you now see home through emerald-coloured glasses? The cows aren't going anywhere; if you want to run home and roll in manure you can. But what's the rush? In the end you have to give London time – there are no shortcuts. But when you eventually get to the heart of this amazing city you'll be so glad you did.

Ask Graham

Dear Graham,
I am a single woman and recently 'met' a charming, funny
man through an online dating chatroom. We get on really
well, spend hours chatting and never run out of things to say.
Romance has blossomed fast; we are always 'HH' (chat-room
terminology for 'holding hands') and signing off 'KOTL' ('kiss
on the lips'). He described himself as 27, tall, dark and
mysterious-looking. I described myself as a 24-year-old blonde,
size 8, with a successful job. In reality, I am 30, size 16, have
frizzy hair and work for a charity. He is keen for us to meet, but
I am terrified he will be disappointed. What shall I do? Is it too
late for a cosmetic and lifestyle overhaul?

Helen T, Hackney

Dear Helen,
You say you are terrified that this man might be disappointed. Trust
me, he will be. You may work for a charity, but he doesn't. Why would
he continue to be attracted to a woman who, far more importantly
than being frizzy-haired instead of blonde, is a big fat liar? Imagine
how you would feel if he had told similar lies to you.

I'm guessing he has been involved in the world of computer-dating
for a bit longer than you. The way he describes himself sounds great at
first glance, but what has he actually told you? That description could
cover anyone from Antonio Banderas to Osama Bin Laden. I don't
mean to be cynical but 'mysterious-looking' suggests that you can't
figure out if that's his ear or his nose.

Take courage from this, and tell him before you meet what you
really look like. Don't admit that you lied, but simply say that you
should describe yourself in more detail, and then paint a slightly truer
portrait. At the same time, you might push him a little about what he
really looks like.

You have been a very stupid woman, but it may not be too late.
Good luck.

Dear Graham,
Among my circle of rather groomed 40-something girlfriends,
I'm the only woman who hasn't had Botox. As a result all my
pals have brows as smooth as Bernini sculptures, while I look my
age (43). Perhaps it's an age thing, or perhaps I really am worn
out, but people keep telling me how tired I look. None of my old
tricks (Chanel lipstick, regular eyebrow shapes, blingy earrings)
seem to work any more.

I'm not keen to go down the Botox route - quite apart from
anything else, it costs a bomb - but it's hard being the only
woman I know who can actually move her facial muscles. Should
I learn to love my wrinkles? Or should I get real: if I don't blitz
those frown lines pronto am I likely to end up jobless, manless
and possibly even homeless?

Sally X, Worthing

Dear Sally,
Time is not our friend. There are no loyalty points in life. Let's not fool ourselves – age brings nothing but humiliation. But your friends who are walking around looking like surprised burn victims don't look any better than you, merely differently old. They have spent hundreds of pounds to humiliate themselves.

My advice is not to pick a fight you know you can't win. Having said all that, it does sound like you look really awful. Are you truly tired? If the answer is 'yes', then get some rest. If the answer is 'no', then wear sunglasses as much as possible and ask your friends if they've had a mild stroke.

I doubt you will ever learn to love your wrinkles but remember that the only nice thing about getting older is that it happens to everyone. I often take comfort when watching bright young things dancing around clubs with their shirts off, in thinking about them bald and smelling of their own wee. If you're really lucky, you might bump into a gerontophile. Look it up in the dictionary. Trust me, it will cheer you up!

Dear Graham,
Do other English males share my horror of dancing? Whenever I
hit the dance floor at parties, I become horribly embarrassed
and self-conscious. Most of my male friends can't dance either,
and they require enormous amounts of alcohol to try, but for
some reason it's me who attracts the most comment. I've tried
parodying myself by dancing in a semi-ironic way, but that
doesn't seem to work either.
  Needless to say, I'm already dreading our annual Christmas
party. Do you have any tips?

Adrian B, Rye

**❝ Flinging myself across the room in my over-
sized silk shirt, I looked like Douglas Bader
being attacked by a swarm of bees. ❞**

Dear Adrian,

Dancing is a mystery to many and certainly to me. I used to be a very
keen dancer until I witnessed myself throwing some shapes in a friend's
wedding video. Flinging myself across the room in my oversized silk
shirt, I looked like Douglas Bader being attacked by a swarm of bees.

Now I tend to avoid all fancy footwork, but sometimes vodka can
still make me think that I'm the love child of Janet Jackson and Justin
Timberlake. If I were you, I would hug the bar as much as possible.
Irony is difficult at the best of times and I'm fairly sure it's a non-
starter when it comes to the dance floor.

Over the years I've learned two tricks. A simple side-to-side shuffle
may be rubbish but no one is going to talk about it in the taxi on the
way home. Attempting to mimic those around you is another option.
Again, it may be awful, but if it's what everyone else is doing it's harder
for the group to pick on you.

When it comes to going out with a group of friends, it is important to
choose your moments to shine. We can't all be brilliant all the time.
Accept that the dance floor is not your arena and look on the bright side:
you'll always find the drunkest girls at the bar. Let the rhythm take you!

Dear Graham,
Am I a sex tourist? I've fallen in love with a Turkish farmhand I
met when I was on holiday in East Anatolia last year. He lives
in a remote hilltop village and has never stepped outside Turkey
(and has no intention of doing so).

I'm in my mid-fifties, widowed with grown-up children; he's
in his early forties. He doesn't appear to be interested in my
money, or to have any desire to come to England, but even so
I'm worried that I'm just like those desperate middle-aged
women who pick up younger men in Ghana. My daughter - who
has never met the man - says that it's 'disgusting' and it's time
I started acting my age.

Although language is a bit of a problem, we understand each
other perfectly. He also treats me like a queen and makes me
feel young again. Men of my age in Britain are either long
married, dysfunctional or busy chasing girls in their thirties, so
over here my romantic prospects are terrible.

I suppose this relationship has no future and perhaps I
am making a fool of myself, but is what I'm doing so very
reprehensible?

Margaret H, Tunbridge Wells

Dear Margaret,
I like sex. I've stayed up too late at night to get it. Fortunes have been
spent travelling across London to find it. But I've never wanted it badly
enough to trek all the way to a remote Turkish village and lie down
with a man whose cologne is stale milk and manure. But you obviously
enjoy the experience and, as you so rightly point out, men in Britain
aren't exactly pushing the pierced-navel lovelies out of the way to get
to the 50-year-olds.

It's all very well for your daughter to call you disgusting, but she has
yet to experience the cruel journey from farm-fresh to stock clearance
at the back of the shop. I think you know the answers to most of your
questions. Yes, you are making a bit of a fool of yourself, but then
sitting around being dignified at the book club hasn't got you chatted
up recently.

Clearly, it will end in a flurry of heartache, but this is where you
must make a decision. If you choose to continue, just go for it and
enjoy the relationship for what it is – until one day he throws a glass

of warm goat's milk in your face and uses words that sound like he's gargling jelly.

If you feel you can't ignore your worries or the opinions of others, then you might as well end it now. I hope you don't, because it must be better going to the grave regretting things you did rather than those you didn't.

But if someone is reading this in an airport waiting for a flight to Ghana with their life savings in a bag, this advice doesn't apply to you. Go home. Shirley Valentine has a lot to answer for.

Dear Graham,

My Greek girlfriend makes such a racket when we make love that I can't look my neighbours in the eye when I pass them in the hall. The last time things got a bit high-pitched, I begged her to pipe down, but she only laughed and accused me of being 'pathetically middle-class and worrying about what the neighbours think'.

The problem is that I am middle-class and do worry about the neighbours. Of course, I'm a lucky man to inspire such fervour in the bedroom, but is there any way of ensuring that the next time we're in the mood things are a little more sotto voce?

Justin T, Manchester

Dear Justin,

This is a situation where I feel sorry for everyone involved: your neighbours for having to listen to your girlfriend scream like Nana Mouskouri having hot moussaka dumped in her lap; your girlfriend for having a boyfriend who tells her off about how she makes love; and you for having a poor-quality flat conversion.

Why not seduce your Olympic screamer during times when other loud things are going on, such as the *X-Factor* results show? Unless you move to a well-insulated or remote home, this situation will never resolve itself. You can't stay in a relationship if you find having sex with your partner annoying.

As she is Greek, why not get her to smash plates when things hot up. Then your neighbours will simply think you indulge in occasional bouts of domestic violence – far less embarrassing.

Dear Graham,

My London-based granddaughter, who's a fussy eater of 13, has just announced that she's vegan. It goes against the grain of everything our family stands for. We're (dare I say it) classic hunting, fishing, shooting types.

I met my husband on a grouse moor in Perthshire 45 years ago and have been plucking game birds ever since. I've spoken to friends and it seems that veganism is all the rage these days among the young. I can't understand it at all. In my day, you ate what was put on your plate and that was the end of it.

Am I expected to put up with this sort of nonsense? Or should I take a stand? They are all coming to us for Christmas and I'm already dreading the cooking. Apparently cheese and eggs are off-limits - and even mince pies are verboten.

Virginia X from Exmoor (I've changed my name - for obvious reasons)

PS No point discussing things with my daughter-in-law. She's what I would describe as a 'hands-off mother'. Rarely lifts a finger and very happy to just let her children run riot.

Dear Virginia,

Your granddaughter's newfound appetite for kitchen waste on a plate seems to have worked you up into a frenzy beyond reason.

Might you be upset about something else? Your daughter-in-law perhaps? Your thwarted desire to see more of your grandchildren? I can only guess.

As for the vegan Christmas, it only takes a phone call to sort it out. Call your granddaughter and explain that silly old granny doesn't know a thing about vegan food so why doesn't she prepare some lovely dishes to pop on the table along with the traditional Christmas spread that you'll be providing.

The worst that can happen is that you may have to try a mouthful of some mushroom pâté served on a bed of boiled hair but at least you didn't have to make it.

The best outcome might be that your granddaughter is too lazy and simply joins you all in an orgy of butter and breast.

Christmas is still quite a way off for a young girl with a faddish diet so who knows what she'll want to eat by then? It is ironic that people with dietary requirements (what we used to call fussy eaters) think it makes them in some way interesting, when in fact it renders them as dull as what they eat. I know there are serious issues about hormones in meat and overfishing but is eating a free-range organic turkey so very wrong? It is Jesus' birthday after all.

Dear Graham,
Is there an easy way to dispense with the services of my hypochondriac Polish cleaning lady? I am beginning to doubt her work ethic. The other day I found an empty gin bottle under the sofa. The surfaces had barely been dusted and my husband's shirts had been ironed haphazardly.

When we first hired her, she worked really hard and everything sparkled. But her husband left her, and she moans about all sorts of phantom illnesses and pains.

I would feel terrible asking her to leave, as she has two children to support and I'm sure she'll just keep drinking. But we can't pay her just to consume our gin and flick a duster over the coffee table.

Tara K, Surrey

Dear Tara,
Those dinner parties where the entire conversation consists of people grumbling about their cleaners are unbearable. 'I don't know where she's from, but they don't have skirting boards there!' How everyone laughs.

However, listen carefully to that smug middle-class chat and you learn that, while no one is happy with their domestic help, nobody is going to get fired. Why? Because at cleaner school, somewhere between the ironing class and basic hoovering, they hold a master class in emotional blackmail.

I don't know anyone who has a cleaner without an awful sob story. Sick husbands, children in jail, a family abroad – take your pick. You can't just ignore what is going on. Talk to her – you are her employer, not her friend – and explain that things need to change or you will have to find a new cleaner. Lock the drinks cabinet and hide the key. Hopefully, your hard worker will return, because if there is one thing worse than a bad cleaner it's having to do it yourself. As the old saying goes: 'Cleanliness is next to impossible.'

Dear Graham,

I am desperate to move to the country, but my wife is making a song and dance about it. She hates the weather and the food and is convinced the natives will be hostile. As a result we're holed up in a tiny London flat when we could be in a rambling old farmhouse with a big garden. I grew up on Exmoor, love country pursuits and am keen that our three children have a healthy lifestyle.

We spend our city weekends traipsing around overcrowded parks with other equally miserable families and have a really pathetic quality of life. I'm convinced we would all be happier living out of London but, although I have my own business, I can't afford to maintain two properties. How can I persuade my stubbornly metropolitan wife to be a little more open-minded?

Josh L, west London

❝ Climbing a tree to look at some cows is good, wholesome fun but it's not exactly *Grand Theft Auto* is it? **❞**

Dear Josh,

You may run your own business but at home your wife is clearly the CEO. The fact that you want to move to the country is never going to get Mrs Josh into a headscarf. The only way the mother of your children is ever moving beyond the smell of designer coffee is if she sees how it can benefit her.

I assume she is thinking that a larger house will simply be more work and that children involved in various outdoor pursuits will mean hours spent in a car ferrying them from one damp hell to another. The real problem here is that she's right: a rural retreat will be lovely for you and terrific for your children while they're young, but what's in it for her?

You might suggest that if you had a bigger house you could get an au pair. Does she like dogs? Horse-riding? I'm clutching at straws. It puzzles me that you went ahead and had three children with someone without talking about this major issue. Weekends away could be a plan, so that she can see how happy it makes your children, but be prepared: they may hate it, too.

Climbing a tree to look at some cows is good, wholesome fun but it's not exactly *Grand Theft Auto*, is it? Maybe you need to learn to love the smell of wet concrete and the sound of hysterical sirens. Focus on what makes city life great. The country may have all the stars in the night sky but we have Starbucks.

Dear Graham,
I can't forget my ex. We split up by mutual agreement almost a year ago and I still dream and think about him every day. Each time I see a man in the street who reminds me of him in some obscure way - his loping walk, funny Tintin hair or Jay Jopling glasses - my heart stops beating and I feel as if I'm being punched in the stomach. I don't believe we would have made one another happy, but somehow I can't move on. He continues to haunt me. Do you have any tips for laying old ghosts to rest?

Hannah D, Humberside

Dear Hannah,
We are odd, shallow little creatures and what we believe are huge gaping holes in our hearts can usually be filled by the smallest flirtation. The reason you can't get over your ex is most probably because you haven't met anyone else. Given that it sounds as if you were dating Timmy Mallett with a bad leg, I'm rather surprised that you have been unable to find a replacement. But then I can't tell from your letter what sort of unclaimed prize you might be.

If, after going out on a couple of dates with prospective beaux, you are still unable to stop thinking about the spikey-haired lurcher, then perhaps there is unfinished business. Knowing that the two of you have no long-term future together isn't the same as reaching an end.

Don't misunderstand me, I'm not suggesting that you start going out with him again but simply that you might want to have lunch to remind yourself why it won't work.

An even simpler thing to do would be to draw your curtains, light some candles and chant quietly: 'The hair, the walk, the glasses, the hair, the walk, the glasses' until you come to your senses.

Dear Graham,

My boyfriend is buying a flat and, six weeks ago, I reluctantly agreed to let him move in with me until the sale went through. Unfortunately, he pulled out of the purchase after discovering that drug dealers were living upstairs. He is now being very lazy about finding a new place and is settling into my tiny flat as if it were his own home. He has even asked if he can move in his furniture from storage.

The problem is that he works from home, and having no space and no privacy is driving me crazy. Before he moved in, we were madly in love, but we now argue about petty things such as unwashed breakfast plates. Sometimes I pretend to go to the shops or for a run, just to get away.

When we didn't live together, I felt gorgeous and desirable but now I'm turning into a shrew. Yesterday, when he finished all the milk (but didn't replace it), I completely lost it. A friend suggests I gently give him a deadline for moving out. But when I raised the subject last weekend, he wept like an abandoned child (he is Turkish). Any ideas?

Jane H, Brighton

Dear Jane,

You don't tell me how long you have been dating your Turkish cuckoo. If it has been six months or less, then clearly you have moved in together too soon and this is a handy *Reader's Digest* version of your relationship. You have reached the end much faster than you would have, but reached it you have. Be sanguine about it: you've lost a boyfriend but saved a lot of time.

Conversely, if you have been dating for some time, the only problem may be that you made this move without enough forethought. Why not go on holiday together? Rent a house or cottage and see if increasing the space you have to share decreases the irritation you feel.

If this relationship is strong, you would be stupid to throw it away over unwashed plates. However, his big boo-hoo act does suggest that your lover may be more interested in having a mummy than a girlfriend. Be strong: you don't want to still be staring at this turkey next Christmas.

Dear Graham,

My brother-in-law (60 and never married) recently went into hospital for an operation. During his weeks away from home, I went round daily to feed his cat at his request.

It was apparent that he does no housework. His home was verging on filthy, with heaps of old newspapers, cat hair glued to the carpet, surfaces littered with dirty plates and so on. I fought with my urge to sort the place out, feeling it wasn't my job to interfere, so I only did the bare minimum.

When my brother-in-law came home, he made no reference to what I'd done and I wished I'd had a real blitz. Now he appears to have allowed the house to turn into a tip again. He seems cheerful enough and is due to go back for a second op, which means I'll be doing cat duties.

How can I sensitively broach the subject of keeping the house cleaner? He is a stubborn yet kind man, very set in his ways.

Fran S, Wiltshire

Dear Fran,

Repeat after me – my house, his house. You seem to be confusing the two things. This man is 60 years old and you tell me that he seems perfectly happy. That is really all we need to know.

I understand that your desire to blitz his hovel is coming from a good place but it's going to be very hard to get into full Marigold and Mr Muscle mode unless your brother-in-law actually asks for help. Depending on what sort of relationship you have, the only thing you might be able to do is to explain the situation honestly.

When he is in hospital next, explain that you know the house doesn't bother him but it's driving you crazy. Would he mind if you cleaned up? Reassure him that you won't throw anything out – people have a strange attachment to canned goods long after they have expired. If he agrees, off you go in a smoke of Flash.

If he says no, then step away from the spray gun. As a man who lives alone, I fully appreciate the old expression that cleanliness is next to Godliness but it is also next to impossible. You are a very kind sister-in-law. Don't spoil it by crossing a line of grime.

Dear Graham,

I feel really bad writing to you with this problem, especially after reading in Weekend about your labradoodle, Bailey. My gentleman friend has an old and malodorous spaniel called Lola. Blind and milky-eyed, she is on her last legs. My friend, who is in his seventies, has very little sense of smell so has little sympathy with my complaint. The stench is so vile that it doesn't make a bit of difference if doors and windows are opened. Lola's abominable pong clings to walls, curtains, hair and skin like an evil vine.

It's got so bad that I won't go to his house. It's beastly of me, I know, and she's a loyal, loving old dog, but I've reached breaking point. He's going to have to choose between me and his hound.

Is it cruel and heartless to ask this of him?

Meredith T, East Surrey

❝ My new dog Madge is a small terrier but, on occasion, she emits a smell like low tide in an industrial town in Eastern Europe. ❞

Dear Meredith,

I used to do a joke in my stand-up routine where I said that children were a bit like farts in that people like their own. Clearly, this also applies to the farts of their children. My new dog Madge is a small terrier but, on occasion, she emits a smell like low tide in an industrial town in Eastern Europe. If someone else did this on a regular basis in my home they would be out faster than Paris Hilton, but, because Madge is my baby, all is forgiven.

You say that Lola is on her last legs, so my question is, do you really want to tear your partner's heart in two when time will solve your problem ere long? The other risk you take if you ask him to choose is that Lola will end up waving a tired paw at the window as you drive away in a taxi like some soon-to-be-forgotten *EastEnders* character.

On a more positive note, perhaps Lola should visit the vet. He might be able to suggest something to improve the stench or even hint that it's time for Lola to make her way to that big park in the sky. Please don't think I'm dismissing the horror of your problem, but old, loving, loyal companions shouldn't be discarded when they begin to stink. Today it's Lola, tomorrow it could be you.

Dear Graham,

I am 26 and have just started seeing a fellow barrister in the chambers where I work. He's a lovely, funny guy aged 33, totally genuine and very bright. My worry is that I'm not as experienced as he is. I've had boyfriends, but I've never actually gone to bed with anybody.

Somehow it never felt quite right, so I just kept the brakes on. Now I've met Dan I feel it would be the most natural thing in the world, but I'm embarrassed at my lack of experience. Should I tell him I'm a virgin?

Emma H, Lincolnshire

Dear Emma,

Usually I only feel old at 3am on a Saturday morning dancing to music I don't know in a puddle of vodka, but reading your letter has made me feel older than Barry Norman's teeth. Being a 26-year-old virgin is in no way a handicap. It is absolutely still a selling point. Wait until you're 30, however, and the virgin tag will be as appealing as 'ex-council' in the property pages.

To be honest, I can imagine it freaking out Dan a little, so choose very carefully the moment to tell him. Don't blurt it out over dinner or even in the taxi home. In fact, I'd wait until after he has removed your bra. By then he will be in full flow and will climb your virginity mountain with all the bravura of Noel Edmonds opening boxes.

When the deed is done, nestle in his arms and whisper: 'Dan, you're the man!' The memory of this magical moment may cheer him when you dump him, because you'll have to sleep with others so that you have somebody to compare him with. I know this sounds harsh but, trust me, it's going to happen.

Dear Graham,

I'm newly married and finding it a bit of a trial. I met my wife in New York (she has now joined me in London), and our relationship has always been a transatlantic one, with long periods doing our own thing. Now we're in the same house in the same country, we seem to have morphed into a hideous version of The Odd Couple.

It turns out that my wife's idea of heaven is to shoot out of bed at the crack of dawn on a Saturday morning and drag me off to a farmers' market, then spend the rest of the weekend having a couply domestic time. What I like doing is playing poker late into the night and having big lie-ins, followed by mega fried breakfasts.

I'm 31 and not quite ready for this very middle-aged life she's proposing. And she's only 26, for goodness sake.

Any ideas on reaching a happy compromise?

Dan W, north London

Dear Dan,

And you got married because...? Did you just fancy a sit-down lunch with some friends and family? You couldn't afford to buy a new toaster? Seriously, I would like to know.

It sounds as if you put less thought into this than someone buying a pink jumper. Couldn't you have figured it out before you dragged the poor woman away from her life in America?

One of the reasons she probably wants to do lots of things with you is that right now you are her life. She has made a huge decision based on her love for you and you can't be bothered to get out of bed for her. Greasy sausages seem to get your heart beating faster than this poor woman does.

Pining for your bachelor days is helping nobody. Action is the key here. You either make the marriage work or you make it stop. So far you have been a chump of award-winning proportions – don't make it worse. She's 26, she can still find happiness with someone else. As for you, consider your future without her. You'll be alone, fat and, as the years tick by, there will be fewer and fewer guys sitting at that poker table. Eventually, no matter how good your hand is, you will feel like a loser.

You didn't put any thought into getting married; think carefully before you end it.

Dear Graham,

I'm marrying an Australian physicist this summer and feel increasingly anxious about our differences. He's not your average beer-swilling, surf-loving Aussie, but is bright and dynamic. The problem is that he comes from a country where sport is worshipped rather than literature or music, whereas it's books and exhibitions that really make me tick.

I'll be giving up my job in publishing and moving permanently to Brisbane in the summer and I'm getting terribly cold feet. I worry that the lack of culture will make me shrivel up and die inside.

He's a great guy and fits in brilliantly with my friends in London, but will I fit in over there? I see a sterile life of palm trees, barbies and cold beers stretching ahead.

Am I being a snob? Or are my fears justified?

Lauren C, west London

Dear Lauren,

Have you actually visited Australia or are you moving there on your first trip? If it's the latter, then I sense disaster. Worry not, I am not going to indulge in a lot of easy Australia-bashing. I like the place. If it was where France is, I'd go all the time. The trouble is that it's just so far away.

In the end, it's not the barbies and pie shops that will get you down, it's the sense of living on the edge of the planet. When I was there, it felt like being backstage while the main show was going on at a great distance. I've a feeling that your physicist husband may not like Brisbane quite so much when he arrives there direct from London.

But the pros and cons of Down Under are simply a distraction from the real issue here. You are moving somewhere for no other reason than to be with your partner. Even if you were moving to Bristol, that is a huge pressure to put on a relationship.

Before you get on that plane, I would urge you to think of some reasons why you'd like to go besides holding hubby's hand. You come from the world of publishing, so perhaps this is your chance to write that book no one wants to read.

I'm sure there are many words to describe Brisbane, but I can't imagine that 'distracting' is one of them. Live your life for you, not your husband, and maybe this move won't be a divorce with airline food thrown in for free. Bon voyage!

Dear Graham,
For my birthday, my beautiful Norwegian girlfriend, Ingrid,
surprised me with a set of nude photographs of herself. An
amateur-photographer friend had offered to take them and
they met secretly at his house one weekend when I was away
on business. Even though I love the pictures, I have worked
myself up into a jealous rage. I hate the fact that he has the
images on his computer and can drool all over them whenever
he likes.

The 'photographer' is gay (I'm told), but I don't believe a
word of it. I'm convinced he leapt at the chance to see Ingrid
naked and is ogling the pictures as we speak.

Should I go over to his place and give him a piece of my mind?
Name withheld, Herefordshire

❝You can't tie a partner down like some hot-air balloon filled with love.❞

Dear Anon,

Judging from your letter, I wouldn't rush to give anyone a piece of your mind, since, frankly, I don't think you can afford to be that generous. Jealousy is a vile and insidious emotion. It grows in the dark with a ruthless and destructive efficiency.

At times there is good reason to be jealous. It could be about friends being chosen over you, or about workplace flirtations and so on, but you are being wildly irrational. Ingrid is clearly a classic Scandinavian and, if this photographer is bothering you, good luck when you go on holiday. It sounds as though the only beachwear you would be happy to see her in is a burka, whereas I imagine Ingrid won't even bother to pack a bikini.

The one thing I would agree with is that the gay snapper shouldn't have the photographs on his computer, but that is Ingrid's fault. It's great that you love your girlfriend but being with someone isn't the same as owning them. What makes it special is that the other person wants to be with you and chooses to stay.

You can't tie a partner down like some hot-air balloon filled with love. Other men may admire and desire Ingrid, but for whatever reason she has decided to hold your hand in public.

Be happy.

But after all that, I feel it would be remiss of me not to add: what sort of person gives a set of pictures of themselves as a birthday present?

Dear Graham,

I have just given up my gym membership because it made me feel old and unlovely. One of the personal trainers is a sort of Adonis - fit and hunky with a permanent Hollywood tan. Even though he's insanely good looking, he is rather leery and is known for putting his hands in unexpected places. There are always endless jokes in the girls' changing room about his behaviour.

The depressing thing is that, despite going regularly to his spinning classes and even signing up for one-on-one training, I appear to be the only woman who hasn't been the recipient of his unwanted attentions. It's not that I want to be, it's just that I hate to be consigned to the shelf. Where could I be going wrong?

Sally K, Basingstoke

Dear Sally,

Seriously? This is your problem? Some creepy lech who works in a gym you don't even go to any more failed to make an inappropriate pass at you. Now you have managed to translate this stroke of good luck into a profound insult that has shaken your self-esteem to its very core.

What other terrible things have happened to you? Did burglars choose another house over yours to break into? Did the drunk guy vomit on someone else on the Tube when you were actually sitting closer to him? Did the vicious dog bite the bloke in the hat instead of you? Getting upset about this man ignoring you at the gym is like a singer getting upset about a bad review written by a deaf person.

Sally, if you feel old and unattractive, then stopping exercise probably isn't the best plan. Join another gym at once and spend more time on the treadmill than standing around the changing room listening to prattle. We are all judged all the time but, before you take it seriously, judge the judge. If Amanda Holden had listened to me, she wouldn't have the glittering career she has today.

Dear Graham,
After I went a whole year without meeting a single new
person, I finally decided to bite the bullet and do some
online dating. A friend advised me to tick the 'sporty' box,
arguing that it would attract a better class of male. Despite
the fact that the only sport I play is ping-pong, I'm now going
out with a handsome, solvent guy who runs marathons and
climbs mountains.

But, like everything in life, there is a downside. We are both
pretty active in the bedroom department (which is great) but
what he really likes is having sex in public places. So far we've
made love in a station car park, the roof of my office, the fire
escape of Peter Jones, the Gorilla Kingdom at London Zoo and a
boat on the Serpentine.

Keeping up this level of excitement is wearing me out, quite
apart from the sheer terror that we might be caught.
I should dump him, shouldn't I? The man can't be normal.

Becky R, London

Dear Becky,

Let's examine the evidence. You ticked the 'sporty' box on your online form, but I don't see how that translates into standing on a fire escape stuffing your knickers into your handbag.

As always, this is a choice between how much you like this man and how much you don't want your bottom to end up on YouTube.

I don't think using words such as 'normal' is ever useful, especially when discussing relationships. Your man likes high-risk sexual situations and as far as he is aware he has found a great woman who enjoys it as much as he does. Just as you have a choice to make, so does he. If you stop the rooftop romps, he may like you enough to accept that or he may dump you in the hope of finding a cross between Ann Summers and Kate Adie.

To be honest, it all sounds quite exciting to me, but I'm sure his alfresco ardour will be cooled by the onset of winter, so why not just make sure you are wearing clean underwear for the next couple of months and hope for some indoor loving later on?

I have to say, though, that I doubt being taken roughly on a ping-pong table will ever do it for him.

Ask Graham

Dear Graham,

I've been with my husband for 16 years and have three lovely children. We have had the usual ups and downs, but no major wobbles. We are antique dealers and recently moved into a gorgeous Victorian country house in Devon. All pink and rosy? Here's where it goes pear-shaped.

My darling husband is a hoarder and his tendencies are getting worse. Nothing is too trivial for him. He even collects the plastic figurines and gadgets in our children's cereals. From Tweety Bird chains to plastic Smurfs and racing-car magnets, his finds are everywhere.

The children are inured to his growing obsession, but I despair at the prospect of living among miniature trolls and plastic frogs for the rest of my days. I've tried to confront him about his problem, but he sees no wrong in it at all.

Not long ago, I invested in a glass dresser to allow him to display his 'goodies' in an orderly fashion. But still I find myself pulling out putty-slime eggs from under the bed covers. What can I do?

Carol N, Devon

Dear Carol,

I don't really know what you expect me to say. You've been happily married for 16 years and have three lovely children – that's great. Your husband collects plastic crap – that's annoying. The two of you need to put this hobby into perspective.

It must be hard for him to understand how much this upsets you, given that you have allowed it to go on for so long. 1 imagine he mistook your gesture of buying a display cabinet as a sign of encouragement, rather than the slap on the wrist you intended it to be. Be firm with him. You are sharing a new house and there has to be some give and take.

A garden shed sounds like it might be one solution. Or slip 20 quid to the removal men so that they 'lose' a couple of boxes in transit. Whatever improvements you and the Smurf-lover manage to make, it will never be as *Homes & Gardens* as you'd like. Focus on what you love about him and try to find it in your tidy heart to forgive him for making you live with the contents of a Tesco Value Christmas Cracker.

Dear Graham,
I've been with my new boyfriend for only a couple of months but already things are going pear-shaped. Our first month together was a whirlwind of marvellous dates and general couply in-loveness. He was up for seeing fringe plays, obscure French films and even going to galleries on Sundays. I thought I'd met the man of my dreams! Football was never mentioned, we never even stepped inside a pub and he appeared to like Middlemarch as much as I do. How wrong I was and how easily I fell into the trap.

It appears my new boyfriend doesn't have a cultural bone in his body. He was just pretending in order to get me to go out with him. Now he's 'got' me, he makes very little effort and most days I can't prise him away from the television screen.

I find the same pattern repeats itself with every boyfriend. The wooing part is always tragically brief and before I know it I've sunk into a depressing Darby-and-Joan scenario - and I'm only 28.

Louisa M, Buckinghamshire

❝ Just as there is joy to be had from a French film about a housewife trapped in a lift, so there is a certain fun to having your boyfriend hold your hair back while you vomit outside a Slug and Lettuce. ❞

Dear Louisa,

I can only imagine how hot you must be. It's only for the most top-quality lovely that any man would endure the string of hellish dates you describe. You have clearly seen one too many Woody Allen films and the women in those all end up sleeping with him. Self-improvement and high culture are all very well, but in moderation.

You seem to be one of those people who go through life as if you're going to face an exam when you die. Surely the greatest joy of life is that living is one of the very few tasks we can't fail at? We can do it differently, but just as there is joy to be had from a French film about a housewife trapped in a lift, so there is a certain fun to having your boyfriend hold your hair back while you vomit outside a Slug and Lettuce.

No one is watching you and no one is impressed. Relax and learn to find pleasure in the simplest of things. Do you like this new boyfriend? If you do, then surely spending time with him is reward enough without having to read subtitles when you're with him.

The reason all your boyfriends become housebound slobs is because going out with you is as much fun as a vegetarian meal with an opinionated know-it-all without wine. Give and take with the men you date. You may be only 28, but continue on your current path and you will morph into one of those poor creatures on *Newsnight Review*. When was the last time Allison Pearson went to Alton Towers and laughed and screamed at the same time? Mix it up, Louisa!

Dear Graham,
My sister-in-law (who is single) has a really noticeable moustache. Since we don't exactly see eye to eye on many subjects, part of me is delighted that she looks like Magnum PI, but I feel that I should say something. What would you advise?
Annie G, Sheffield

Dear Annie,
What a delicious problem to have. You can pretend to be a nice person by torturing your sister-in-law and her Groucho Marx special. I have so many suggestions I hardly know where to begin. If you want to go the überbitch route, tell her that female facial hair is going to be huge this autumn and you're jealous of her because you find it very hard to grow. A gentler approach would be to complain how sore your upper lip is after waxing, then to ask what method she uses.

Sending an anonymous gift certificate for a free hair-removal session at a fancy spa is another slightly subtler way to stop people mistaking the poor woman for Des Lynam. Finally, a sister-in-law-running-in-tears-from-the-room approach is to take some photographs and then have them digitally altered so that her moustache is very visible. Don't go for a comedy handlebar style, because this will just make her angry. Be subtle and watch her sob into her shaving foam.

Of course, all of this effort may be for nothing. Your hirsute sister-in-law may simply be a radical lesbian. Now who's laughing?

Dear Graham,
My boyfriend came out of a rehabilitation centre (for
alcoholism) six weeks ago. Unfortunately, during his time there
he fell in with a really druggy crowd, who seem to have escaped
the law by the skin of their teeth.

All of them treat me like a sort of earth mother and on Sundays
I find myself spooning caramelised parsnips on to the plates of
former junkies. They are all insidiously charming, eloquent people
- the situation is utterly surreal. One of them, a recovering heroin
addict, even has to have his food cut up for him.

I understand that they share an important bond from their
time in rehab, but I would rather not have them in my house.

My boyfriend has sworn not to drink again and so far he has
stuck to his promise. I want to support him, but must I take up
his friends, too?

Lily U, London

Dear Lily,

I've never been to rehab – yet – but I imagine the friends you make there are a slightly more intense version of friends you might make on a cruise. You've been through it together and can talk about things that other people cannot fully understand or share in. On the one hand, a battle with personal demons; on the other, how they ran out of king prawns on the Tropicana buffet. You get my point.

Eventually, your boyfriend won't need these people around and they won't need him. You and your sober partner can walk towards the future in a straight line. I have no idea how long this will take, but it will happen.

A word they use a lot in rehab, I'm told, is 'enabling' and right now you are enabling your boyfriend and his posse. They treat you like an earth mother because you behave like one. Enough with the caramelised parsnips. Make plans on a Sunday, not a medieval feast. Cook it and they will come; stop and so will they.

Try to be patient, though. If you want your boyfriend to stay off the sauce, then accept that these creatures, as unappealing as you may find them, can give him a kind of moral support that you simply can't.

It has only been six weeks and you are working towards a lifetime. Good luck.

Dear Graham,

I'm desperate to be a grandmother but my 38-year-old daughter (and only child) is being rather selfish. She doesn't seem to care when I point out that it's high time she got on with it.

What's wrong with all these young men? Why can't my perfectly attractive daughter find someone? There she is with a good job in London and a lovely flat on the river, and there never seems to be any kind of man in tow. Where did we go wrong? Did we over-educate her? She can't be happy alone - or is this generation different? Could she be a lesbian?

On a serious note, it's not just a matter of my wanting grandchildren; I worry that she's missing out. But if I talk about it (assuming I can get her on the phone, because she is constantly out), she just thinks I'm nagging.

As a last resort, I have started a computer course in the hope that my daughter and I can start exchanging emails. Any advice?

Vanessa T, Tunbridge Wells

Dear Vanessa,

If your daughter doesn't want children, perhaps it is because she fears she might turn into the same sort of mother as you. Maybe she wants children, maybe not, but whichever direction her life takes she must do it for herself, not you.

You say that you worry she is missing out, but on what? After 38 years, the poor creature still can't please you. If you don't want to lose the child you have on top of the imaginary grandchildren, then you must allow your daughter to live her own life in a way that suits her.

Don't you realise that she isn't out all the time but is just screening her calls? Who can blame her? With your daughter's biological clock ticking louder and louder, the pressure you are piling on her is about as useful as an anti-war protester living in a tent outside the Houses of Parliament.

Your baby girl is all grown up and what she needs is for you to be a shoulder to cry on, not a pain in the neck.

Ask Graham

Dear Graham,

My boyfriend, a retired racehorse trainer, is in his early seventies and I'm in my mid-thirties. I'm desperate to have a child. He isn't. I never expected to fall in love with a man so old but I did. In addition, I've managed to pick someone not just with baggage but also with a long line of ex-wives and children trailing in his wake.

Although he's only a couple of years younger than my father, I'm totally smitten and can't imagine being with anyone else. I couldn't care less about his money, though his exes think I'm a gold-digger. I just want commitment and the chance to start a family.

Should I give him an ultimatum? Try to get pregnant 'by accident'? Or just hold on tight in the hope that he eventually comes round to my way of thinking?

Hatty L, Northamptonshire

Dear Hatty,

I'm not sure waiting for your 'boyfriend' to eventually come round to your way of thinking is really an option. I'm in no position to judge anyone for having a May–September relationship – we all find love where we can – but you can't just pretend that it's the same as going out with someone your own age.

Your boyfriend is fast approaching 80 and he's retired. Why on earth would he want a screaming baby in the house? Whatever the joys of fatherhood may be, he's had them already.

Michael Douglas might have put up with late fatherhood for the sake of his Welsh lovely, but I'm guessing he didn't even bother putting a stair-lift in the nursery wing of the mansion.

It's selfish of you to think that a new baby is the right thing for your relationship. You need to decide: motherhood or the last of the summer wine? You can't have both.

Of course, looking on the bright side, if you do stay with your man, it won't be that long until your life is all about mashing up food, bibs and the smell of pee anyway.

Life has a funny way of working out.

Dear Graham,

Pepe, my Spanish boyfriend, is a last-minute sort of person, who likes to improvise. His spontaneity is part of why I find him attractive (he's so much more fun than your classic risk-averse Brit), but at the same time it drives me nuts that we can never make proper plans. More often than not we get to cinemas only to find the film has sold out. And when we go on holiday, we're always the sad losers paying through the nose to fly easyJet or Ryanair, having left the booking to the very last minute.

Apparently in Madrid, when you throw a party it's quite normal to invite everyone on the day. But in Manchester, if you don't plan ahead, things tend to go pear-shaped. I don't want to change him but sometimes I wonder whether this aversion to planning hints at a deeper problem and isn't about being Spanish at all. What do you think?

Bella S, Manchester

> **'At first, I loved her disciplined love of order and planning, but lately it is like living with General Franco in a bra.'**

Dear Bella,

I think it is fair to say that what we at first most love about a new partner is in the end what we most hate. Crazy European spontaneity that once made you feel like you were in an exotic sub-titled art-house film now appears like lazy incompetence that makes you feel like you are living with John Candy in *Planes, Trains & Automobiles*. Pepe, if he wants to, can change, but you must let him know how annoying you find his behaviour.

But be warned, if you really do insist he change, then I can imagine him composing a letter to a Spanish newspaper to ask some Señor Grahamio what to do about his girlfriend. 'At first, I loved her disciplined love of order and planning, but lately it is like living with General Franco in a bra.'

Camels' backs have been broken by less and I wonder if one more visit to www.lastminute.com won't result in www.finalmoment.couple.

Ask Graham

Dear Graham,

I met my new boyfriend on the internet. We are both divorced and in our mid-forties with children away at university. In many ways, things are perfect between us - he is loving, funny, attractive and generous - everything, in fact, which my ex-husband wasn't. The problem is I appear to have fallen in love with a man with next to no libido.

I've never considered myself to be highly sexed, but, now that I don't get much of it, I do miss it. Needless to say, he'd rather peel 1,000 Brussels sprouts than talk about it. Whenever I bring it up, he skilfully changes the subject, or teases me affectionately about my 'voracious' sex drive. I have, of course, tried all the usual feminine tricks - to no avail. Perhaps we should volunteer for a Trinny and Susannah makeover?

Becky P, Grinstead

Dear Becky,

You are in your mid-forties and have one failed marriage behind you. Surely by now it might be beginning to dawn on you that no relationship is perfect?

True, it can be depressing living with someone who, it seems, doesn't find you sexually attractive. But, so long as he isn't finding an outlet for his libido elsewhere, perhaps his other assets can suffice.

Do you really want to give up this man for sex? Sex that will tail off after a couple of years anyway? It sounds as though you are always the one trying to initiate the love-making, hence his description of you as 'voracious'. Back off for a bit and see if he comes to you.

If he doesn't, then try to talk about it once again. He might never be enough for you in the bedroom department, but remember how funny, generous and attractive he is and how available vibrators are. As for Trinny and Susannah... please. I think their taste is seriously suspect now. They thought they'd look good on ITV. Wrong.

Dear Graham,

I'm always getting rejected. Getting dates isn't a problem, but somehow I never seem to get beyond a first or second rendezvous. Is the modern male lethargic?

One friend says that extended periods of peacetime kill the male libido and it would be a different story if we were living in a war zone. I wish I knew where I was going wrong. My New Year resolutions (to lose weight, drink less, do more cardio) have long since fallen by the wayside and I've been feeling so discouraged that I didn't give anything up for Lent. What's the point when men are so picky and unenthusiastic? Please tell me how to get a man interested - and keep him so.

Milly C, Tooting, south London

Dear Milly,

I fear I have bad news. Look at the bigger picture. You can't get a second date. For this you are blaming all mankind. Is it not a little more possible that the problem is not every man you date, but you? Other women manage to date, get married and have children without having to start a third world war.

If this letter was from a man, I would suggest that he was choosing the wrong women to date, but these men are selecting you. I don't think people can be called 'picky and unenthusiastic' when they bother to pluck up the courage to ask you out on a date.

There is clearly something that initially attracts them and then, upon closer examination, repels them. Your girlfriends are not going to help you if the 'move to a war zone' advice is anything to go by, and yet you must do something.

The only plan I can think of is extremely painful and borders on humiliation. Deep breath, Milly. Try contacting one of the men who rejected you. Choose one that you thought really liked you.

Explain that you are fine about the date not going any further but you would like to know why. Assure him that you don't care how personal or possibly hurtful the reason is but you'd just like to prevent it happening again in the future.

I've no idea if this will work, but the bottom line is either you change or you just wait for the very rare lid for your quirky pot to come along.

Ask Graham

Dear Graham,

I'm feeling a little crowded by my new girlfriend. I was struck down with flu the other day and not only did she bombard me with food parcels, she also deluged me with phone calls and text messages offering to come round and look after me. Yesterday I got back from the doctor's surgery to find a cardboard box on my doorstep containing three lamb chops (from a dinner party I failed to make), an enormous slice of plum tart and a gushy note.

It's all a bit much and I told her to back off, which she has, but I'm worried her OTT behaviour is a signal I should beat a hasty retreat.

What do you think?

Oliver U, London

Most young men are desperate to be mothered, but if you want to lie in bed shivering with flu, picking at a lukewarm Pot Noodle, who am I to stop you?

Dear Oliver,

Truly one man's meat is another's poison. I can think of few things that would make me happier than coming home to find lamb chops on my doorstep, but clearly you are happier finding nothing juicier than cards for a local minicab firm and a leaflet for cheap pizza.

This young lady has done nothing wrong. She has feelings for you, so, when you were ill, her natural inclination was to care for you. When she discovered that you found this a bit suffocating, she did what you asked and backed off. So far, so blameless.

I think the real problem here is that you simply don't like this woman very much and your flu has just fast-tracked the issues. Good. End it as soon as possible. All over London, young men are desperate to be mothered and to trip over meat. If you want to lie in bed shivering with flu, holding a silent phone and picking at a lukewarm Pot Noodle, who am I to stop you? Enjoy.

Dear Graham,

I'm a fairly normal single bloke in my late twenties. I split up with my last girlfriend about a year ago and since then have had no luck finding a new one. The problem is that every girl I ask out gets really drunk on the first date. The last one passed out (from alcohol) on the dance floor and the one before that was so drunk that I had to carry her into her flat and tuck her up in bed. I'm a gentleman and wouldn't dream of taking advantage, but this hasn't exactly done wonders for my confidence. Is there something wrong with me, or am I just picking the wrong girls?

Jim D, Newcastle

Dear Jim,

I read your letter with a growing sense of bewilderment, and then I saw where you live and it all fell into place. If you don't want to meet hordes of drunk women, I suggest you move.

Dear Graham,
My grandchildren object to my husband (86 and full of vim)
smoking his pipe. Brainwashed by their parents, they say that it
is a filthy habit and that my poor husband, whose only vice is
the occasional puff in his library, is 'killing' himself. The other
day, when we were on Marlborough High Street, my five-year-
old grandson tugged my sleeve, pointed at a complete stranger
and said: 'Granny, please tell that man to stop smoking.'
    What makes the young these days so self-righteous and
intolerant? In my day, we believed that what didn't hurt us was
none of our business.

Patricia L, Wiltshire

❝ Next time your grandson mouths off about someone in the street, remind him that the person he is talking about doesn't still wet the bed, is allowed to stay up late enough to watch *South Park* and is big enough to go on all the rides at Alton Towers. ❞

Dear Patricia,
There is no one quite as priggish and full of self-certainty as a child.
I suspect it has always been thus, but what has changed are the
attitudes of grandmothers. Don't try to reason with the Nazis
in nappies, just tell them to shut up and give them bags of snacks
with enough E-numbers in them to keep their parents awake for
several days.

Have a bit of backbone. Your husband didn't live to the ripe old
age of 86, smoking his pipe, only to spend his twilight years being
hectored by objectionable children. Your argument is really with your
own offspring. They should be instilling in their children respect for
their elders. Failure to do so is a far greater danger to society than
passive smoking.

Next time your grandson mouths off about someone in the street,
remind him that the person he is talking about doesn't still wet the bed,

is allowed to stay up late enough to watch *South Park* and is big enough to go on all the rides at Alton Towers.

Remember there is no law stating that you have to like your grandchildren. It is possible that they are simply not very nice little people.

Dear Graham,

My freeloading cousin, Miles, recently moved in with me and my wife, while looking for a place of his own. He is a lazy slob and within days had succeeded in turning our house upside down. About six weeks into his stay, my wife called me at work. That morning, after I had left, Miles, dressed in only his underpants, entered our room while Polly was still in bed and offered to give her some 'good and proper loving'.

Naturally, on hearing this, I threw Miles out. But now Polly has confessed that she made the story up to get rid of him. She has apologised, but says she was at her wit's end.

Just as I never expect to be forgiven by Miles, neither can I excuse my wife. Our relationship now seems tainted.

Charles H, Shropshire

Dear Charles,

The good news is that you and your wife seem perfectly matched. The bad news is that you are both morons. How on earth did either of you allow something as simple as an unwelcome house guest to spiral into this hideous mess?

Your wife's solution was as overblown as someone who wanted a drink of water calling the fire brigade to come round with hoses. Please don't feel that I'm placing all the blame on Polly, though. You allowed this intolerable situation to drag on for six weeks, and clearly there was no end in sight. Miles is your cousin and, therefore, on some level, your responsibility.

Your challenge is to learn from this and move on. Polly must communicate her needs to you and you must respond to them.

Charlie and Polly, a marriage made in bedlam.

Dear Graham,

My husband has been out of work for nine months and is being rather lackadaisical about finding a new job. So far he has applied for only a handful of nebulous-sounding managerial jobs on the internet - with no success.

We have four children and I have had to start dipping into my savings to pay the mortgage every month. I don't feel we can go on like this and, secretly, I'm furious with him. Part of me is quite old-fashioned and, even though I work (part-time), I was brought up to believe that men provide.

The truth is I'm feeling terribly let down. How dare he sit on his bottom all day when we have bills to pay and a family to bring up?

Although he's doing lots with the children and really helping around the house, there are days when I just want to kick him out of the door in the morning.

Please advise.

Bridget P, Harrogate

Dear Bridget,

What a horrible situation. Although you've written to me, I'm sure your husband is just as miserable. You didn't want to end up married to Mrs Doubtfire and, as sure as Robin Williams has a back hairy enough to shave into a map of Barcelona, your husband never wanted the role either.

I imagine his confidence is at an all-time low and that is why he is being a bit lazy about applying for jobs. Without doubt he will know how disappointed you are in him and that won't be helping his state of mind. What must be truly frustrating for both of you is that this problem has such a quick easy fix – get a job!

Keep the faith because he will and then, like magic, the hell you are both going through will be a distant memory. Talk to your husband, don't nag him. Does he want to start looking in different areas? Does he want to learn new skills? Is it time he changed direction?

I know that a 'yes' to these questions will mean you have to dip further into your savings, but, if this isn't the rainy day, when will it be?

You sound like a strong woman, Bridget, so hang in there. This will pass.

Oh, and if all else fails, tell him to get in touch. I need a part-time dog walker.

Dear Graham,

I came back from work early one day to find my husband of seven years standing in front of a mirror dressed in my fishnets and high heels and in the midst of wrapping himself up in one of my Diane von Furstenberg dresses. I was so shocked, I was literally speechless. Curiously, he was so absorbed in what he was doing that he didn't even notice me in the doorway. What on earth could have possessed him to dress up in my clothes? He is a devoted husband, loving father and, until now, has displayed no strange sexual tendencies. If anything, he's straighter than most men (Army background, partner in a law firm, etc).

I'm feeling very confused and couldn't possibly talk to anyone I know about it. Can you help?

Pamela T, Cheltenham

Dear Pamela,

It's Diane Von Furstenberg I feel sorry for. She probably has no idea that her lovely dress is being squeezed over the hips of an ex-Army lawyer and, even worse, worn with fishnets. And in Cheltenham! I certainly hope that your husband didn't get his sense of style from you, Pamela.

After seven years of marriage, a little cross-dressing in the privacy of your own home shouldn't threaten your relationship. I imagine that there is a little corner of his mind that wants to feel sexy and special, which by implication means that is how he feels about you.

Doubtless, he will be mortified if you mention your discovery. But I think you must, or the secret becomes yours instead of his and you don't need or want that burden.

Apart from stretching some expensive gowns, I can't see what harm he is doing. And you never know, a night between the sheets with him in some silky underwear might just scratch the seven-year itch.

Dear Graham,

Did you see Boris Johnson's recent column [Daily Telegraph, 12 July]? Did you read about all those poor girls nurtured on the meringue-laden pages of Brides magazine who long to have a ring on their finger?

Boris blames the dating crisis on the growth in the number of underachieving working-class men - the ASBOs and the hoodies. But I'd say the lack of decent chaps is just as common in the middle classes. Perhaps even in the upper?

My (middle-class) mother wasn't allowed to go to university because her father believed it would make her 'unmarriageable' (she married her first boyfriend at 21). Savage and politically incorrect though it might sound, did my grandfather have a point?

I'm typical of my generation of middle-class girls, ie highly educated (university degree plus PhD), averagely attractive, still young enough to have a family (33) and permanently single. I'd like to know what's going on. Where are all the men? What are we supposed to do if we want marriage and children?

Helena F, Suffolk

Dear Helena,

I despair of you. You think that it is your enormous intellect which is frightening men off and yet you are so stupid that you are taking something that Boris Johnson said seriously and, what's more, writing to me and expecting me to do the same. How on Earth do you think that hoodies with ASBOs are causing a dating crisis? Have you and Boris not noticed that for every spotty-faced youth breaking car aerials there is a greasy-haired lovely with pink and grey marbled legs leaning against a nearby wall, fag in hand?

There is a lid for every pot or, in this case, a hood for every thug. If you really want to date, spread your net wider – or lower your standards. Finding a partner isn't like filling in a job application. The old adage about kissing a lot of frogs is true except it's highly unlikely that you will ever find a prince, merely an acceptable frog – step forward, Boris.

There is no dating crisis, just a generation of people who have been lied to and promised more than our parents' generation. Harness the intelligence you claim you have and realise that men are simple creatures and always have been. Send out the right signals and they will come. Laugh at their jokes, find them interesting and most of all, on the first few dates – don't compete!

If that sounds unbearable, then enjoy being single because it really is your choice.

Dear Graham,
My 33-year-old boyfriend is being posted to Luxembourg for two years and has asked me to go with him. Apparently it's one of the dullest places on earth - full of very rich, very old people and their very small dogs. I simply can't face it. If it was Paris, New York or even Madrid, I'd go like a shot. But Luxembourg? He's very excited about it but then he grew up in Lincolnshire.
Please let me know how I can stay put without breaking up with him.

Oriel D, Herts

Dear Oriel,
I can't quite put my finger on why I find your letter annoying, but I do. Let's be brief. Tell him the truth. You have made a complicated problem out of something that is very simple. He's moving somewhere for two years where you don't want to go. I don't think you are being that unreasonable since I'm assuming you have a job and friends.

It's simply a case of planning your holidays together and doing a couple of weekends a month. He's not going to the moon and it's only 24 months. If he takes the hump and dumps you, then it probably wouldn't have lasted anyway.

Maybe that's why I found your letter irritating – it's not really a problem.

Ask Graham

Dear Graham,
I fear my 52-year-old wife is becoming a laughing stock. The problem is that she has started using the same 'street' slang as our 15-year-old daughter, who, like all her privately educated friends, is currently going through a 'Jafaican' phase. The other evening she described a mutual acquaintance as 'butters' and she peppers her conversation with words like 'sick' and 'bare', which I have deduced mean 'great' and 'very'.

Quite apart from the fact that I find it a horribly embarrassing affectation in an otherwise sensible middle-aged woman from Berkshire, she is becoming almost as difficult to understand as our daughter. How do I tell her she is making a fool of herself?

Anthony P, Chilton

Dear Anthony,
You are so distracted by the 52-year-old Ali G getting the reusable Waitrose bags out of the boot of the car that you have missed your first problem – your 15-year-old daughter lives in Berkshire but she is speaking like a Jamaican drug dealer. What happened to Pony Club? Have the Girl Guides become the Ku Klux Klan with berets?

Your family is spiralling out of control and all you do is write to me. Put down the paper, Anthony, and act!

How do you tell your wife she is making a fool of herself? She is over 50 and I presume you have been married for at least 15 years. You say: 'Darling, you are making a fool of yourself.'

Personally, I would be tempted to follow this with: '…and I want a divorce', but you are clearly a nicer person than I am. Happily, your spouse has handed you a secret weapon in your battle against your daughter's stupidity. Take her aside and ask her how pathetic she thinks her mother sounds. Then reveal to her the awful truth – that she sounds that lame to the rest of the world.

If this doesn't bring her to her senses, then I fear the only realistic option is for you and your family to emigrate to Jamaica.

Ask Graham

Dear Graham,

When does a tipple in the evening become one drink too many? I live on my own and when I take the bins out on a Tuesday evening I'm always a bit shocked by the number of clanking bottles in my orange recycling bag. Somehow no evening is complete without a lovely glass or two (or three) of vino. And thanks to my giant balloon-shaped Riedel glasses I can (almost) fool myself I'm keeping within the recommended limits.

It's a rare day that I practise any kind of temperance and among my friends, all 30-something professionals with hectic social lives, my drinking is normal. None of us is ever drunk, in the rowdy, destructive sense of the word. We don't run wild in town centres, terrorise our neighbours or beat up our loved ones. We just consume an awful lot of Rioja and then talk an awful lot of rubbish.

Without giving up completely (no AA meetings for me!), I'd like to quietly cut down. Any tips?

Patsy T, west London

Dear Patsy,

I admit to a certain self-consciousness as I attempt to give you advice. I've lost count of the number of times I've been at the bottle bank unloading the debris of my own personal consumption when a passer-by has asked: 'Been having a party?' Too often I wake in my house in rooms that aren't my bedroom and there are nights when I wouldn't like to stand in a court of law under oath and describe exactly what happened.

Do I have a problem? I don't ever cancel appointments due to hangovers, show up at work with vomit on my shoes or wake up in the street, so I choose to say no. Should I cut down? Probably.

Of course, the question we should both be asking ourselves is: can we cut back? There is an attitude with drink that it has to be all or nothing, but that seems as if you are giving alcohol all the power. You need to learn to control it and not the other way round. An obvious thing to do would be to invest in smaller glasses. Spritzers are an option for the white-wine drinker, but perhaps the easiest thing to do is bring in some rules. No wine before 8.30, perhaps, or no drinking alone.

If you have real trouble doing any of these things, maybe your problem is more serious. It's hard to say what the difference is between a bon viveur and a drunken slag. Tread carefully.

Dear Graham,

I'm a 39-year-old gay guy who runs a thriving investment firm. I have a good group of friends, most of whom have been happily coupled off for seven years or more. Meanwhile, I struggle to get a decent date with anyone remotely compatible. A lot of the guys I meet seem content to be single and short-termist.

I go to gay social groups and bars in the right part of town, but it doesn't seem to help. Internet dating has also failed. Potentially part of the problem is that I'm a little on the serious side, nearer Owl than Tigger, with perhaps a dash of Eeyore. I'm not exactly hunk material - not a Shrek but more than a hint of Mr Bean.

I ought to be satisfied with the prosperity my career has brought me, but the absence of a companion is really getting me down. I can't get a dog because I travel too much. Any advice?

Simon J, Manchester

Dear Simon,

Stop. Deep breaths. You seem to know a great deal about yourself and practically nothing about other people. True, a bookish Mr Bean won't fly off the shelves, but it can't help matters when you equate getting a pet with having a relationship with a fully functioning human being. Boyfriends tend to be slightly more complicated than a dog that is able to feed himself when you are away.

You might also consider how attractive it is for someone who is nearly 40 to describe everything in terms of children's cartoon characters. Not cute.

The reality is that you may never meet the man of your dreams because he only exists in dreams. You need to get on with the life you're actually living. How many happy marriages have been eaten away waiting for the baby that never arrived? How many fabulous people judge their own lives a failure because they haven't got a partner?

Don't waste all the happiness you could have in your life by pining for something that may never happen. We can't pick and choose the lives we lead. There is no emotional equivalent of 'must have outdoor space' and so I suggest you embrace the here and now. You don't have to lie about it to yourself or others. Yes, you'd like to be with someone, but it seems that isn't on the cards.

The only practical bit of dating advice I can give you is to leave Manchester, where there are far too many gay men. Move to some little town where, because of a lack of choice, you may find someone willing to go out with you. Nobody would choose canned vegetables, but if that's all there is in the cupboard...

Dear Graham,
Just after New Year, I met a handsome 30-year-old American in the electrical department of Peter Jones. He was buying a SCART cable for his plasma TV, I was buying an iPod. We ended up going for drinks at the Royal Court, then dinner at Tom Aikens, and each of our five dates since then has been brilliant. The problem is nothing has happened, even though he's obviously keen. We are both in our early thirties. What should I do? Should I pounce? Would he be shocked? (He is teetotal and from Boston.)

Jules L, London

Dear Jules,
One word screams out from your letter and quite frankly explains everything – teetotal! Without a little vino in the Garden of Eden, the Bible would have been a very short book indeed. I'm afraid to say that, short of plying him with a sneaky sherry trifle, you are going to have to speak to him about it.

Let him know that he is on to a dead cert, tell him that you find him attractive and then ask him how he feels about your relationship becoming physical. The answer, of course, may not be what you want to hear – he may only want you as a friend, there might have been a tragic accident on the climbing frame as a child or there is always the possibility of the old gay chestnut, but at least you'll know.

Then you'll either have a happy and rampant sex life or you can return to the electrical department and see what else it stocks.

Dear Graham,

My girlfriend is always having a go at me. It seems she can't accept that I'm just an average 30-something man who likes relaxing with a cold beer in front of the telly. I'm never going to be able to give her the kind of banter she gets with her girlfriends, nor do I want to. Like most men I'm pretty straightforward and only talk when I've got something to say. Why can't she leave me in peace?

Everything is fine between us and we have a good time together, but these days she's always nit-picking. If it's not my clothes that are wrong, it's the job I do (computer analyst), or the food I like eating (meat and two veg). Her latest campaign is to get me to join a gym and eat more fruit. Every time I go past the fruit bowl, she badgers me.

She's a great girl, but I'm getting really cheesed off. How can I get her to calm down and stop nagging?

Simon C, Totnes

❝ A girlfriend is for life, not just half-time. ❞

Dear Simon,

Your letter makes me nervous. Perhaps your girlfriend is being unreasonable, or – and this is what I fear is true – perhaps she is going out with a fat, sullen drunk.

If she really is a 'great girl', then I suggest you listen to her a little or she will find a man who doesn't just slump in front of the TV not speaking to her and slowly turning into Les Battersby in *Coronation Street*.

I'm not sure you are ready for a relationship. If your girlfriend does stray and you end up in the boyfriend equivalent of the Battersea Dogs Home, I can't imagine girls rushing to take you home. A girlfriend is for life, not just half-time.

Ask Graham

Dear Graham,

My younger sister is dating a merchant banker, who picked her up in the bar at Sketch and has been plying her with Dom Pérignon and Tiffany jewellery ever since. I can see the attraction - it's the old chestnut of her looks and his money. The problem is the man is divorced (with kids), twice her age (she's 22) and deeply unpleasant. Where to begin? He's arrogant, pompous, offensively right wing and very sexist.

He is in every way the antithesis of her sweet and gentle ex, who grew all his own veg and led walking tours in the Pyrenees for a living.

My husband, who is a human-rights lawyer, won't have him in the house. I've tried not to interfere, hoping it was just a rebound, but my sister appears to be moony-eyed with love. What do I do? Do I interfere and risk alienating her? Or do I just lie low and hope she eventually sees sense?

Sophie B, London

Dear Sophie,

Here's a handy fact. Your sister isn't you. A human-rights lawyer or a vegetarian wandering around Andorra may push all your sensitive buttons, but perhaps the younger sister is the yin to your yang. This new man may be hideous in your eyes but who else was she going to meet in the bar at Sketch? It's not exactly the sort of place where she was going to bump into a male nurse with an interest in butterfly conservation.

I'm not saying that she is lost to you for good, but you should allow her to enjoy her money-fuelled walk on the shallow side. Clearly, it's a reaction to the endless dreariness of her last boyfriend and it could even be her way of saying that she doesn't want to end up living your life.

It must be horrible to see this woman you thought you knew drifting into a world you hate, but there is nothing you can do. Only she can realise that she is making a mistake.

Ask Graham

Dear Graham,

My boyfriend seems to think that I'm the new nanny. He's divorced with three children of his own and last weekend - just six months into our relationship - I found myself having to single-handedly host a birthday party for 19 five-year-olds.

Just minutes before the party was due to start, he fled to work, saying he had an urgent deadline, leaving me to organise endless rounds of musical bumps. When he reappeared several hours later, looking distinctly sheepish and clutching a bunch of garage flowers, I could barely speak for exhaustion and fury.

He has joint custody of the kids with his ex-wife and I think he's struggling to cope. I understand that things are tough for him but I feel as if I'm being taken for a ride. What's your view?

Faith L, Whitstable, Kent

> **❝** Dating a single father-of-three was never going to be a picnic, but nor does it need to be the opening 20 minutes of *Saving Private Ryan* with facepaints. **❞**

Dear Faith,

My view is that you don't really need me to tell you what you already know. Garage flowers? Your boyfriend has behaved appallingly. This in itself doesn't make him a monster, but you are going to have to lay down so much law that perhaps this relationship isn't worth the effort. Only you can decide.

This man clearly can't cope. I am sympathetic to a point – I'm sure being divorced with three children isn't as easy as an afternoon at the aquarium followed by pizza, but he is doing nothing to help himself.

By ignoring his inability to manage, he is not giving you the choice to help him.

If he had admitted how much he was dreading the birthday party, you could have stepped into the breach and helped him through the crisp-packet hell of it all. Dating a single father-of-three was never going to be a picnic, but nor does it need to be the opening 20 minutes of *Saving Private Ryan* with facepaints.

Talk to him. Explain that you are willing to help but he has to take the lead, and remind him above all else that garage flowers should only ever be purchased when going to visit someone in a coma – and even then, you'd better pray that they don't wake up.

Dear Graham,
I'm a 31-year-old American financial analyst with no life. Most nights, I get home too late to do anything but hit the sack. At weekends, all I do is sleep, watch bad movies and eat take-out food. I won't be going home to Wisconsin for Thanksgiving because I can't take time out of my job.
I don't have a social life unless you count client meetings.
After living in Britain for a year, I've only got to know my ground-floor neighbour, a hilariously uptight Englishman who is always complaining about my drumming (I took it up in college - it's good for tension).
Am I a loser? How do I get out of this rut?
Michael W, east London

Dear Michael,
This isn't rocket science. Leave the house. I understand that during the week all you do is work and sleep but, come the weekend, you should brush your teeth and do something.

While it's true that an American accent isn't exactly a passport to popularity in London, I'm sure there must be some percussion workshops going on somewhere in this great capital of ours. Personally, I'd rather watch Jodie Marsh's wedding video than attend such an event, but I'm guessing it'll be right up your alley.

Remember that society doesn't owe anyone friends – you have to make the effort. Later in life, when the only person you see all day is the man delivering meals on wheels, you'll be sorry that you wasted all the amazing opportunities that London can offer.

Oh, by the way – buy your neighbour a bottle of wine.

Dear Graham,

My beloved only daughter, Joanna, went off to Venice last weekend and got married secretly. I am heartbroken. From the day she was born, I've been looking forward to planning a wonderful wedding for her. It's dreadfully upsetting that she's gone and tied the knot on the sly, excluding me. And in a foreign country where she knows nobody.

When I confronted her about it afterwards - in tears - she said she hadn't wanted any hassle or stress. She argued that it was a private thing and I would have wanted a big, noisy, splashy wedding, packed with relatives she never sees and doesn't particularly like.

I suspect her other half - a chippy Northerner - is at the bottom of all this. What really worries me is that he's going to make her miserable. Call me old-fashioned but it seems such a shabby way of marking such a momentous event.

My husband, who is disappointed, too, but is pretending not to be, says that at least we didn't have to 'fork out'. But it's not about money, is it?

Maureen P, Somerset

Dear Maureen,

No, it's not about money and by the way the other thing it isn't about is you. This was Joanna's special day and if this is how she chose to celebrate it then so be it. An event that you view as penny-pinching and tight could be seen by many others as wildly romantic.

Venice isn't exactly Skegness with a fish-supper reception, is it? Judging from your egocentric sobfest in front of your daughter, I'm guessing you aren't the kind of woman who hides her feelings that well. Your new son-in-law is probably painfully aware of your low opinion of him. Why on earth would he want to spend his happy day with you?

The good news for your dream wedding plans is that the chances of any marriage lasting are extremely slim. Next time round, keep your mouth shut and maybe, just maybe, you'll get to wear your big hat. Try to make it about yourself again and I promise you that Joanna will end up tying the knot in front of some sweat-stained Elvis in Vegas.

Dear Graham,

My trustafarian landlord, who is unfortunately also my flatmate, thinks he's Damien Hirst and keeps preserved tarantulas in glass. Most of the time he's away building mud huts in Africa, but when he's home he pulls all his artefacts out of the bedroom and starts attempting to 'decorate' the house with his macabre collection.

I am really scared of spiders - even dead ones - and have to flee the house, gibbering all the way to the bus stop to keep myself calm. It only takes a glimpse of a tarantula while I'm eating my cornflakes in the morning to make me scream with terror.

I've asked him to remove the spiders, but within days they always pop up again in some unexpected place, whether it's above the lavatory cistern or next to the tennis rackets in the hall. Perhaps he thinks it's funny, but it's genuinely upsetting.

Short of moving out, what would you do in my place?

Fanny M, London

Dear Fanny,

The first thing you must do is stop writing to me. You have a morbid fear of spiders and you decided it was a good idea to rent a room from a man who collects them? Are you the Mayor of Idiot Town?

I think you'll find that Jeremy Clarkson doesn't have a vegetarian roller-skater as a lodger. And I long ago stopped sharing a house with men who like home-brewing and have lap-dancing-club loyalty cards.

If he was your roommate, you might have some right to complain, but this man owns the apartment. The only tiny bargaining tool you have is the rent, but it doesn't sound like that would really be an issue for him. I'm not defending him – he does sound like a howling moron – but you chose to move in with him. Short of moving out, there is only the vague hope that he might get eaten by some wild beastie while building a mud hut. Next time, Miss Muffet, examine the tuffet a little more carefully before you unpack your curds and whey.

Dear Graham,

I am a three-times divorced 56-year-old woman with an unusually open attitude to men and dating. My last boyfriend was a 28-year-old Lebanese student who I met on the number 10 bus. It didn't last, but it was very romantic all the same, and he still sends me wonderful handwritten letters from Tripoli where he lives. I am currently seeing a 35-year-old basketball player from Baltimore and the age gap isn't an issue for either of us.

The problem is that it's an issue for other people – friends, family, society at large. My friends don't approve at all, my daughter finds me 'embarrassing' and people tend to stare at me and my new boyfriend in restaurants, especially if we hold hands or act smoochily.

If men can date younger women without raising eyebrows, why is it so appalling when things are the other way round?

Violet T, London

Dear Violet,

What's the real problem here? Is the disapproval of others really that disturbing or is it more to do with your nagging fear that they might be right? One of the great joys of being alive is how mysterious the ways of love can be. But, Violet, I do feel that at the age of 56, with three unsuccessful marriages under your belt, you should perhaps have solved some of the mysteries.

Going out with young guys can be wonderful – the feel of young skin, the excitement of their virility. But I fear it will always end in humiliation. You know that no matter what he says or does, he is looking at the 25-year-old waitress. The reason it seems to work better when the sexes are reversed is that women have a different set of priorities to men.

Catherine Zeta-Jones can stay married to a tortoise because he is a multi-millionaire and father of her children, but people look on in horror when they catch sight of some young Lothario kissing a bag of prunes in a dress. I fear that, deep in our psyche, it is all about fertility. The sight of an older lady with a young buck breaks some rule of nature.

Please don't think for one second that I am telling you to stop, but don't expect other people to like it.

I imagine your friends and family are just worried for you and wary of problems further down the road if these relationships continue.

I hope you are finding happiness in all this unconventional dating but, to be honest, Violet, I find something heartbreaking in the phrase 'wonderful handwritten letters from Tripoli'. You deserve so much more but I'm not sure you are going to find it in the places you are looking.

Dear Graham,

My boyfriend and I split up in October after a seven-year relationship but we still sleep together. We don't go on dates or anything like that, nor do we cook each other dinner or even share a bottle of wine. We just meet up, usually very late on a Saturday or Sunday evening, and have sex.

Physically, we are very in tune with each other, but it's always incredibly soul-destroying in the morning when he acts as if nothing happened and we go back to not being together. It always takes me a few days to pick myself up and banish the severe misery that engulfs me.

I guess I'm just clinging on, aren't I? Is my secret hope that we rekindle things properly a foolish one?

Imogen C, Glos

Dear Imogen,

If you continue to give this man unconditional sex on a regular basis, not only is your hope of rekindling this relationship a foolish one, it is borderline psychotic. I understand how confusing it must be for you because in that moment he seems to be so full of love and desire for you, but the low value you are placing on yourself and your needs means that I doubt he is taking any of it seriously at all.

Right now you are a sexual 24-hour garage – you need to become an organic farmers' market. If you really do want him back, withhold sex and not just for a month: let him wait six months to a year.

If he still wants you then, there is hope. If not, he will have moved on. Either way, you will have your answer.

Dear Graham,
After watching that Asian marriage broker on television
[Aneela Rahman, Arrange Me a Marriage, BBC2], I've decided
to be more open-minded about men in the hope that this year I
can find a boyfriend. So, even though I'm an attractive 35-
year-old, I'm no longer going to expect to land a tall,
handsome man who can dance, drive, doesn't snore, has a job
and is under 50. I'm going to be open to all-comers and be
non-judgemental.
  But what do you think should I be looking for instead?
Aneela talks about the importance of families getting on but, as
half of my family don't speak to one another, that's just not an
option. What in your view are the real deal-breakers?
                                    Penny B, Bury St Edmunds

❝ The very best we can hope for from the people we choose to spend our lives with is that, when we are with them, we feel like a better version of ourselves, not an edited highlights package. ❞

Dear Penny,

I don't know how long you've been single but you sound desperate enough to make a monumental mistake. Using phrases like 'be less judgemental' conjures up images of you writing to tattooed lovelies on Death Row. Friends who are in relationships often berate their single friends for being too fussy, but this is really just their way of urging you to be as unhappy as they are. Being with someone will always be about compromise but the trick is to learn when you have given away too much. The list you give means nothing. Meet the right man and you would throw it out the window – equally you don't want to become too open. There is nothing very attractive about turning yourself into a fleshy version of Cinderella's slipper by trying on a lot of men until you find the right one.

  For me, there is only one real deal-breaker. Does being with the person in question mean that you cut good friends out of your life or alter the food you eat, the movies you watch, the music you listen to?

Never lose yourself in a partner because ultimately we are all alone. I think the very best we can hope for from the people we choose to spend our lives with is that, when we are with them, we feel like a better version of ourselves, not an edited highlights package.

It's a new year, Penny – make it the year you become happy in your own company and others will surely follow.

Dear Graham,
On my birthday I received a card and letter from a girlfriend whom I split up with 30 years ago. In her letter, she explained how I had been the love of her life, why she thought our relationship of nine months had ended and how her life had been miserable since then. I have no wish to have anything to do with her, but am at a loss as to how to respond. Do I ignore it, or write and explain that it is a part of my life I would prefer to forget?

Tony O, Chippenham

Dear Tony,
Don't pretend – you are thrilled to have received this letter. Your concern suggests that you think these are the thoughts of a well-adjusted human being. I can imagine you reading it aloud to anyone who will listen. Of course this woman wasn't able to get over you for 30 years. Who could blame her?

Don't flatter yourself. Clearly this letter has nothing to do with you. The writer is deeply unhappy and, in her desperate search for joy, she has recalled a time in her life when she wasn't quite so miserable. You could ignore it, but that seems rude.

Why not send a short reply saying that you are very flattered and that you remember that time fondly? Explain that you would prefer not to meet up because you will have both changed so much it could destroy your precious memories.

Of course, we could both have got this wrong. Maybe she has sent this letter to every guy she ever dated in the hopes of getting a 'for old times' sake' shag. I've heard of worse ideas.

Dear Graham,

I'm dreading my summer holiday in Rhodes this year. I'm overweight and feel the problem is so bad that I'm beyond help. I refuse to let my husband see me naked so you can imagine how I feel about hitting the beach in a bikini. Sometimes I envy those Arab women in their burkas, able to cover up all their wobbly bits.

When I was younger I had a lovely slender figure, but since I've had three children the pounds have piled on. I'm also plagued with nasty thread veins and very bad cellulite. I hate hospitals so liposuction is out of the question and it's too late for Weight Watchers (we leave in two weeks' time). Although I've been frantically scrubbing my legs with one of those prickly loofahs, they're just as bumpy as ever.

I'm not dangerously fat - only a size 16 - but my confidence is really low at the moment. Beach life is the last thing I feel like, but it's too late to change our holiday. Tell me what I should do.

Stella P, North Yorkshire

Dear Stella,

I understand how much you must be dreading your holiday. In your mind lurks that woman in a bikini who advertises every bottle of sun protection, every flight and every hotel. The good news is that she is busy modelling for ads – she won't be there.

The beaches will be packed with women like you with a variety of imperfect lumps and limbs. The beach is a great leveller – I refer you to every cover of *Heat* magazine. Learn to love the body you have because I'm not really getting the impression that you want to change. Someone who was really unhappy would be taking more serious measures than waving a loofah at the problem.

Let it go and have a great holiday.

Ask Graham

Dear Graham,

I have appalling taste in men. I've lost count of the number of bounders, rotters and good-for-nothings I've dated over the years. One boyfriend abandoned me at midnight at Lagos airport (he snaffled the last seat on an outbound plane). Another dumped me at my own birthday party, then spent the night with my former best friend. Now that I've reached the grand old age of 32 I'm absolutely determined to pick a solid, loving, dependable type, who will father my children and love me even when I'm grizzled and hoary.

There are still quite a few decent men out there, but the problem is I never fancy them. Torn between a weekend hill walking in Wales with a nice, normal guy and an illicit, no-strings weekend in Paris with a man who will never hold my hand in public, it's a no-brainer. I can never resist the charm of the cad. How do I go about rewiring my brain before it's too late and my eggs dry up?

Minna D, Essex

Dear Minna,

Excuse me while I pop on a wig, slip into a fat suit and go all Oprah on you. This has nothing to do with men and everything to do with you. For some reason you think that these rubbish boyfriends are all you deserve. Or perhaps you have fallen into the trap of believing that, because these cut-price Colin Farrells are so miserly with their affection, the little bit they bestow on you is somehow worth more than the straightforward generous love of a decent man.

True, the bounders and rotters can be exciting, but the sad truth is that, as you are 32, they will probably quit before you get a chance to outgrow them.

There is a series of questions you must ask yourself. Why do you apparently enjoy being unhappy? What is the reason you crave drama? What makes you smart enough to spot a pattern but too stupid to stop it?

Kate Moss is a supermodel and even she's managed it. I understand the attraction you feel, but I beg you to try to break the cycle before you end up doing a photo-shoot in *OK!* with Darren Day.

Ask Graham

Dear Graham,

Over the past year I've met a lot of new single people and we've become quite a gang. I've grown close to several of them and it feels like it's more than just a new crowd of party people. I really value them because, until I met this lot, life was quite quiet. All my old friends are married with kids.

Very gradually I've fallen for one of the chaps. I let myself think that it might even come to something, though I don't have much confidence in that department. He was very tactile, always sitting close and putting his arm around me, to the extent that other friends were wondering what was going on. So the other day I declared myself. Reaction: total surprise.

He was charming about it, saying he was flattered but the spark wasn't there for him, though he thought I was wonderful. I'm very upset as I had allowed myself some ridiculous projections into the future. Still, I'm a seasoned enough campaigner to know I've got to move on and I'm already doing well on that front.

What worries me more is how I could have got it so wrong. What am I missing? I thought that if a chap sits or stands close, strokes my hair and rubs my shoulders as we chat to friends, it's a sign that he's interested. Is that a normal way for 'mates' to behave? How can I do better next time?

Ada (40), London

Dear Ada,

You are 40 and the great thing about getting a little bit is older is that we learn nothing. The only thing age teaches us is new ways for our heart and loins to humiliate us. While some man is shifting uncomfortably and assuring you he is very flattered, this, of course, is scant comfort. But wouldn't you rather let your heart be a ping-pong ball in an under-15s amateur tournament than always be certain of the emotional outcome?

You did nothing wrong and you can do nothing better next time. Who knows what was going on with Mr Touchy-Feely? Maybe he was trying to pluck up courage. Perhaps he was making a point to someone else in the group. Maybe he's gay. The point is, if we choose to, we can imagine that a bowl of soup fancies us. 'Oh the steam was blowing

80

towards my face. When I put my spoon in the bowl the soup lapped right to the edge.'

Don't be put off by this knock-back, Ada. The heart is the Jordan of the human body – fearless, resilient and stupid.

Dear Graham,

My boyfriend and I are planning our first holiday and can't agree on what to do. I've had a juicy invitation to Italy from friends who have hired a fabulous villa in Ravello overlooking the sea, but he doesn't want to go. He says our first holiday should be 'just us'.

My worry is that, if we spend an entire week alone together, we might not get on. It's so much easier to sparkle when there are other people to perform for, don't you think? It is also more expensive doing the hotel option than sharing a villa with friends, and we are bound to end up somewhere grim.

How do I persuade him to change his mind?

Tara W, Hemel Hempstead

Dear Tara,

This isn't really about a holiday, is it? I fear your tan will last longer than your relationship. I admit that your option does sound a lot more fun, but it is sweet that he wants to spend time alone with you.

Even before you've stepped on a plane, I suspect you two are in very different places. It sounds as if he wants a girlfriend he can gaze at on a candlelit terrace marvelling at her skin and the way a gentle breeze has caught her hair – while you are still looking for a boyfriend to hold your drink while you go to the loo.

Changing his mind won't help. Even if he agrees to the villa, he'll hate it. Far better to delay your first holiday together until you are coming from the same place. If you ignore me, remember this: pack your clothes in separate suitcases, because the chance of you travelling home together is slimmer than Calista Flockhart.

Dear Graham,
The vanity of the young shocks and saddens me. My pretty
31-year-old daughter is obsessed with her appearance to an
unnatural degree, as are most of her contemporaries. She
doesn't have anorexia, but she calorie-counts obsessively,
behaves as though the world is coming to an end if she spots a
grey hair and spends a fortune on clothes, beauty treatments
and hair salons.

Every aspect of her appearance upsets her. I hate to think of
the money-grabbing cranks, facialists, pedicurists and Botox
practitioners who have built careers on my only child's
multiple neuroses. I know she is upset about being single - I
suspect this is what drives her into beauty salons - but I worry
that focusing on her appearance in such an obsessive, shallow
way, rather than developing lively interests that engage others,
puts men off.

How can I convince her that she's lovely as she is?
Katherine M, Suffolk

❝ Beauty may be in the eye of the beholder, but that also holds true for the person looking in the mirror. ❞

Dear Katherine,

You can't. Simple as that. Your daughter is 31, and if nothing you've said or done up to this point has had any effect, I doubt you will stumble upon a magic spell now.

I hope you aren't trying to make amends for any parenting mistakes you may have made earlier. Many a mother has crushed a daughter for ever with a thoughtless 'not with your skin' comment or a throwaway reference to 'thin hair like yours'.

I understand that it must be miserable to sit back and watch your adult child stumbling through life where once you could have rushed in and swept her into your arms to protect her from the corner of the table or the pan of hot milk, but it must be done.

Flatter your daughter as much as you want, but, until she believes that she's beautiful as she is, then the trips to the salon and beyond will continue. Beauty may be in the eye of the beholder, but that also holds true for the person looking in the mirror.

Maybe she should have a couple of drinks before she does her make-up – it works for me.

Dear Graham,
My brother recently let me know - I think by accident - that he and his wife, who is heavily into genealogy, regularly record telephone calls without informing people that they are doing so. When I asked why they found it necessary, my brother became angry and defensive.

I now strongly suspect that they also record face-to-face conversations. This thought has made me very wary of talking freely to them and I wonder if I should be sharing my suspicions.

Should I tell my other siblings that these recordings are being made and give them the chance to modify what they say? Or should I remain quiet?

Fred O (no address supplied)

Dear Fred,
I can only imagine what an interesting life you lead that your brother and his wife want to record every word you utter in their presence. Your brother isn't Tony Benn by any chance, is he? Granted, their behaviour is odd but, unless you are a master criminal or working undercover for MI5, I really can't see why you or anyone else should worry. They can tape away to their hearts' content, but who on earth is going to listen to it? A slide show of holiday photos from a month in Utrecht couldn't be more boring than listening to phone calls about the window cleaner not showing up, or what one should get the children for Christmas.

Maybe you should have a kind word with your sibling and explain that 'Big Brother' is just an expression and not a description of the duties of the first-born son.

Ask Graham

Dear Graham,

I know it sounds bad, but I absolutely hate my stepmother. My dad married her two years ago, but they have been together for five years. Because I live with my dad (who is a great guy), I have to live with her, too. She is a total witch and finds any excuse to blame me and shout at both me and my sister.

What makes it worse is that my dad doesn't seem to notice how she treats us. He is often out of the house when she's having a go at us. How can I tell him what she is doing without him hating me for it?

Jemma M, Surrey

Dear Jemma,

You don't tell me how old you are, but I'm guessing you are getting a harsh lesson in life far too early. It turns out that some things that seem very straightforward, such as love and loyalty, turn out to be very complicated. Just as you can hate your stepmother and love your father, so he can love both of you at the same time.

Trust me, your dad knows all about the tensions between you and his new wife. He is simply choosing to ignore them. If you confront him, he won't hate you but he might get annoyed or even angry, because you have forced him to acknowledge the situation.

I think you need to ask yourself what you want him to do. Surely it makes more sense to try to find some way of getting on with your stepmother, since it doesn't look like she's going anywhere fast. Try being nice to her. Remember she, too, is bound to find all of this very difficult.

You seem articulate, so I'm sure you could sit down and talk things through, so long as you make it clear that you aren't attacking her. I doubt the situation will ever be ideal, but if you all admit that to each other then I think it will make it at least bearable.

If nothing improves, perhaps ask to speak to a counsellor through your school or college. I'm sure he or she will be able to help you more than me. I'm guessing from the number of times the words 'evil' and 'stepmother' have appeared together in myths and legends over the years that this situation has never been very easy. Good luck.

Dear Graham,

I'm a grandfather (and theatre director) in my early sixties and what I want now is lots of casual sex, not a serious relationship.

I broke up with a long-term girlfriend recently and I feel years younger. It's a joy to be on my own and have huge fried breakfasts and wear the same socks for three days in a row. Now that I'm (not so) young, free and single, I can even smoke in bed. My children are a bit critical of what they describe as my 'gallivanting'.

But fortunately for me, my job throws lots of attractive and rather lonely women in my path. What man wouldn't make the most of it? Surely if I make it clear at the start that I don't want anything serious, I'm not hurting anyone?

My ex-wife (long remarried) is very forgiving and tolerant. Oddly it's our offspring who disapprove.

Seamus O'M, Surrey

❝ Frankly, I'm amazed that with your socks smelling like the cheese counter at Waitrose you can lure anyone into your love nest. ❞

Dear Seamus,

I think the pensioner doth protest too much. It seems to me that the person who needs convincing about your tarty, silver-haired approach to life is you. Frankly, I'm amazed that with your socks smelling like the cheese counter at Waitrose you can lure anyone into your love nest, never mind these young lovelies you describe.

If you are happy being (smelly) footloose and fancy-free, then I wish you well, but, perhaps when you focus on your heart and head rather than your nether regions, you'll realise that it is probably wiser to tend to your long-term relationships with your children than having one-night stands with young women who might be gorgeous, if a little nasally challenged.

Sexual gratification is marvellous at any age but, when you take the word 'young' away from free and single, it can all seem a little tragic. It might be time to keep your hands to yourself and stick your feet in a bath.

Ask Graham

Dear Graham,

When I lost my job six weeks ago, I couldn't bring myself to tell my wife. Every morning I shower, shave, dress for work, kiss my wife goodbye and drive to Tesco (my wife shops at Waitrose), where I stock up on drinks and sandwiches. I then drive to Windsor Great Park, where I spend most of the day sitting in the car listening to Radio 4 and reading P G Wodehouse. Occasionally I go for a walk, but I'm too nervous I'll be spotted to do more than a mad dash round one of the quieter bits of the park.

My wife is very attractive and 22 years younger than me, and I'm worried that when she discovers I'm broke she'll leave me for someone her age (35). We have always lived a rather glitzy life, funded mostly by my job, and by choice decided not to have children. I fear that her love for me is linked to my ability to provide. She gave up work when she married me and has a happy time playing tennis and seeing her girlfriends.

Given my age and the fact that the industry I work in, banking, is on its knees, I'm not optimistic I'll find a new job soon. Any advice?

David L (not his real name), Surrey

Dear David,

If only 'older and wiser' was more than just an expression. Whatever chance you have of finding a new job, I'm pretty sure you won't stumble on it in Windsor Great Park unless you've always longed for a career involving a lawnmower.

It is time to face up to the difficult situation you find yourself in. Your attractive wife will eventually notice that you have been living a lie. Who knows what might give it away: pockets full of Tesco receipts, deer poo on your tyres? Much better that you control how she hears the news and then you may discover that she actually loves you and not just your credit cards.

I feel it is my duty to point out that, charming as it is that you find her so attractive, at 35 you wife isn't exactly one of the Pussycat Dolls. She may have fewer options than you think, but if she does choose to leave you because you are no longer a cash cow, is that such a bad thing? You don't have children and clearly her wedding veil was so thick it impeded her ability to hear the marriage vows.

Let's not prejudge your wife, though. The best-case scenario is that you discover she has hidden strengths and a deep love for you, and together you face your uncertain future. The worst-case scenario is that you get to read Wodehouse in your kitchen instead of the car. Good luck!

Dear Graham,
Why are men so rubbish at talking on the phone? My fiancé is working in Houston for six months and, whenever we speak on the phone, it always feels as if I'm rabbiting on while he's not really there at all. He tends to just grunt, rather than want a proper two-way conversation. Normally, we talk for hours without running out of conversation, but that's when we're in the same room, rather than thousands of miles apart.
We do email and send texts but it's not the same as hearing the voice of the person you love. Can you train a man to be more phone-friendly?

Alex B, Kent

Dear Alex,
Progress can be made but you may as well accept right now that no straight man will ever be as good on the phone as you'd like. The training is simple – ask questions that require more than one-word answers. Chat about things that you know will provoke a response. Never ask him, for instance, if you think you should get your hair cut, instead just tell him how much it is going to cost.

Deliberately say something ill-informed about a subject he is very knowledgeable about. If he sees a movie or reads a book, then make sure you do too so you can talk about it. Above all, though, the golden rule is to shut up. The more you speak the less he will feel the need to. Also, don't worry if conversations are very short. All you really need to do is remind him you are alive and that he still loves you.

Remember, people rarely fall in love with someone who works in a call centre. Love is meant to be physical and he'll be home before you know it.

Dear Graham,
This is the third New Year in a row I'm spending on my own,
with a couple of bottles of excellent Médoc, a fine ready-meal
(partridge or wood pigeon from Waitrose) and a rather good
book, all accompanied by some Handel. To my annoyance, some
friends of mine have got wind of my unfashionably solitary
celebrations and keep badgering me about going to a small
dinner they're holding on New Year's Eve.

Fond of them as I am, I can't face the prospect of drinking
cheap Prosecco with them and their very dull neighbours, Sue
and Colin. On any other day of the year I would be willing to
be the sacrificial lamb - and haul myself over to their grim
house in Willesden - but New Year can really get me down in
the dumps if I'm with the wrong people.

I wonder how I can refuse their invitation without causing
offence?

Rupert L, north London

Dear Rupert,

I fully understand your hermit tendencies during the holiday season. A good time is all very well but the forced jollity of events such as New Year's Eve can be as much fun as a walking holiday in the Brecon Beacons with a vegetarian. Does anyone really enjoy looking around a room at midnight wondering if they are having a good time?

I must admit, however, that the evening you have planned for yourself does sound duller than puréed cardboard, but each to their own. Not going to the dreaded dinner party couldn't be simpler – you just need to hold your nerve.

The most straightforward plan is to accept the invitation, and then cancel because of illness on the day. This is incredibly rude, but it gets the job done.

The other option is to decline the invitation because you already have plans. Assure your friends that you would much prefer to spend the evening with them, but some obscure family member has suddenly insisted that you attend their party – maybe throw in an aunt visiting from Australia or Canada. Job done.

Just remember to draw your curtains very firmly and don't answer the phone. May auld acquaintance be ignored. Happy New Year!

Dear Graham,

Do all women want children? I'm a single guy of 35 and find the dating scene has really changed since my twenties and early thirties, when parties were rife with stunning available girls, none of them intent on marriage and motherhood.

Now that so many of my university contemporaries are hitched, there's a small but vocal pool of single girls in my circle, all apparently desperate to have a baby. Every time I go out I feel as if I'm being sized up for my breeding potential.

The truth is that I don't want children of my own, but it's not something you can say to a woman, is it? I broke up with my last girlfriend over this very thing. She wanted them, I didn't. Every now and then she rings me - drunk - in the middle of the night to tell me what a bastard I am.

Next time I meet someone I like, what's a delicate way to indicate that I'm not on for kids to avoid any awkwardness later on?

Andy, London

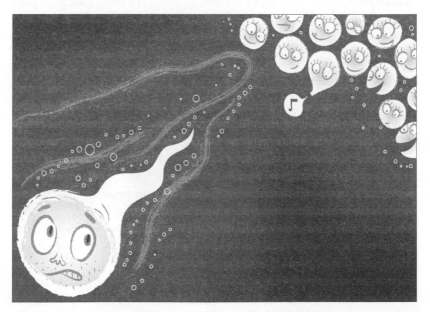

Every time I go out, I feel as if I'm being sized up for my breeding potential.

Ask Graham

Dear Andy,

You have every right to not want kids but you must accept that it's not something that will endear you to many. You don't make it clear what is so great about your life that having a child would spoil, and maybe you would change your mind if you met the right woman.

It strikes me that the internet and small ads were designed for this very situation. You are interested in niche dating so it makes sense to set out your stall immediately rather than waste a second of any woman's ticking womb clock.

Alternatively, you could wait 10 years before you settle down and all the clocks will have stopped.

Dear Graham,

I'm spending the Easter holidays in a Landmark Trust house with a group of friends, all single and in their early thirties. None of us has been in a relationship for years and - to put it mildly - we've all become a bit eccentric. The problem is that the host is the stingiest person I know. He is famous for disappearing whenever there's a cash till in sight in case he might be required to open his wallet. He's insisting on organising the food and I'm worried that we'll all starve - or worse - find ourselves miles from a shop or pub, forced to eat the mouldering contents of his London fridge.

What can I do to gently prise this job from his iron grip?

Anna M, Glos

Dear Anna,

Bring food! Pack lots of things that you can take home again if your friend turns around and surprises you all with a feast worthy of Delia before she discovered the microwave. Ham, pâté, vegetables, cheese and crackers all travel very well. I do not advise packing eggs or fish.

Encourage your other friends to do the same. Oh, and just a thought, you say that you have all become slightly eccentric. Do you think the others refer to you as the one who is obsessed with not having enough to eat? You are spending Easter in a Landmark Trust property, not on the moon – I promise you won't starve or start having to eat each other.

If all else fails, fill up on chocolate!

Dear Graham,

I am heavily pregnant, I feel fat, bloated and ugly and I find I just cry all the time, especially when people are rude. The other day I got on to a crowded bus heaving with schoolchildren and tourists and asked a man if he would mind giving up his seat for me. 'Why?' he said, staring at my bump rudely, as if it was the most disgusting thing he'd ever seen. 'Because I'm seven months' pregnant,' I replied. 'But isn't that just like being fat?' he said.

By the time he gave up his seat I was sobbing uncontrollably. Nobody said a thing - they all hid behind their newspapers and pretended nothing was happening. When things like that happen, I feel as if I don't want a child any more. What sort of world will our baby be born into when people are so cold and heartless? Whenever I try to tell my boyfriend how upset I get by these encounters, he just laughs and makes a mocking reference to my 'crazy hormones'.

Lottie I, Chelsea

❝ It is probably an inappropriate thing to say to a woman who is seven months' pregnant, but I do think you need to grow some balls. ❞

Dear Lottie,

Hopefully, most of this is to do with hormones, otherwise it is quite hard to justify blaming all the ills of humanity on one very rude man riding a bus. I understand it can't be nice being spoken to in such a manner, but, rather than give up on the entire human race, perhaps just make sure that you do a better job raising your child than that man's mother did of raising hers.

It is probably an inappropriate thing to say to a woman who is seven months' pregnant, but I do think you need to grow some balls. If you think things are bad now, just wait till you try breastfeeding in public. You need to learn to stick up for yourself.

The truth is, no one will ever be as interested in your pregnancy, or indeed your baby, as you'd like them to be.

People on the bus didn't react to the huge drama because it was in fact a tiny incident in their lives. All they saw was a man being rude but then giving up his seat. The end.

They weren't to know that you were experiencing the end of civilisation as we know it.

I understand that your new baby is your whole world. I hope that you have a great birth and that your new family is everything you hoped it would be. Just don't expect anyone else to care. Harsh but true.

Dear Graham,
I am a very happily married lady with an urge to be spanked by an older man, but not by my husband. I am not interested in anything sexual with these men (who are queuing up to do it), just the spanking. Do you think that this is being unfaithful or would you say just enjoy it? Would anything be gained by telling my husband, who is very liberal in all sorts of ways?
Marjorie M, Leeds

Dear Marjorie,
Why not try shoplifting in Singapore and see how much you like being spanked by a strange man in a non-sexual way? Fantasies are fine but imagine the reality of you bent over the arm of the sofa, Noel Edmonds on *Deal Or No Deal* talking in the background, while some bored neighbour slaps your bum. You have to admit that there is something depressingly Channel 5 about the idea.

Is there no way that your husband can satisfy your spanking desires? Maybe he could wear a disguise? It seems crazy to risk your marriage for what you describe as a non-sexual urge. You may have other men 'queuing up' to spank you but, trust me, if you act on your urges, they will expect some sort of sexual gratification eventually. You are playing with fire and if you continue on this path more than your bottom will get burned.

Dear Graham,

I am blessed, or should I say cursed, with the figure of a Page 3 girl, despite the fact that I am a very serious person and have a PhD in physics. For all my adult and part of my teenage life, I have had to endure the wolf whistles, jokes and building-site mockery that no normally shaped woman encounters. Men always expect me to be a party girl - big breasts mean fun - and when I'm introduced to people I don't know, they always talk to my boobs, not my face.

A friend advised me to go to Rigby & Peller, the lingerie shop, but, since I got fitted out there, my bosom has become more buoyant, rather than less.

Needless to say, I try to keep my cleavage under wraps, but, however primly I dress, it is almost impossible for me to walk down the street or enter a pub without being met with a volley of leery stares and inappropriate remarks. It seems that nature has played a cruel joke on me. The combination of a vast poitrine and the height of a leprechaun (5 ft 3 in) makes me pure pornography in men's eyes.

I have always despised plastic surgery, but now I'm starting to wonder: should I go under the knife?

Lucy N, Tunbridge Wells

Dear Lucy,

You may have a PhD, but I'm guessing you are not nearly as smart as you like to think you are. The reality is that your bosoms are bigger than either your brain or personality, so they are what people will respond to first, but that doesn't mean that, given a little time, they won't see the rest of you.

I do understand the frustration you feel as people constantly judge your book by its very fleshy cover. Try to see this as a plus rather than a negative. Your true persona is your secret and you should savour it as others make fools of themselves whistling and dribbling down their ties.

Plastic surgery seems like a very extreme step to take, especially since you'd be radically changing your body for other people rather than for yourself. In this instance, going under the surgeon's knife is closer to expensive self-harming than cosmetic self-improvement.

Why don't you start showing a little cleavage? If you give people permission to enjoy your body, maybe you will begin to as well. Having breasts just makes you a woman, not Jodie Marsh.

Dear Graham,
My wife and I took my 91-year-old widowed grandmother on
holiday to Seville recently. At 12.20pm at Gate 20 she
announced she was peckish (no matter that our flight had been
called) and said she wouldn't board the plane unless she had a
proper lunch first. Spotting a Garfunkel's, she insisted on going
there and promptly took over the whole establishment,
complaining loudly about the plastic menus and paper napkins
and quizzing the waiter about the 'fish of the day'.

While our flight was on last call, the saintly Brazilian waiter
served her salmon - where he found it I don't know. We did
catch the plane but the holiday was a failure as no hotels met
her exacting Edwardian standards.

My grandmother has now announced she would like to
move in with us. My wife says she'll divorce me if I agree. Even
though I get just as irritated as she does, I feel responsible for
the old girl and we do live in a large house. What would you
do in my shoes?

Dominic L, Cheshire

Dear Dominic,

If I were in your shoes, I'd look down and wonder where my trousers were because clearly you aren't wearing them in your house. Which idiot thought it would be a good idea to take a 91-year-old woman to Seville for the weekend? And how hard is it to say no to an old lady when there's a plane to catch? If she wants a sit-down lunch after a flight has been called, there is only one appropriate response – tell her she can't. This woman is your grandmother, not the Queen.

The thing about old ladies like your grandmother is that most of their pleasure in any given situation is derived from telling other people what's wrong with it. Think of her constant moaning as the purring of a cat.

The idea of your grandmother moving in is of course much more complicated than surviving a weekend in Spain. I do wonder why this has all fallen into your lap and not your parents', but maybe they've already made it clear they won't have her.

If your wife is serious about divorce, then you just have to decide which woman you prefer to live with. Your house may be large but having someone of your grandmother's age move in is very different from having a lodger. Perhaps you think you're being kind, but, if you aren't equipped to care for her, then is it really for the best?

I understand your dilemma, but isn't living with guilt easier than living with someone who is older than most of your furniture?

Dear Graham,

Why do all the single men left in Britain work in IT? I have been internet-dating energetically for about six months now (without success) and find that every man I meet works in this dreary, dandruff-laden profession. There are no doctors, lawyers, bankers, publishers or indeed anyone on the net with the sort of job I can relate to. Or, if there are, I haven't found them.

If a man tells me he's in IT, I'm afraid I get put off instantly. I want a boyfriend who's socially skilled, not a geek who prefers talking about bytes and links and URLs to having a normal conversation. Is that too much to ask?

A friend says you never know, the man might end up founding something like Google. Perhaps I'd even get to live in California. Or Seattle. But I'd so much rather stay at home with a nice, handsome publisher who loves dogs and Jane Austen.

Have I missed the boat? (I'm 33.)

Sarah-Jane N, Bradford on Avon

Dear Sarah-Jane,

You are looking for love via a computer and wonder why you keep meeting people who like computers? You cannot figure out why this should be? It's the equivalent of trying to buy a kitten by flicking through the small ads in *Dogs Today*.

I wonder if it's really a boyfriend you want or a different life, where you are played by someone else – a young Jane Asher perhaps.

Try living the life you actually have and see who turns up. It's unlikely that you'll meet the hero from a Joanna Trollope novel if you don't even own an Aga.

There is a particular sort of person who ends up missing the boat because they were looking for a plane – don't let that happen to you.

Dear Graham,

My 20-year-old son had an affair during his last year at school with a Brazilian dancer 10 years older than him, and they split up after just a few weeks. A couple of months later, she called to tell him she was pregnant with his child. At my insistence, he asked her to have a DNA test, but she got so upset (and he felt so guilty) that he moved back into her life. The baby - a boy - is now 10 months old and my son is trapped in an unhappy relationship that had already ended long before the child arrived.

I have done all the right things - helping the mother get proper medical care, ensuring she ate the right foods when she was pregnant, but I would like to know if the child is my son's - and my grandson. Given the mother's general demeanour (stacked heels, hair extensions, vampy make-up, scant clothing), I don't have a lot of faith that my son is her only conquest.

Although he adores his boy, it breaks my heart to see my son sucked into something that may not even be his responsibility - and at such a very young age.

I would never abandon the child - I just want to know the truth. A friend has suggested I take a sample of the child's hair from his hairbrush for DNA testing. Would that be a very immoral thing to do?
Patricia L, Stoke-on-Trent

Dear Patricia,

Ask yourself a few questions. Who is trapped in an unhappy relationship? Who may or may not be the father of a Brazilian dancer's child? Who is a fully fledged grown-up who needs his mother to back off big time?

I think you'll find that the answer to all these questions is your son. This is his life and his problem. I can only imagine how frustrating and upsetting it is to watch your child stumbling through life like a drunk in a pub car park but that is what you must do. Remember when he asked for a DNA test and ended up moving back into her life? Who's bright idea was that?

Patricia, you aren't helping. Stop obsessing about the child's paternity; it is irrelevant in this situation. DNA holds no answers and if you continue to act like a badly written character from *Footballers'*

Wives, I fear you may end up losing your own child. Again I say, Patricia, you aren't helping.

If I was to advise your son, it does sound like he should get out of this non-relationship. The little boy will gain very little being brought up around all this unhappiness, but it is your son's decision to make. I also wonder if things are quite as bad as you paint them. If the dancer is the man-eating vamp you describe, surely she could do better than shacking up with a 20-year-old student?

Unless, of course, that guy has a busybody mother who pays for everything.

Dear Graham,
For the past six months I have been exchanging emails with a girl I met through a mutual friend. We have been 'cyber-dating', but whenever I suggest meeting up she makes excuses, even though the emails she sends are bright, funny and suggestive, with lots of innuendo.

I know she was hurt in her last relationship. Do you think she's afraid of taking the plunge again?

I feel that if she just gave me one chance to impress I would be able to bring her some happiness. But how can I persuade her to meet for real?

Peter B, Worcestershire

Dear Peter,
Six months? I'm not sure if your persistence deserves praise or derision, but I love a challenge – let's smoke her out. First, for at least a month, make no mention of meeting – it's the cyber equivalent of moving downwind. Then try to get some really juicy bait, such as hard-to-get tickets to an exhibition. Casually mention that you have a spare ticket, but apologise that you won't be able to take her to lunch afterwards because you are very busy.

The chances of her believing this are slim, given that you found the time to spend six months emailing her, but it is vital that she doesn't feel trapped. If this softly-softly approach doesn't get results, give up or give her an ultimatum. If that fails, delete her email address and get on with your life – or perhaps just get a life.

Dear Graham,
I recently remarried after five years struggling to bring up two
children on my own, with very little support from my ex. The
problem is my new barrister husband has never been married
before. The noise and chaos of a family of three moving into his
house has been a major shock for him - and six months on he
may even be regretting taking us on.

I'm desperate for things to work out but it feels as if I'm caught
between two opposing camps. On the one hand I've got the
demands of my two kids, on the other I've got my new husband.

My son and daughter are seven and nine - and are both
sensitive and vulnerable. I worry that he is making his negative
feelings towards them quite obvious. How do I draw the two
camps closer?

Lydia L, Herts

Dear Lydia,

Are you familiar with the expression 'out of the frying pan into the
fire'? I fear that five years of wandering through an emotional and
financial desert has led you to the first oasis you could find, but I
worry it may have been a mirage. Where once there was a lonely,
unhappy barrister and a desperate and unhappy single mother now
there are four unhappy people and that makes no sense. It's like *The
Brady Bunch* directed by Mike Leigh.

Having said that, it has only been six months and the huge change
to his bachelor life will take some getting used to. Equally, your
children will have to learn that they are now going to have to share
their mummy with someone else.

As the go-between, I'm afraid it is up to you to take the strain. Make
time to be alone with your new husband. Get baby-sitters as often as
you can and remind him why he wanted to marry you.

Much harder, but surely not impossible, is to find things to do
together that both your children and the barrister will enjoy. Does he
have any outside interests? Sailing? Cycling? Kite-flying? The point is
to show him that having kids can add value to his life – they aren't just
noisy messy drains on his bank account.

Surely both of you realised this was never going to be easy and sure
enough it isn't. Tenpin bowling? Good luck!

Dear Graham,

My girlfriend chucked me two weeks ago. She had been feeling low for quite a while and, although it was a bit of a shock at the time, I now feel I'm partly to blame.

I ignored her distress signals in a typically male way, thinking it would pass and not really sure what I could do/say to make her feel better.

I really care about her and blame myself for the break-up. I should have listened to her and offered support. I miss her terribly. How can I win her back?

Christian B, Canterbury

Dear Christian,

Isn't hindsight a marvellous thing? My gut says you don't deserve this girl back and you should just get on with your life and apply the lessons you have learned to your next relationship, but there is a pale winter sun in the sky and I don't have a hangover, so here goes.

The first rule is not to tell her that you want her back. Simply be available to her. Text her and email her just to make sure that she's feeling OK. Then do those things you failed to do when you were together – listen and support. If she responds, there is still some hope, but if you encounter a firewall then it's a question of waiting or moving on. Imagine she gives you a glimmer of hope, then wait a few weeks before suggesting a meeting. Don't refer to it as a date, just a quick drink before you have to go and do something else that's close to where she works. After that, just see what happens.

What's interesting is that by then you may have gone off the idea of getting back together. There must have been a reason why you didn't care about her enough when you were together. Do you really miss her or just the idea of a girlfriend? Is it your heart that is hurting or your pride because she dumped you?

Taking things slowly will hopefully answer these questions and make the future clearer for both of you.

Dear Graham,
My wife - an attractive woman - has always been obsessed with her lack of volume in the bosom department. She is determined to have surgery in order to increase her breast size from an A to a D. The problem is we're rather short of cash - we're currently putting two children through private school - and at £ 2,500 a breast we can't really afford it.

You'd think that would be the end of the matter, but my wife is determined to push ahead one breast at a time. She says she's 'too desperate to wait' and has her heart set on getting one breast done this year and the other in twelve months time.

Needless to say, the surgeon has advised against it, but when my wife gets a bee in her bonnet she's a very tenacious woman.

Quite apart from the cost, I am very perturbed at the prospect of sharing my life for 12 months (possibly longer) with a woman who is built like a Page 3 girl on one side and a pancake on the other. What is a man to do?

Philip O, Manchester

"When it comes to plastic surgery and sushi never be attracted by a bargain. "

Dear Philip,
Although the operation may be called 'a' boob job, I think we all assumed the plural was implied. It's good you recognise that your wife's plan is an odd one, but I'm not sure you completely understand how barking at the moon, running naked down the high street, drinking your own pee, bonkers it is. If she has found a surgeon willing to agree with her, then I would search carefully for their name on the medical register.

I understand the need to budget, but a good rule to remember for life is that when it comes to plastic surgery and sushi never be attracted by a bargain. It's all very well to say your wife has a bee in her bonnet but that isn't quite as acceptable when it looks like she has the Andrex puppy in her other bonnet. Is all of this a threat because you have been promising her the operation for years and she has finally run out of patience?

I can't believe any woman or doctor would go through with this lunatic plan so either you call her bluff or you cough up the extra £2,500. The Government is desperate for the banks to start lending again and this might be the sort of investment your bank manager would be interested in. Not all inflation is bad but remember when it's all over it's not just the books you want to balance.

Dear Graham,
I've been with my girlfriend for 10 years and now, even though we're still in our twenties, she is dropping hints about marriage and babies.

We've been together since university, but I know that I don't want to marry her. Deep down I've always felt that things weren't quite right, even though she's gorgeous. It's not very admirable, but I've stayed with her partly out of laziness and partly because she cooks delicious meals, organises our social life, books our holidays and so on.

I guess I should grit my teeth and end it. But is there a nice way of dumping your girlfriend, without causing terrible distress?

Jake S, Bristol

Dear Jake,
Let's be clear here. 'Not very admirable' doesn't cover how you have behaved towards your girlfriend. You have stolen the best 10 years of her life and now you plan to replace her. She isn't a fitted kitchen – she's a woman who understandably believes you want to be the father of her children. You deserve to die alone in a ditch with a tramp's dog chewing off your ear.

Your girlfriend is gorgeous and does everything for you – how much better can a girlfriend get? My heart breaks for the poor woman but, trust me, you could never dump her, only release her from her prison of deceit. Do it now – there isn't a moment to lose. A nice way of breaking the news to her might be to show her these letters. I know that there will come a day when you realise what you've lost and perhaps even beg her to come back to you. That thought makes me smile.

Dear Graham,

One of my closest friends is married to a man who is in the throes of raging cancer and I feel enormously guilty about my failure to support her.

I am a youngish (49) widow and lost my husband 11 years ago in a similar way. Having spent over a decade trying to get over my own loss, I simply can't face going through the whole thing again.

It's terribly difficult, of course, to say this. And I know it will come across as totally heartless when my friend is going through such hell. But I simply can't be there for her. And because I've been there before myself I know just how helpless her situation is. I feel I'm incapable of saying those supportive, but essentially untrue things that she might want to hear.

Despite our long-standing friendship I would almost rather sever all ties now than get caught up in the untold misery and heartache that lie ahead for her. Even returning her calls is a tremendous effort for me.

Your advice would be so very welcome.

Celia D, Suffolk

Dear Celia,

You are dealing with very complicated emotions and it is clear that there will be no happy endings. I think the only thing you can do is be honest with your friend. Explain why you have been distant and you may be surprised at how understanding she is.

Perhaps your friendship won't survive since you won't be able to hold her hand as she goes through her personal hell, but surely it's far better if she at least understands why you have had to abandon her.

Once you have explained your own pain, you may find it easier to cope with hers.

Since you have been through this bleak time, it seems a real shame that your experience couldn't be put to some sort of good use. Knowing how far she has to fall and spotting the emotional pitfalls will maybe mean that you didn't suffer for no reason.

Could you ever consider that helping your friend – simply allowing her to voice her worst fears to someone who knows – might salvage something positive out of your pain and the loss of your husband? I hope the suffering ahead is brief and that your friendship can somehow survive.

Dear Graham,

My son has had a succession of very attractive girlfriends since his first year at Cambridge, almost 20 years ago.

Each time he brings a girl home I find myself praying fervently that she might be the one. But in his quiet, understated way he appears to be a bit of a Lothario. There is no actual 'type'. He's tried everything. I've liked most of them, especially the last one, who was less pretty than her predecessors but very sweet-natured and helpful in the kitchen. My husband, who rarely agrees with me, liked the French girl who looked a bit like Sophie Marceau and pouted energetically at breakfast.

Why can't he just settle down like his friends and make a proper commitment? In my day we didn't endlessly swap partners, we just got on with it.

My husband says he'll find the right one eventually (will he?), but I worry that he'll never make his mind up. What if he wakes up one day to find all the nice girls have gone and married other people? I am - it goes without saying - desperate for grandchildren. Our other son is homosexual so there's no hope on that front.

Eileen J, Devon

Dear Eileen,

You brought two children into the world. Congratulations. Neither of them is living the life you wanted them to. Commiserations. The only deal you make when you raise your children is that there is no deal. They are living their lives for themselves not for you.

The best thing you can do is to back off because I doubt that flicking through back issues of *Brides* magazine every time your son brings a girlfriend home is helping matters very much.

Hopefully, the problem is that you are so fabulous he cannot find a girl to measure up. Take it as a compliment and be glad you brought your son up to be the sort of man who doesn't just settle. You may yearn for grandchildren but surely not if they are the product of an unhappy marriage. And you never know, even your gay son may surprise you one day by bringing home a little bundle of joy.

It's a very modern world we live in, Eileen. I'm sorry things haven't worked out the way you hoped but allow your sons to find their own versions of happiness in their own way.

Dear Graham,

My son appears to be going off the rails. He split up recently from his girlfriend - a lovely girl who is the daughter of old friends - and has fallen in with a bad set at university. They are a gloomy lot who don't wash their hair, wear black from head to toe and favour body piercings of various kinds. On his last visit home, our son walked through the front door with a pierced eyebrow. My wife nearly wept.

Although I'm told that the Royal Family has made body piercing chic, my wife and I are quietly appalled. Our talented, healthy son, who was captain of his school cricket team, now looks like the sort of person who mugs grannies outside Tesco. What makes young people mutilate themselves in this way?

Far more worrying than his rather alarming appearance, though, are his job prospects. He graduates this summer from one of Britain's best universities, but will employers look kindly on a young man with mutilated eyebrows?

Nicholas L, Shropshire

Dear Nicholas,

I suggest you and your wife take a few moments and sit down together to watch an episode of *Hollyoaks* on Channel 4. While you've been living on Planet Clueless, the rest of us have been seeing children behaving like your son since the dawn of time. Some cavewoman probably wept when her son came home in shoes and told her he was a vegetarian.

Although what your son is doing is quite extreme, all it means is that he is stating his independence from you and his mother by joining another clan. You don't understand or approve because you're not supposed to.

I urge you to remain calm. You may have lived your life according to a preordained plan, but clearly your son has decided to shake things up a bit. When he leaves university, he may not even apply for the jobs you think he should. Don't be surprised to find him working in some alternative record shop or announcing that he's going to go travelling. It doesn't mean he'll never settle down, just that he is living his own life, not yours. Neither is better or worse, it's simply about choices.

Keep the faith. As long as your son knows you love him, no matter what, it seems to me you are doing your job as a parent. You decided to have a child rather than a dog and now you must live with the consequences.

Dear Graham,
I have been invited to a friend's birthday party at a karaoke bar and I know that a girl I really fancy will be there, so it is the perfect chance for us to get to know each other better. The only problem is that everyone in the party has to sing a song and I am possibly the world's worst singer. If I refuse to sing, I will be seen as a bad sport. But if I do pick up the mike, I might just empty the bar. How can I win this girl's heart without making an utter fool of myself?
Tim W, Edinburgh

Dear Tim,
You poor thing – stop worrying. Everyone is terrible at karaoke, that's the whole point of it. If people wanted to hear good singing, they would have hired a band or popped on a nice bit of Norah Jones.

Choose something nice and easy that everyone will join in on, so that your voice will be drowned out. 'Waterloo' by Abba springs to mind. Just remember that the people who are very good at karaoke are the sad, slightly annoying ones.

Surely the best way to win a girl's heart is by being brave enough to make an utter fool of yourself? Sing out, Tim, and perhaps your heart will sing as well.

Dear Graham,

I'm in my late twenties and go out a lot with a childhood friend who behaves like a single girl because her boyfriend is often away on work trips. She's always up for going out on the razzle and we usually have a brilliant time together. She's a bit more confident than me so she makes me braver than I would normally be.

She's always giving me words of encouragement and telling me I look 'gorgeous' and saying that guys fancy me. The problem is that whenever I start to get keen on anyone they always seem to prefer her, even though she's not available. I do understand that she's probably more attractive than I am but I can't help blaming her a bit. It's almost as if she's using me to prove that she's still desirable, or perhaps even to prove that men will always prefer her over me. It's weird though, because she's really loved up. I just don't get it.

I've been trying to be a bit more independent generally and see other friends, but she calls constantly, wanting to make plans.

What would you do in my place?

Tilly S, Essex

Dear Tilly,

I feel for you. This is a very tricky problem. If you say or do anything, you'll seem like a petty, insecure child. Your friend isn't doing anything so wrong that it makes her a monster and yet she is blighting your life.

However you manage it, you have to see less of her. This is sad, given how long you've been friends, but what for her is just competitive fun is costing you dearly.

One approach could be to work on the trusting out-of-town boyfriend. Does he know how she behaves when you go out? Why not bring a disposable camera one night 'for a bit of fun'? Take lots of shots of her with all these men who are attracted to her like babies to Angelina Jolie, and he may give his girlfriend a few more ground rules. Start planning nights out when you know she's busy and don't plan them all around the pubs and clubs. Try activities or groups where you can shine on your own.

The trouble is, once you find the man for you, your friend won't be able to leave it alone. The problem is clearly hers, but you can't solve it for her.

This friendship is from childhood. Perhaps, like wetting the bed and pink jewellery, it's time to put it behind you.

Dear Graham,
To my dismay, I'm spending Christmas with my boyfriend's family. They're a pretty dysfunctional lot – they don't talk to one another and have the telly on full-pelt at all times. The heating is always sauna-like, no one goes for walks and no one comes to visit. The men of the family tend to sit around being slobby and telling unfunny jokes, while the women do all the cleaning and cooking in a furious, martyred way. There are no children to cheer things up.

I guess these are normal relationship compromises (we're spending New Year with my family), but the problem is that, when he's at home, my boyfriend morphs into adolescent mode and becomes moody and monosyllabic. Any advice?

Rowena G, London

Dear Rowena,

I think many readers will be surprised to learn that the family you describe is dysfunctional. A quick life-on-planet-Earth update for you: they are perfectly normal. The mulled wine, Labrador-walking, 'let's have a goose this year' crowd are the freaks. I understand you aren't going to enjoy it much, but you have a choice: don't go, or go and make the most of it.

Since Christmas is all about family, why not just give into it? Standing around like Princess Margaret at a farting competition will only make things worse. Imagine how much your boyfriend's poor family must be dreading your arrival and try to appreciate the effort they are putting into it all.

Do yourself and everyone else a favour, and have a drink. Have several drinks. Shove wine down your neck as if your stomach was a flaming Malibu mansion. Everyone can tolerate a drunk at Christmas – no one can ever bear a snob.

Dear Graham,

I am dating a vegetarian called Melissa who happens, unfortunately, to be a truly dreadful cook. When I go round to her place, there are all these depressing beans - chickpeas and the like - soaking in little glass bowls or bubbling furiously on the stove. I don't know whether it's her cooking or my delicate digestive system, but her food is barely edible. Things get a little windy - and I'm not talking about the weather.

I wonder if a carnivorous, red-blooded male can have any sort of future with a strict vegetarian?

Nick C, Ealing

> **❝** Breaking bread with another human being is such a basic pleasure but if it's pitta bread with beans, then the only things that will be broken are teeth and wind. **❞**

Dear Nick,

Vegetarian food is one thing, badly cooked vegetarian food is another. I'm afraid this can never be anything more than a fling. Breaking bread with another human being is such a basic pleasure but if it's pitta bread with beans, then the only things that will be broken are teeth and wind.

Relationships can survive all sorts of compromise but, maybe because I'm a greedy pig, food seems like an insurmountable problem. Consider the future – sitting in lay-bys hurriedly shoving cheeseburgers into your mouth and forgetting to clear the wrappers out of the car, a wedding reception comprising a meal that smells like wet dog. Just call her right now, finish it and get a pan of sausages on to the stove to celebrate.

Welcome back to the world of blood and fat!

Dear Graham,
I have too many friends and it's stressing me out. I wasn't
popular at school - I was overweight, painfully shy and generally
a bit lumpen - but before going to university I signed up with
Weight Watchers, lost three stone and pulled myself out of the
mire. Since then (I'm now 32), I've been frantically collecting
friends. There are so many people in my life now, I feel
overwhelmed. Every time anyone is friendly towards me, I'm so
pathetically grateful I never stop to think about whether I like
them or not. Ludicrous as it sounds, it's making me depressed.
Sometimes I want to turn off the phone and go into hiding. I
can't remember the last time I had a call, or invitation, from
someone I was actually excited to hear from. And I can't
remember the last time anyone attractive asked me out.
   My life seems hectic, cluttered and pointless. Do I need
therapy?

Lily A, Shropshire

Dear Lily,
It is one of the great truths of modern life that the people who call and
email us the most are the ones we never want to hear from again.
   The answer is simple – you must make the calls and send the emails.
Contact the people you truly like and make plans to see them. Then,
when the less-loved get in touch, you won't be free and slowly they will
fall by the wayside. Obviously, some will be more tenacious and you
may end up having the odd night out with them, but the situation will
at least be better.
   To stop the hectic clutter of your life, why not have a couple of
nights each week when you don't go out? There's no need to tell lies or
make excuses. I think most people will find it perfectly acceptable that
sometimes you just don't want to go out.
   As for therapy, I think the last thing you need in your life right now
is someone who pretends to be your friend in exchange for cash.

Dear Graham,

Like most people who write to you, I'm single, but my problem isn't boyfriend-related. Maybe this is an un-PC thing to say, but I'm fed up with picking up the pieces for my female colleagues. They leave work for months on end to have babies and then, when they do come back with their shrunken, baby-addled brains and la-di-dah attitude, they might as well not have bothered.

I've lost count of the number of times female colleagues have left the office - in the midst of a major crisis or deadline - at five, with the excuse that little Freddie has to be picked up from nursery. And it's not even just the women - the men think they can bunk off because the wife's having a meltdown and they have to take the baby to Tumble Tots. They even seem to think I should find that appealing and new-mannish. Because I'm childless I'm expected to drop all my plans but my married colleagues can just go home and make wriggly snakes out of Play-Doh.

Worst of all, it seems I'm now supposed to arrange my holidays around theirs. I'm not meant to be off between Christmas and New Year because they all need to be. I daren't complain, but it's really getting to me. And the biggest irony of all? I'm a newly qualified employment lawyer.

Charlotte S, Exeter

Dear Charlotte,

As I read your letter – and this is probably wrong of me – I was expecting to find that it was written by a man. I presumed that, as a woman, you might understand that when children enter someone's life their priorities change. Getting to hear sausage-fingered Bruno's piano recital is suddenly far more important than the Harrogate figures on Nigel's desk.

For a lawyer, you seem to have missed out on a very simple fact in this case – it isn't about you. People aren't trying to be mean to you. They don't care about you. Their main focus is now outside work.

You have a couple of options. Move to a company with a younger, older or gayer workforce where this will be less of an issue, or have a baby. Failing that, take up smoking: then you can take lots of breaks while those health-conscious parents are chained to their desks.

Ask Graham

Dear Graham,

My girlfriend and I have been together for five years now. This year, as usual, we're going to my parents in Lincolnshire for Christmas. They know I'm gay, but we don't talk about it. When my girlfriend and I visit we're given separate rooms, but only for appearance's sake.

The problem is that my parents are wildly sociable. For them, Christmas is a hectic round of drinks parties and get-togethers with the vicar, the neighbours and just about every Tom, Dick and Harry within a 50-mile radius. Every year I get grief from their friends along the lines of 'Have you met a nice young man yet?' or 'What's a lovely girl like you doing on her own?' It's utterly maddening. I am 35, gay and in a serious long-term relationship.

Do I really have to put up with this kind of thing year after year? I don't blame my parents for keeping schtum, but would it really be so awful to let the cat out of the bag?

Jessica C, north London

Dear Jessica,

I completely understand how this situation came about, but enough is enough. Nobody wants to talk about sex – whether hetero or homo – with their parents but, this once, briefly, I think you have to. The fact that you spend time at home suggests that you don't want to lose contact with your family altogether, but I fear that unless some difficult nettles are grasped that may be what will happen.

The discussion doesn't have to be long. Simply inform them that you aren't comfortable about being unable to acknowledge your sexuality or your girlfriend when you are out socially.

Accept that they want you to sleep in separate rooms because, after all, it is their house. If even this seems impossible, then just make a unilateral decision to come out.

When someone asks about you being single or not finding a man, just point out your girlfriend and tell them who she is. There may be a few sausage rolls spat on to the carpet, but the world won't end. As soon as your parents see that their friends don't really care, it will be a burden lifted from all of you. Then everyone can get back to not talking about anything even vaguely personal ever again.

111

Dear Graham,
My career is on the skids and I'm not even a proper mother.
Technically, I'm back at work (as a barrister), but I've got
hardly any work at the moment. I feel guilty all the time that
(a) I'm not at home looking after my one-year-old and (b) I'm
employing a full-time nanny I can't afford.

My husband's salary isn't enough to cover our monthly
outgoings and already I've had to dip into my savings to hide
how little I'm earning. My average working day is spent sitting
in Starbucks around the corner from my chambers, staring out
of the window.

The guilt is dreadful. When I'm away from my child, I feel I
should be doing virtuous things such as earning money,
rather than reading Vogue and drinking skinny cappuccinos.
But I'm ambitious and know I just couldn't cope with being a
full-time mother.

Please don't tell me to talk to my husband - he's desperate for
me to give up work.

Eleanor B, London

Dear Eleanor,

What is going on in your head? You are too ambitious to contemplate being a full-time mother but you are content to drink coffee and flick through magazines all day? There are receptionists at funeral homes with more get up and go than you.

Think about what you are doing. You're not spending time with your child when you could be, you are lying to your husband and you are wasting time and money.

I hope your family can bounce back from this weird lie you are living.

The bottom line is you need a new job. Start looking. Although you don't want to, you must confess to your husband the reality of your daily schedule. Once he knows what's going on, you can work together to sort things out. Keeping it all bottled up will only make matters worse. He can't force you out of the job market, especially since you say you can't afford not to work.

You have been an idiot, but it's not too late to wise up. At this point, it's no longer about having a career but simply putting a value on your time. Not being paid much is better than earning nothing, and when you get home you can enjoy your baby and husband without feeling guilty.

Just a thought, but if your kid is cute maybe it could do some modelling so that at least someone will be bringing home the bacon.

Dear Graham,

I'm fast sliding towards 50 but feel youthful, both in outlook and looks. I'm using an internet dating site, have oodles of contacts via email and have met several men. While the ones I've met are pleasant enough at the first meeting, I've yet to meet anyone who lights that special spark in me.

My quandary is this: should I continue to meet up with these pleasant men and widen my social life, or should I say 'no thanks' after the first date and only go on a second date with the man who induces that melting feeling in me?

Faye W, Gloucestershire

Dear Faye,

My gut instinct has always been not to go on a second date unless I felt that special melting feeling. What was the point? If I was looking for 'the one', why would I want to spend time with someone who was just another one? However, as I get older, I find that experience has taught me to be more cautious. I don't simply give my heart to someone who is likely to leave it in the back of a taxi. I need to get to know people first and maybe reduce my chances of being hurt or disappointed.

Don't underestimate the quiet pleasure of simply socialising with pleasant company over a nice meal. What is the alternative – nights in front of the television learning how to train a dog you don't own? I don't want to get brutal here, but you're 50, and most women in your situation if asked on a first date – never mind a second one – would be thrilled.

The young are brave and foolish: they don't fall in love, they jump. We, on the other hand, have learned to be scared. We step in carefully, and that takes time. That melting feeling might still arrive – it just takes a bit longer to turn up the heat.

Dear Graham,
I've fallen in love with a guy who comes from an incredibly
musical family. My problem is, I'm practically tone-deaf. I
absolutely dread the family get-togethers - lots of singing
around the family Steinway and impromptu string quartets - as
I can't join in. Instead, I sit there like a lemon, knowing that
his parents are not impressed.

Although I am quite successful in my own sphere, I have no
artistic talent. My fiancé's Jewish family are the kind who play
the French horn before breakfast. The atmosphere in their house
is always incredibly competitive. If it's not cellos whining
miserably at all hours, it's debates about the US presidential
race over the kitchen table. I feel like a fish out of water when I
visit them, and I know that my future mother-in-law (retired
surgeon, resolutely undyed grey hair, zero interest in clothes)
disapproves of me (I am blonde, work as a fashion buyer and
grew up in a non-musical, non-Jewish household).

So grim are these evenings that I often wonder why I bother
going. Last time I went to his parents' house for one of their
Friday suppers, I was spectacularly ignored by everyone, except
my boyfriend's seven-year-old niece, who admired my butterfly
hairclip, and the family Pekinese, which clambered on to my
lap. My boyfriend is usually too busy fussing over his mother, or
tuning his flute, to notice how left out I am.
Any advice?

Katy S, Olympia

Dear Katy,
You are not alone in wondering why you bother going. Clearly, this
family are just playing a nasty waiting game. Your boyfriend may love
you, but his family obviously don't like you much at all. That dog is
only paying you attention because he recognises in you a kindred
spirit. He's probably shocked to see you sitting at the table rather than
sniffing around the floor for scraps.

When a seven-year-old is trying to make small talk because she feels
sorry for you, it really is time to move on. Not spending Friday nights
with the Von Trapp family doesn't mean your relationship with your
boyfriend is over, but, if he can't see why you hate it, then I would
think long and hard about how much of a future you really want with

this man. For most of us it's bad enough that we have to spend time with our own families, never mind long swathes of quality time with our partner's clan.

Be honest: you hate them, they hate you, then see where things go. You may lose your boyfriend, but on the plus side, you'll never have to spend time with the Waltons of Radio 3 again.

I would never encourage anyone to do this, but I wonder if you might feel a little better if you dribbled the juice from a can of sardines inside their piano before you left for the last time? Just a thought.

Dear Graham,
I recently went out to dinner with a gay male friend and we both fancied the wildly attractive waiter, who seemed keen, although he went home with neither of us. We couldn't tell whether he was gay or straight. Is there a clever way of finding such things out, while simultaneously eliminating the competition?

Penny S, London

Dear Penny,
I am deeply embarrassed for you. The sort of people who talk about picking up the waiter are the same ones who shriek about how naughty they are being when they order dessert, as if eating a bit of meringue was on a par with war crimes.

Thinking the waiter fancies you puts you in the same league as people who think a hairdresser finds their hair interesting, or that the lady at the check-out is admiring their choice of groceries. These people are doing a job, and if they do it well we all have a nicer life – nothing more or less.

Oh, and by the way – of course he was gay.

Dear Graham,
My parents refuse to help out with our children. So do my
husband's parents. This is despite the fact that they have reared
six children between them and are comfortably set up in homes
with plenty of spare room. I'm not talking about being regular
unpaid childminders while I swan off to work, or even monthly
baby-sitting. I just wish that once or twice a year they would
offer to have the children for a day or even, dare I say it, a
weekend from time to time.

As it is, if my husband and I want to have a night away by
ourselves, we have to fork out vast quantities of cash to get our
nanny to move in for the weekend. Meanwhile, all my friends
seem to be beating their parents off with a big stick and
refereeing arguments between various grandparently
contingents all craving extra time with their clan.

Why have I got such a raw deal?

Sarah G, Devizes

Dear Sarah,

What a lot of self-pitying drivel! Luckily, any single parents out there probably don't have time to read this column, but try to imagine for one moment how little sympathy you'd get from them.

Your parents and in-laws have already brought up six kids between them; there is no earthly reason why they should start bringing up yours as well.

Your children are precisely that – yours. No one owes you any childcare apart from the nanny that you are blessed to have. Raw deal? Millions of mothers up and down the land dream of having it as good as you.

I have only two suggestions for you. Try asking your parents to baby-sit once in a while, rather than waiting for them suddenly to turn into the grandparents from *The Waltons*.

If they refuse, that doesn't make them evil people. It sounds as if you don't enjoy spending that much time with your kids, so why would anyone else?

My other suggestion is to pack your kids into a large crate with some nice snacks and a bottle of Sunny D, then send them off to Angelina Jolie. Problem solved.

Dear Graham,

What do you do if you have a peeping tom? The other day I was doing my ironing in my undies and, to my utter horror, spotted a man in the building opposite looking at me through a pair of giant binoculars - the sort you'd see on a Benny Hill programme. I felt sick and disgusted and closed the curtains immediately, then rang the police. They arrived within minutes and were very helpful and sympathetic. They rang the bell of the flat opposite, but were told by the Portuguese woman who opened the door that they must have the wrong flat - no man lived there.

Imagine my dismay when, last weekend, I was spied on again. This time the man was pointing an enormous video camera directly at my bedroom window. My daughter says he's probably planning to launch me on YouTube. It seems there is nothing I can do to stop this odious man, short of confronting him myself. I am too embarrassed to call the police again.

I am not, as you might think, a nubile beauty who prances about in Agent Provocateur, but an overweight 53-year-old housewife with varicose veins. My admirer is at least 70, bug-eyed and earth-shatteringly ugly.

Cynthia J, Edinburgh

Dear Cynthia,

This is how you deal with a peeping tom: stop wandering around your flat in a bra and knickers with the curtains open and he'll get bored and train his sights on someone else's window. Given that you are 53, I'm slightly surprised that you haven't figured out what curtains are for or learned that standing around in your underwear in full view of your neighbours isn't really the done thing.

Part of me suspects that you may enjoy all the attention. I notice his binoculars were 'giant' and his video camera was 'enormous'. I wonder if you don't really want any advice at all, but just enjoy retelling the story in all its gory detail (did we really need to know about your veins?). Your outrage can scarcely mask your thinly disguised delight.

Invest in a dressing-gown, Cynthia, and spare a thought for the poor Portuguese woman who has a man break into her flat on a regular basis just to get a better view of your wobbly bits.

Dear Graham,

When I broke up with my boyfriend at the age of 37, he told me gleefully that, if I ended things with him, I'd never have a child and was unlikely to find another man. Three years on, I am still single and childless. So is he.

What I'd like to know is, should we try to revive things? We bumped into each other recently at a friend's 40th birthday and ended up talking late into the night. His view is that, although things weren't perfect between us - the sex, in particular, wasn't quite right (his words, not mine) - given that we haven't found anyone else, we should get back together again.

I can't pretend life hasn't been a struggle on my own and part of me feels this incredible joy at the prospect of being in a couple again. The other part feels really downhearted about the offer. Is this all I can get: a lukewarm male who doesn't love me properly and wants me back only because he hasn't found anyone else?

Ruby Wax would tell me that at 40 I am gathering dust so quickly that I'm practically a museum exhibit. No single, solvent male should be turned away, even if he's an ex-boyfriend. What's your opinion? Should I go for it? Am I crazy to go on waiting for some mythical figure to come charging in on a white stallion?

Emily S, Gloucestershire

Dear Emily,

I understand that you would like a baby and a partner, but getting back together with this guy is like someone who is so desperate to be a home owner that she moves into a cardboard box. This man wasn't good enough for you once and he won't be again. Imagine the years of staring at him across dinner tables, the Christmases, the holidays – all with this man who will slowly but surely become a living, breathing symbol of your life as a failure.

Yes, you want a kid, but do you really want that child to grow up in a house devoid of love and full of compromise and regret? You are 40 years old, Emily, and, without trying to be controversial, may I suggest that you have probably lived half of your life? Isn't it time to stop dreaming and get on with accepting and enjoying the life that you have?

Having a baby and a partner might be the ideal way you would like to live, but not getting them doesn't mean you can't share your life with others in a thousand different ways. We get only one life, Emily. Don't waste it in a fog of fruitless yearning.

Dear Graham,
I came back early from work one day and found my husband in bed at 4pm with a female colleague. I threw him out and only just managed to resist the temptation to cut up his suits and put petrol into his much-loved, diesel-run convertible Merc. Now, a month later, he's begging me to take him back, saying it was all a terrible mistake and it's me he really loves.
* Why do men betray us like this? And how can I ever trust him again?*

Zara P, Kent

" Love is like a tame tiger, beautiful and awesome. But in the blink of an eye, and without warning, it can rip your heart out. "

Dear Zara,
Love is like a tame tiger, beautiful and awesome. But in the blink of an eye, and without warning, it can rip your heart out. I can tell from your letter that against all your better judgement you are about to get back in the cage with the beast. Don't worry. If we all went through life being sensible, we'd probably never feel pure joy – and no one would buy any of Stella McCartney's clothes.

The questions you ask go to the very root of what separates the sexes. Your husband wasn't betraying you, he was satisfying himself. The fact that he probably never gave your feelings a second thought will doubtless sound depressing but it could help when it comes to your second question. You can trust him only if he knows that he will suffer as a direct result of his afternoon delight. My advice is to stay strong and don't just let him buy you a few dinners and forget what he did. I'm thinking here of his love for his convertible Merc. It has to go. Somewhere in his subconscious, that car says he has not accepted being married. If he refuses to get rid of it, then your decision is made: get rid of him.

Ask Graham

Dear Graham,

I had a miscarriage a couple of weeks ago at four months. It was my first child and a shattering experience. My husband has been really distant since it happened, burying his sorrow in frantic DIY projects. Most weekends he charges off to Ikea, Homebase and B&Q, and I don't see him all day. In the evenings, he builds shelves and walks about the house muttering about how the floor needs revarnishing or the bathroom needs retiling. He isn't a builder and didn't show any particular inclination for DIY before we lost the baby.

I really want to share my grief with him and talk about it, rather than pretend nothing happened, but I can't seem to communicate with him any more. He's developed a ridiculous cheery whistle, which sounds completely fake and is designed, I think, to keep me at bay. I feel alone and grief-stricken.

Laura S, Bristol

Dear Laura,

My heart goes out to you both. What a miserable situation. Grief is never a welcome guest and we all deal with it in different ways.

It sounds as if your husband thinks his gorgeous wife and beautiful family are broken and he needs to fix them. If he makes everything else perfect, maybe the pieces will fall into place and you can be happy again. It sounds crazy, but that poor man is searching the shelves of Homebase for something to help him mend his broken heart. I doubt it is you that he is trying to keep at bay, it's the pain.

It must be incredibly difficult for you, but don't try to rush him. In strange ways, it might be easier for you to cope with all of this because at least it happened to you, whereas no matter how much you reach out to him, he feels like he's on the outside looking in. In the days of cooking by candlelight and drinking warm milk, you'd have simply tried to get pregnant again as quickly as possible. While there is much to recommend that solution, in the end I think you need to be ready to move on and clearly neither of you is.

I would urge you both to get some professional counselling before things become too deep-rooted. The only good thing about grief is that it does eventually leave; when it does, take a moment to look around your house and admire all the home improvements it has left in its wake.

Dear Graham,
I can't cook, my flat is a tip and I find myself in the awkward
position of owing an awful lot of people dinner. Even though
I'm pretty good at singing for my supper, various friends have
started to drop heavy hints that they have yet to clap eyes on my
place. It's rude, I know, not to reciprocate, but I would rather
eat a live cobra than host a dinner party of my own.

I fear that New York-style decamping to a restaurant would
be seen as lazy and inhospitable, even if I did pick up the bill at
the end.

My ex-girlfriend has refused to step in with her fish pie. And to
be honest, I fancy one of the girls I owe dinner to so it wouldn't
be a good idea to have my ex there, creating an atmosphere.

How can I get around this problem while ensuring I remain
on everybody's party lists?

Ben L, Edinburgh

Dear Ben,

A letter? You had to sit down and write a letter? Pick up a rag and
some spray that says 'shine' on the bottle somewhere and clean your
flat. Your friends are justified in being irked by you because you are a
lazy lump.

No one expects your apartment to be something from *Grand
Designs* and the meal need be nothing more than a selection of the easy-
cook ranges that all the supermarket chains do now – they just want
you to go to the effort of breaking bread with them in your home.

Cooking isn't some sort of medieval witchcraft – even Delia has
discovered the joy of the microwave – and if the food is less than
marvellous then at least people won't be so keen for a second invitation.

If your home really is something from a Channel Five documentary
– I'm thinking two-seater leather sofa and a dead plant – then why not
hire a Landmark Trust property or a cottage and invite everyone away
for the weekend? Your chances with the prospective girlfriend are also
increased unless you happen to be in love with Kim or Aggie from
How Clean is your House? Do you think I watch too much television?

Dear Graham,

My husband's parting shot to me when I returned to work recently after 10 years at home bringing up children was: 'This had better not interfere with family life.' Even though I still manage to get everything done, he misses no opportunity to have a go at me. Last thing at night, when he's checking his BlackBerry and setting his alarm, he will say something to me like, 'Don't expect me to go to Tesco at the weekend' or 'Don't think I'm going to organise our holiday this year'.

It's true that there's no economic reason for me to be back at work. My husband - all alpha-male machismo - earns big money in the City and we have more than enough. It's really about me striking out on my own and pursuing my ambitions, rather than just being a mum and wife for the rest of my life. Our daughters are seven and nine, busy and happy at school, and I do feel that there's more to life than walking the dog, doing Pilates and looking decorative at corporate dinners.

Am I being selfish? And if I'm not, how do I soothe my husband's huge and very fragile ego, and keep our marriage on an even keel?

Samantha H, London

Dear Samantha,

You are right to assume this is all about your husband's ego. No self-respecting bread-winner wants to come home and discover the family eating cake. Presumably one of your husband's major sources of job satisfaction is simply derived from providing for you and his little princesses. In fairness, it does sound like he is being very thin-skinned about it all, so tread carefully.

A man might understand your desire to work more if you gave him a financial reason, or goal. Obviously, your contribution isn't required for the day-to-day running expenses of your lives, but perhaps you could put your wages towards a spectacular family holiday that you organise. If you don't have a country house for weekends, perhaps that's where your money might go. If your wages don't quite stretch to that, then a simple trust fund for your children's education might ease his anxiety.

Of course, all this advice may soon be redundant, like your husband

and all his friends. In a world of cutbacks, Mummy going to work might seem like a very good idea. Not wanting to go to Tesco is very different from not being able to.

Dear Graham,

I have a work colleague who is driving me crazy. As the newest person in the company, I have been put next to the office PA, a competent but brassy woman, who never stops talking in between frantic bouts of nail-painting, internet shopping and crisp-eating.

Every day I have to listen to her tittle-tattle to her builder boyfriend, Kevin, who is always up to no good. Typically, the conversation goes like this: 'Did ya?' (Gasps of disbelief.) 'Could ya?' (More gasps.) 'Why did ya?' (Fascinated horror.)

It is incredibly distracting. How can I get her to pipe down without alienating her completely?

Ian S, Hemel Hempstead

Dear Ian,

Tread very carefully. Fall out with the brassy, competent PA and you might as well resign the same day. An obvious solution would be to pop on your iPod and get through the day in a haze of Genesis and 10cc, blissfully unaware of the marathon monologue in the cubicle next door... but then you'll also fail to notice your boss trying to get your attention, or your phone ringing.

Whatever you do should make her want to be quieter. Perhaps make it clear that you are listening to every word. If she cracks a joke, laugh way too loudly. Should she offer any opinion on something, shout over the partition: 'You're right there!' In the kitchen, always talk to her about her phone calls, starting every conversation with: 'I couldn't help but overhear...'

Eventually, she will grow self-conscious and turn down the volume. If she doesn't, rip your computer from the desk and throw it at her. You will be sacked, but the security camera footage will make you a YouTube star!

Dear Graham,

Why are women so messy? My girlfriend, like all my exes, lives in a state of permanent chaos, which she calls 'bohemian' and which I think is more like 'freshly burgled'. Remember that ad on the telly? It should have been the other way round, because in my view it's women, not men, who are the messy ones.

I'm not guilty of any of those crimes that men are so vilified for - wet towels on floor, dirty pans in sink, lavatory seat left up - but you don't even know the half of my girlfriend's squalid habits. We love each other and get on brilliantly, but I get exasperated with all her mess. Tissues, Post-it notes, knickers, felt-tip pens with lids missing, bank statements, lipstick - somehow the whole lot always end up on the floor or inside the bed.

In her flat, she has a boxroom stuffed to the rafters with her mess. The vacuum cleaner lives in there, as does an old Amstrad computer. How can she bear to live like that?

Marcus S, Bath

❝I don't think you have a right to complain or use the word 'messy' until a friendly rat is helping out with the washing-up, or that strange moving pattern on the carpet turns out to be a talented group of line-dancing cockroaches.❞

Dear Marcus,

I am a gay man who lives alone and even by my standards you sound as if you are on the wrong side of Anthea Turner home management. Lipstick and bank statements are simply the normal debris of any human being getting through each day. Well, maybe not lipstick, but you get my point.

I don't think you have a right to complain or use the word 'messy' until a friendly rat is helping out with the washing-up, or that strange moving pattern on the carpet turns out to be a talented group of line-dancing cockroaches. Try to relax a little. The minute someone else starts spending time in your space, it will cease to be exactly the way you want. You could provide the adult equivalent of a toy box where you stash any of her stuff that you find lying around your home. I warn you now that your girlfriend will find this wildly annoying, but it may save your sanity.

I urge you to seriously consider your future as a heterosexual, because, if you think your girlfriend is bad, I fear that children may make your head explode.

Dear Graham,
What's the gentlest way to end a relationship? I have been chucked twice, including once in the middle of an Alpine snowstorm. But I now find myself in the position of having to end things myself. My (soon-to-be ex) boyfriend is handsome, thoughtful, rich and titled, but as dull as ditchwater. I cannot face another weekend in his stuffy French family's crumbling château, drinking stale port and talking about the weather.
I have no wish to behave like the cowardly men I've dated. Is there an elegant way to end things?

Jessica P, Paris

Dear Jessica,
Rather late in the day, it seems you have stumbled upon a universal truth: there is no good way to be dumped. Even if (and I speak from experience) you have been praying that your boyfriend would end things, it is still about as welcome as a shoe full of vomit. Key things to remember when dumping are: keep it short and blame yourself for the relationship failing. Truth in this arena is neither helpful nor appreciated.

Avoid doing it over dinner: there is no need to waste another evening on this corpse of a romance. A mid-morning coffee seems about right. Not a word about his dullness or the rural crusties. Talk about past relationships still having a hold on your heart, or how your parents' awful marriage has left you phobic about commitment and how unfair that is on such a great guy. And insist on paying for the coffee.

Dear Graham,

I seem to be out of sync with my generation. Everyone I know is obsessed with their position on the ladder but I'm just not ambitious. I don't want a job where I have to be clever and on top of my game. All I want is to be paid to phone someone up and ask when they are going to post 'that thing' (or whatever).

At the moment I'm working as a picture editor, calling in pictures from libraries, clocking off at 5pm on the dot and tootling home on my bicycle. But my City-based friends make me feel inadequate and ashamed to be doing such mundane, menial work.

I have lots of time to read novels, bake cakes, entertain friends and just have a good time but I'm made to feel like a lesser mortal for not wanting to thrust my way into a trendy media job or a large London bank.

Am I?

Verity S, Stow-on-the-Wold

I have time to read novels, bake cakes and tootle around on my bicycle, but I'm made to feel inadequate by my City-based friends.

Dear Verity,

Somewhere in a parallel universe, someone is writing a letter to an agony aunt describing a friend who bakes cakes and reads novels and makes them feel awful about wanting to build their career and earn more money. Life is all about choices and when our friends make ones that are very different to ours we are disconcerted.

Reassure your friends, praise them for their ambition and marvel at their success in tackling the corporate ladder. In turn, they will pretend to envy you your simple flour-covered life. For a while, this may keep you all fairly close but, as business trips to Hong Kong and expensive skiing holidays begin to dominate their lives, I'm afraid you may be forgotten.

The truth is, you'll start to make them feel uncomfortable. 'Did anyone remember to invite Verity?' or 'How can I get out of going to Verity's on Sunday?' will become questions heard more and more frequently. This isn't a bad thing because you'll soon grow tired of going round to see someone's new integrated sound system or sitting mute while everyone else talks about an uber-hot new restaurant that you will never go to.

Soon all you'll have in common is that you used to be friends and your only contact will come at weddings and christenings followed by a bit of a gap and then funerals.

This isn't meant to be some bleak *A Christmas Carol*-type warning. The point is that there is more than one recipe for a happy life. You're lucky that you've found one that works for you. Lick the plate.

Dear Graham,
We are in something of a diplomatic quandary. My wife and I are great friends with a couple who were at university with us. To our surprise and sorrow, they got divorced a year ago. Over the past few months, we've made a big effort to keep up a separate friendship with both of them, inviting them to dinners and parties at our house.

Our male friend has just announced he has met someone he would like to introduce to us. We would, of course, love to meet her, but are worried this would upset his ex-wife, who remains the aggrieved party. My wife thinks it would be 'disloyal' of us to have the new girlfriend over and we can't be certain she won't hear of it. What would you advise?

Nigel A, Wiltshire

Dear Nigel,

No matter how hard you try there will always be some situations in life – like running over a neighbour's cat – that are socially awkward and this is one of them. Someone is going to get hurt and if I were a betting man my money would be on everyone.

Seize the nettle and be honest. Call his ex-wife and tell her that you have invited the new woman over and that you didn't want her to hear about it from someone else. If you wanted to, you could throw her a bone by agreeing that it does seem way too soon, but you don't want to be seen to be taking sides. The important thing about the call is that you are telling her what's going to happen and not asking her if it's OK or if she minds.

If you ever feel they are asking you to take sides, then step away from the friendship. Unlike the CD collection or the Christmas decorations, friends cannot be simply divided in a divorce. Perhaps if you accept the new girlfriend, it will help your friend to accept her, too, and move on with her life.

> ❝ There will always be some situations in life – like running over a neighbour's cat – that are socially awkward and this is one of them. ❞

Dear Graham,

The other day I went to a lunch party where all the guests were married apart from me and an interior decorator with boyish looks, who was my age (36). Everyone kept teasing him about a 21-year-old girl he was wining and dining who lived at home with her parents. I suggested - gently - that he might do better if he focused on his own age group. His reply? 'Oh no, my cut-off point is 29. Any older and they want to move in after two weeks, get married and have babies. And they expect to be taken out for expensive dinners.'

I told him I thought that was ridiculous and he said you had to think about 'CPI'. When I pressed him, he told me it stood for 'cost per insertion'. Have you ever heard anything more vile? It's a horrible way to look at women. I went home in floods of tears and thought, 'Is this all that's left on the market?'

Do all men think like this when they take women out - but they just don't say it? Am I doomed (and naive) to expect better? Gabi S, London SW7

Dear Gabi,

An interior designer with boyish good looks who speaks like that about women in mixed company? Have you met my friend the closet homosexual? This guy is a joke with his posturing and meaningless macho mantras. Presumably he can only date kids because anyone else would just politely ask him to stop the car and get out.

I'm sure guys laugh about CPI up and down the land but usually in locker rooms or down the pub – not at lunch.

I can only imagine that the amount of wine consumed led to his obnoxious remarks and you leaving in floods of tears.

Seriously, why would meeting one jerk at a party upset you so badly unless, of course, you fancied him? It's only in fairytales that frogs turn into princes – in reality it's usually the other way around and this is one slimy toad. Forget this guy and his sub-Jeremy Clarkson *bons mots*. Men may not be very nice but it's safe to say that most are better than this.

Dear Graham,

My problem is a small but distressing one. I blush all the time. I have the kind of pale, thin-skinned English rose complexion that shows every emotion. Whenever boys talk to me, I go red. Whenever I'm embarrassed, I go red. Sometimes I go red for no particular reason. I feel the heat rising up my neck and cheeks, and if other people notice - usually a cruelly delighted 'You're blushing, aren't you?' - I go an ever-deeper, shaming shade of magenta. If I'm about to go into a potentially blush-inducing situation (meetings at work, parties and suchlike), I wear lots of foundation, but the flushing is so bad that it storms through even the thickest war paint.

Other people think it's rather sweet, but I find it humiliating. It means you don't have the same armour - the veneer of cool sophistication - that other people have. No matter what I say or do, my rosy Anglo-Saxon complexion lets me down.

Will I blush till my dying day? (I am 29.)

Lizzie H, Framlington

Dear Lizzie,

Presumably you have already sought medical advice for this problem, so all I can suggest is that you learn to live with it. Some people have big ears or a laugh that sounds like a drunk dolphin, but their lives go on. Think of your blushes as something that makes you special rather than the mark of a freak.

The only other thing you could do is live your life in a permanent state of embarrassment, so that people understand why you are blushing. Try always tucking your skirt into your knickers before you leave the house, or perhaps attaching some lavatory paper to every pair of shoes you own. Just imagining how grateful you are to read these wise words is making me blush!

**❝ Some people have big ears or a laugh
that sounds like a drunk dolphin, but
their lives go on. ❞**

Dear Graham,

Am I a lost cause? I'm 19 and like to think of myself as an optimistic and outgoing person, but I'm not really. I often feel low and unsure about my future. When I think about what I might do in life, I get these great ideas, but then give up, convinced I'm bound to fail. I say to myself: 'Look at the statistics - what are your chances of being remotely successful?' Meeting people is another problem. I rarely socialise because I'm afraid of how others will respond. Will they be mean? Will they be nice?

What will they think of me? How do I step outside myself, shut down my negative thinking and just go after whatever it is that I want in life?

Nicole M, no address supplied

Dear Nicole,

Being 19 is truly fabulous and seriously awful at the same time. Your whole life is ahead of you and filled with possibilities, but the thought of actually living it seems exhausting and filled with pain. I know there is very little more annoying than middle-aged people telling you things they wish they'd known at your age, but I'm going to do just that.

This too shall pass. That's it. All you need to know. When you are in a funk of depression, it is impossible to imagine that the sun will ever shine again or you will laugh out loud without a care in the world but of course you will.

Similarly, when you are giddy with joy, remember to treasure it because storm clouds will gather once more.

Life isn't lived in a straight line because that would be boring. It's more like a series of peaks and troughs, some higher, some lower, some brief, some long, but the point is nothing lasts for ever. When it comes to success or failure, I think you should fill your life with smaller goals.

If you set yourself the challenge of becoming prime minister (you think you feel bad now!), that will seem impossible, why not start with getting a letter published in the *Telegraph*. Don't decide to read the complete works of Shakespeare – pick one play and finish it. Life isn't a firework, it's a slow burn with flashes along the way.

Of course, none of these words will actually help you – only experience will teach you that when you were 19 you shouldn't have been so down on yourself. If the clouds in your life are stubborn or seem to be getting darker and darker, don't be shy about asking for help. A professional counsellor will be able to help you in ways a man of telly who is very jealous of your youth simply can't.

Trust me, there will be a day when you won't even recognise the woman who wrote this letter. Strangely, that will make you a little sad.

> **❝ Life isn't a firework, it's a slow burn with flashes along the way.. ❞**

Dear Graham,

My boyfriend and I are considering moving in together but I am worried about his Siamese cat, Britney, whom he adores. She follows him around the house, eats off his plate and often sleeps on our bed - in fact, I have woken up to find her snuggled up on his pillow. I am sure that she sees me as a threat - she has shredded two of my cashmere sweaters - and quite rightly, because, although I love cats, I want to ring her scrawny neck. I really think it's her or me, but which one will he choose?

Sophie F, St Andrews

Ask Graham

Dear Sophie,

Read this aloud: 'I am going to move in with a man who owns a cat called Britney.' Repeat it a couple of times. Now, ask yourself, does that really seem like a good idea? The problem is not the cat, it's the bloke. Leave any cashmere sweaters you have left where they are. Moving in with him isn't just covered in cat hair, it also has disaster written all over it.

Dear Graham,

My father had a heart attack a year ago and was rushed from his office to hospital. I raced to his bedside, along with my mother and two brothers, only to discover that a whole unknown family had already gathered there: a woman, roughly the same age as my mother, and one boy and a girl, both in their twenties. The girl looked oddly like me, just a slightly younger version with a different haircut. But the resemblance isn't a freaky coincidence, she is my half-sister.

It turns out that, all through his marriage to my mother, my outwardly conventional father has had an established mistress in London and fathered two other children. And do you know what really rankles? He didn't even bother to give his second family different names. The son is called Adrian, just like my younger brother, and the daughter has my name - Eleanor.

When he was discharged from hospital, my mother refused to let my father come home. She has since changed the locks and cut off all contact with him.

My father is in his mid-sixties, recovering well according to his doctors, but still very frail. None of us is speaking to him. I have no idea what the situation is with his other family, but presumably they are more forgiving, given that his mistress must have known he was married. Perhaps he has moved in with them and they are all playing happy families at last?

I'm very, very angry but I miss my father, even though I'm not sure I can ever forgive him. But I'm tortured by the thought that he might have another heart attack - this time a fatal one - and I won't even have said goodbye to him.

Eleanor P, Hampshire (all names have been changed)

Dear Eleanor,

I know I'm supposed to be an agony aunt but agony doesn't even begin to cover the sort of pain you are feeling. To discover such betrayal and deception at any time would be devastating, but to learn about it as you rushed to hold the hand of a father who might be dying is almost too much to bear.

The only good thing is that you have found out now rather than, as many families do, standing by the side of a grave looking across a muddy hole at people who aren't quite their mirror image. Your brothers, your mother and yourself must all decide how best to react, particularly as time may be of the essence.

I think you know what you want to do so go ahead and contact him. It's not a question of forgiving or even understanding; indeed, I doubt talking to him will answer any questions for you, but at least you won't live the rest of your life with this huge bit of unfinished business trailing behind you like loo paper stuck to a heel.

Please don't let your father's legacy of secrecy become part of your life as well – tell your mother that you are planning to talk to your father, not because you are sympathetic or on his side but because you need to. Your mother may be unhappy and why wouldn't she be? Her entire life was based on a lie told by a man who didn't even trust himself to remember more than two children's names. It's amazing he wasn't rumbled years ago.

What's important is that your decision to see your father doesn't distance you from your brothers. The one good thing that should come out of this mess is that you will become a much closer family unit. Just because one part of your family and personal history was a lie doesn't mean that none of it was true. Sometimes love is a very fragile thing but at other times it is tough as an elephant's foot. Only time will tell how much survives. Good luck.

❝ Sometimes love is a very fragile thing but at other times it is tough as an elephant's foot. ❞

Dear Graham,
Have you ever split up with anyone on holiday? I recently spent a disastrous week in Majorca with a new boyfriend, who I thought was my dream man. He booked it (I gave him a cheque for half the money) and he picked this horrible high-rise hotel full of drunk people from Manchester.

Our room was dark and dingy, we found cockroaches in our bed and the 'balcony' backed on to a wall. Meals were just awful - greasy and tasteless - and because he had signed us up for full board my boyfriend wouldn't try any of the local restaurants.

Apart from the bugs, he didn't see anything wrong with the place and refused to move, saying he wasn't 'shelling out a second time'. Even when I said I'd pay, he told me to 'get real', and stop being 'such a princess'.

I stuck it out but I had a really miserable time. He kept putting me down and telling me how boring and middle-aged I was (I refused to do karaoke or swim in the hotel pool). He dumped me on the plane home, saying he would have had more fun with a robot.

Now I'm back at work I feel my self-confidence is in shreds. I know he probably wasn't right for me, but am I too fussy for my own good? Everybody else in the hotel seemed to be having the time of their lives.
I am 26.

Jo L, Nottinghamshire

Dear Jo,
They were having the time of their lives? They were drunk people from Manchester. Give them a clean bus shelter and some warm chips and they'd be happy. I really don't know why this whole experience has affected you so badly. You had a horrible holiday and the man you went with has left you. Problem solved.

There is nothing wrong with you or your boyfriend. You just weren't compatible and your Majorcan version of Guantanamo Bay has simply accelerated the end of the romance. Be grateful. You are only 26: the chances of this being your worst holiday, or indeed boyfriend, are pretty slim.

Try Cuba with a man who won't eaten frozen fish and doesn't like rum.

Ask Graham

Dear Graham,

I moved into my boyfriend's flat three months ago. I'm very easy-going and relaxed, but my boyfriend is really uptight. Whenever we cook anything, it's as if we're preparing for Carla Bruni's visit to Buckingham Palace. The fruit and vegetables have to be sliced in a particular way and certain dishes demand certain plates. Everything has to be perfect: candles, silver, flowers, crystal.

I always use the wrong salad bowl or wrong glasses. One night we were making salad and I squashed an avocado (very ripe) straight into the bowl, rather than cut it into half moon slices and arrange them in a fan shape. I was hungry and couldn't be bothered. My boyfriend lost it, I got bored and furious, and we almost split up.

We are both in our late thirties and in every other area we seem compatible. We just drive each other nuts in the kitchen. He thinks I'm a barbarian and a slut. I think he's a sad, nit-picking old maid who's in love with Gordon Ramsay.

How do I avoid more Avocado Nights?

Nico D, Earl's Court

Dear Nico,

You get on with your boyfriend everywhere except the kitchen, so try this radical piece of advice: avoid cooking together. Clearly, how things are prepared and presented matters a great deal more to him than to you, so let him do it. If you insist on being a sous-chef, do it his way. Doubtless, he should relax and be less Anthea Turner about it all, but, trust me, it'll be easier this way.

My warning is that, once he has his way in the kitchen, you may have problems in new areas. The difference between a squashed avocado and a pretty green fan seems to indicate two very different people and soon his attention will turn to how you put magazines on the coffee table or open letters. Once this happens, he will have to let go of some control or you will have to move out before you find yourself wrapped in clingfilm and stored in the cupboard under the stairs.

You have been warned.

Dear Graham,
When my weight shot up to 14 stone, I was mocked so cruelly by
a gang of schoolchildren at the bus stop that I decided there
and then to do something about it. It's been a long and
arduous slog and I still have some way to go, but the hardest
thing is the lack of support from friends and family. It seems
everyone prefers me fat and cuddly.

When I invite friends over, they bring boxes of chocolate, even
though I ask them not to. 'Oh, go on. One won't do you any
harm,' they say. People - my slimmer friends, especially - make
me feel I'm being controlling and obsessive by dieting. And
some days it seems as if all the world is conspiring to make me
the obese, self-loathing 33-year-old woman I once was.

I sometimes wonder if it's jealousy that makes them behave
this way. Most of my friends are still single and perhaps their
biggest fear is that I will meet someone and leave them behind.
What do you think?

Debbie S, Swansea

Dear Debbie,
Congratulations and hurrah for bored schoolchildren. I'm sorry you
aren't getting the level of support you'd like, but you must understand
that your strength of character reflects badly on the rest of us. Am I the
only one who has breathed a sigh of relief when a friend who has been
on the wagon picks up the wine bottle once more? Don't we all feel like
pigs when someone refuses the offer of bread in a restaurant while
we've already started slapping the butter on ours?

We can all sympathise with short bursts of self-discipline – such as
losing weight for a wedding or not drinking because of antibiotics –
but any encounter with pure unmitigated self-control leaves most of us
feeling very unsettled and slightly judged, even if it is only by ourselves.

I hope for your sake that these are the reasons your friends are less
than enthusiastic and that, by giving you tempting foods, they're not
trying to cut down the competition for the cream of Swansea
manhood. People are also very resistant to change and in their eyes you
are Fat Debbie. You must admit it has a certain ring to it and rolls off
the tongue faster than Debbie Who Lost all the Weight or, worse still,
Gorgeous Debbie.

Joke about your diet when you are around family and friends and don't let them see how seriously you are taking it. Accept the boxes of chocolates with a smile, but then give them away to the schoolchildren at the bus stop. Revenge can be very sweet indeed.

Dear Graham,
I haven't had full-blown sex since 1997. I've got a great life, with an exciting job and lots of lovely friends but I haven't been in a relationship for years. Having lived like a nun for the best part of 12 years, I feel terrified at the very thought of taking my clothes off in front of a man.
There's a guy I like, who fortunately doesn't know about my lack of a track record. I think something might happen, but I'm worried my technique is going to be a bit rusty.
I'm 39 and my friends tell me I'm attractive. None of them is prepared to say why it's been so long since I've seen any action.
Any advice to ensure the man doesn't run away afterwards (or during)?

Jules M, Bristol

Dear Jules,
It may be 12 years, but, unlike mobile phones, I'm here to tell you that there really haven't been that many technical innovations. Not to belittle your problem, but I imagine it really is like riding a bicycle.

Typically, I tend not to spend much time between heterosexual sheets but surely a red-blooded male would be rather turned on by you simpering some plea for him to be gentle because it has been some time since you were with another man? Fan your hair out on the pillow and apply copious amounts of lipgloss to complete the effect.

Presumably, men prefer their sexual partners to have slept with fewer men rather than more. They won't feel as if you are comparing them to others and there will be the feeling that it's special for you rather than another notch on a bedpost that is starting to look like a wooden comb.

Don't be nervous – be delighted! Just remember, no man likes to find cobwebs. Have fun!

Dear Graham,
My husband (a peppy 63) and I live in such different time frames
we might as well be on different planets. At dinner parties he tends
to nod off before the cheese course, and at weekends, when other
couples have sex, he is up at the crack of dawn, usually engaged in
noisy DIY projects. I grew up in France and Italy and am very
Mediterranean in my hours.

We've been married for a few years - no children and no
plans to have any (I am 42) - but, as the years roll by, things
only seem to get worse.

I fear that by the time he is 70 we will be living like strangers.
What would you advise?

Felicity T, Beds

Dear Felicity,

Thank you for taking the time to write to me. I do feel, however, it would have been quicker and simpler for everyone had your letter just said: 'Me 42, him 63. Problem?'

I can't understand how you have wandered blithely into this situation without figuring out that an age difference of 20 years might become an issue. It is almost touching that you can write a sentence like, 'as the years roll by, things only seem to get worse', as if this was some sort of insight on your part. Wait until he's 83 and see how different your time frames are then.

I'm not saying that your relationship is doomed, but you must accept that your expectations are wildly unrealistic. You have fallen in love with a much older man and you must figure out how to live happily with that fact. So he doesn't stay awake for the cheese course, but I'm sure he's great at the history questions in the pub quiz. Enjoy what you can enjoy together and allow each other to do things separately.

If you continue to demand that he keeps up with you, he will grow to resent you or you'll kill him. Either way, I can't imagine it will make you any happier.

Dear Graham,
What is a decent interval to wait before you go to bed with
someone? I've had a few (unintentional) one-night stands and
it has always ended in tears with me sitting miserably by the
phone, wondering if I should ring BT to check the line is still
working. Men can be so very hard to resist, particularly when
they show interest rather than banging on about cars,
computers or football.
   I'm about to embark on a second date with a very attractive
man (a cross between Colin Farrell and an Italian waiter) and
I'm determined to hold out for a bit, rather than seem 'easy'. I
want a boyfriend rather than a quick shag. I turned 30 last
week. What would you advise?

Natasha M, Worcester

Dear Natasha,
Well done! After a mere 30 years on Planet Earth you have figured out the male of the species. On a first date, going all the way usually translates into going nowhere at all. The trouble is that the giddy world of dating often involves late nights and strong drinks and that can lead to a lady behaving like no lady should.

The trick is to plan ahead. Put brakes in place before you even go on the date and certainly before you are halfway through your second bottle of mid-range wine. Don't clean your flat, leave your legs unshaven and even resort to wearing old underwear. Make an early-morning appointment that you can't break. Arrange for your mother to come round for breakfast. Draw something embarrassing on your breasts with eyeliner.

My list of deterrents is endless. Remember that when you give a man your very special gift he should feel incredibly honoured and lucky, not like you've just shoved a free newspaper through his car window at the lights. Value yourself and others will follow suit.

Dear Graham,

My 71-year-old mother is hard of hearing, but in denial about it, and it's driving me bananas. The frustration and intolerance I feel towards her deafness (she refuses to wear a hearing aid) is unbelievable. It drives me nuts that she doesn't understand anything I say. Our conversations are utterly surreal. If I mention 'granola', she'll think I'm talking about 'Dracula'. I get a blistering headache just trying to keep the conversation on a sane, rational level. Sometimes I get so furious that I have to leave the room.

One thing she does really gets me every single time. On each occasion I go to see her, she will leap up sporadically with: 'Oooh! What a fright!' The noise? Just the usual one of my mobile going off in my pocket. But my mother behaves as if al-Qaeda are storming the house.

How do I get her to put that blasted hearing aid on and become human and normal again?

Toby C, Wiltshire

> **❝** Distance may make the heart grow fonder,
> but gossip makes the ears grow sharper. **❞**

Dear Toby,

Mothers find pleasure in the strangest of places. For some it is keeping the grouting clean, for others it is counting the years a light bulb has continued to work, and, when it comes to your mother, it is clearly winding you up with her refusal to wear a hearing aid. Your job – and it is a very tricky one – is to find things she'll enjoy more than watching steam coming out of your ears, but that require her to hear.

Your mother isn't very old, so one hopes she still has some sort of social life. I'm surprised she enjoys not being able to fully participate in conversations with friends. Perhaps get them to tell her she needs a hearing aid. She might take it better from them than you: let's face it, she could hardly take it worse.

The problem, I imagine, for your mother is that admitting she's getting deaf is admitting that she's getting old. You becoming annoyed is only prolonging the agony for all involved. Once you cease to react, she may get bored and decide to rejoin the world in all its loud glory.

One thing is for sure, and that's that no one is going to regret going deaf if their visitors discuss things like granola. Arrive armed with dirt and gossip and you may see a 71-year-old lady change her mind. Distance may make the heart grow fonder, but gossip makes the ears grow sharper.

Dear Graham,

I got married a couple of years ago to a divorced man with two children. Sadly, he has little contact with his children, who now live in Sydney. Being separated from them has given him untold agony, but he feels there is very little he can do as they appear to be happy with their new life.

I really grieve for him, but at the same time I resent his not putting more effort into our marriage. We live in my flat and he shows little interest in our home, or our friends, and is down in the dumps most of the time.

It's too late for me to have children with him (I am 48), but I'd like us to build a proper life together. What can I do to raise his spirits and help him move on?

Robin L, Hertfordshire

Dear Robin,

What should have raised his spirits and helped him move on was you. I don't quite understand how he could have made this huge commitment to you when his heart was obviously occupied elsewhere. Perhaps he thought that marrying you would make things better, but it clearly hasn't.

I doubt that even moving to Sydney would cheer him up, even if it did bring him closer to his children. What you describe as down in the dumps is what many call depression. Perhaps he should seek professional help.

Don't give up on this man too quickly. If you love him and are strong, there's every chance the two of you can get through this. Good luck.

Dear Graham,
Isn't the internet marvellous? I have met a wonderful second-hand bookseller on a dating website and things are going unexpectedly well. We live near each other and spend a lot of time together. The only blot on the landscape is that he's a chain smoker. He's considerate about it and smokes out of the window and up the chimney and - most of the time - empties his own ashtrays, but as a non-smoker I really loathe the smell. It hangs in the air and clings to everything - hair, nails, skin, clothes. I am permanently opening windows and airing rooms just to get rid of the odour. And even though I find him very attractive, often I don't want to kiss him because the smell of cigarettes makes me nauseous.

I wonder what I can do to encourage him to give up without meddling too much?

Neither of us is a spring chicken. He is 64 and I am 62.

Janice L, Nottinghamshire

Dear Janice,
You are in your sixties with a new boyfriend and you're worried about a bit of smoke? Most women your age are either trapped in a loveless marriage, alone, or getting a tattoo of Westlife. No one is that keen on ashtray breath but it doesn't seem to be that big a price to pay for the happiness you have found.

Don't turn into the sort of nag who makes the bookseller long for his days of being single. But equally he'll never know how much his smoking bothers you unless you tell him. The vast majority of people who are in relationships don't do that very simple thing of asking for what they want and then somehow it becomes their partner's fault for not guessing what you'd like them to do.

Explain that if he could cut down on his smoking it would make you very happy but equally you understand that it is an addiction. Don't ask him to choose between you and cigarettes because I'm not sure your ego could bear the result. If he really can't cut back, just stock up on scented candles and chewing gum and count your lucky stars through a romantic haze of smoke.

Ask Graham

Dear Graham,

All my close friends are hitched and having babies. My problem is that while I'm thrilled for them I don't have the ability to be endlessly fascinated by my friends' children. I hope the time will come when I have one or two of my own, but until it does I'm just not interested in nappies, breastfeeding, nanny problems or anything like that. Even doing minimal godparent duties are a massive effort for me as I find small children quite boring. Is that a shameful thing to say?

My friends keep asking me over to dull, smug, married evenings and I feel so mean making my excuses.

Am I making a terrible mistake putting these friendships on the back-burner? Or is it normal to want to seek out new people?

Sarah-Jane P, Middlesex

Dear Sarah-Jane,

Of course other people's babies are boring – they can't read menus and have no interest in discussing the red-carpet body language between Brad and Angelina.

You don't have to stop being friends with people because they have children, but you have to realise that those relationships will become harder to maintain. Lives change and so do we and there sometimes comes a point when we have to accept that all we have in common with some people is that we used to be friends.

When that happens, it's time to let go and that's not a bad thing, it's just about the choices you've made on your journey. Don't pretend to be someone you're not just to please others because ultimately that's in no one's best interest.

If you become a mother one day, you'll develop an interest in nappies and nannies, but until then let the only mention of 'pampers' be when someone gives you a full-body massage followed by champagne.

Ask Graham

Dear Graham,

How do you stick to New Year resolutions? Last year I vowed to give up drinking, stop eating after 6pm, and take up kick boxing and samba dancing. I joined a very chic gym and bought myself some glam kit.

The kick-boxing class was oversubscribed so I went for the most expensive swim of my life in a pool the size of Paris Hilton's handbag (annual membership £500). Somehow I never made it back and the Stella McCartney leggings are now being worn by my skinny younger sister. Yes, I've got to the end of the year even fatter and more unfit than ever. How do other people do it? Is there some shortcut I don't know about or is it just that I lack self-discipline?

What are your top tips?

Bella X, Middlesex

(no boyfriend - still)

Dear Bella,

Willpower isn't a magic spell. You'll find the resolve to diet and exercise when you truly want to stop being fat. The problem is that may not coincide with New Year's Eve.

The other problem is that the resolutions you made were wildly unrealistic. Don't give up drinking – cut it back. Allow yourself a dessert on a Friday night. Approach the gym as half an hour of increasing your heart rate rather than an episode of *Gladiators*.

Measure your progress in terms of things you have achieved – I walked to work twice this week – rather than cataloguing your failures – I didn't run up Ben Nevis.

I manage to get to the gym because I don't have the luxury of a personal trainer, but since you can afford to throw money away on Stella McCartney leggings perhaps you could hire one. This is the equivalent of buying willpower.

Whatever you do – do something. Slow steady improvement will mean change that you can maintain rather than some sort of manic extreme makeover that is thrilling for a couple of months but one year on leaves you fatter than ever, depressed and defeated.

Who knows? If you get your confidence back, next Christmas Santa might leave a boyfriend under your tree.

Ask Graham

Dear Graham,

I'm one of those rather fashionable, or so my wife tells me, older men with a wife of 36, who has two young children by her previous partner. We are hoping to add to the family - my wife has just embarked on a course of IVF - so, if everything goes according to plan, there's a strong likelihood I'll be a first-time father at 62. Quite how I'll cope, I simply don't know.

The thing is, much as I love my wife, I'm terrified of becoming a grey-haired Zimmer-framed old boy, with a mutinous toddler in tow. Yes, I'm fit and healthy now, but who knows what the future holds. What if I suddenly start sliding rapidly downhill and falling asleep with my head in the soup?

I haven't confided my fears to my wife but I've been having panic attacks about the whole thing. Is it fair for our child to have a geriatric dad?

Christopher J, north London

Dear Christopher,

What isn't fair is that you are willing to discuss your fears with me but not your wife. You do realise that the woman is having serious medical treatment just to give you a child you aren't sure you want? How has this happened? Presumably you talked about it at some stage or did you not think it polite to ask what she was intending to do with the sperm?

Hopefully, you did at some point think it was a good idea and what you are experiencing is the 'jitters'. The point is you are currently healthy so why not enjoy life as it is rather than living in fear of an unknown future?

I'm not sure why you think you will suddenly turn into a Zimmer frame-owning narcoleptic but, if you did, isn't the thought of your 36-year-old wife having to look after you just as upsetting with or without the mutinous toddler? It doesn't take Einstein to figure out that, when this new baby is leaving school, you'll be 80 and your wife will be in her mid-fifties.

No doubt your lovely bride has done the maths and is willing to take a gamble on the future so why don't you relax and do the same? Perhaps there is method in her madness – since you'll soon be getting up to go to the loo during the night quite often, you can nurse the baby while she sleeps through the night.

Seize life and don't shy away from it. This new family may not be picture perfect but it can be picture happy.

Dear Graham,

When my daughter (and only child) recently announced she had met someone, I was delighted. Despite being pretty and highly intelligent, she has been without a boyfriend for most of her twenties.

To my horror, though, it turns out she is romantically involved with a married male colleague 10 years older than her. The man in question is a father of three, who clearly has no intention of leaving his wife.

It makes me weep that my marvellous daughter is throwing herself away on this wicked man. And, although she insists colleagues don't know about it, I worry they'll find out and lose all respect for her. And what will happen if some nice (unattached) young man comes knocking on her door in the meantime? Presumably he won't get a look-in.

I've been sworn to secrecy and haven't told her father, as he is sure to hit the roof. But what can I do to help her see the light? I fear there's only going to be one loser in this sorry tale and it's going to be my daughter.

Vanessa F, Bristol

" A heart that has never been broken has also never swelled with love. The scars on our hearts are just signs that a life has been lived. "

Dear Vanessa,

I feel for you. Of course you don't want to see your daughter get hurt. You held her when she was small enough to sleep in a drawer using your knickers as a pillow, and, while your love for her remains unchanged, the fact is that she has. She's a woman now and is living her life to please herself, not you, and that includes making mistakes.

I fear your reading of the situation is completely correct but all you can do is be there to dry her tears when it all goes wrong. By all means, tell her what you think but do it in a calm 'just for the record' sort of way. There is no point falling out with your daughter over this.

Hard as it may be to accept, you can't protect your child from all the hurts that life deals out, but look at it this way: a heart that has never been broken has also never swelled with love. The scars on our hearts are just signs that a life has been lived.

Just as you can see this affair ending badly, surely you can also see that she will meet someone else. One day you will both be able to laugh about what she ever saw in that pig from the office. Difficult as it may be, surely part of being a mother is taking the training wheels off the bike and watching your child freewheel down the hill.

Dear Graham,
My boyfriend spends hours and hours in the bathroom with the door bolted. Is this a male thing? I have no idea what he does in there. I don't hear the chain being pulled, or even water dripping from the taps. He helps himself to my Jo Malone bath oil and I'm pretty sure he's now dipping into my Crème de la Mer. Should I be worried?

Georgina B, Chipping Camden

Dear Georgina,
What sort of paradise syndrome are you living in? Have you ever read the letters readers send me? They have problems – you have a minor irritation. You might as well have written to me complaining about how difficult you find it to open the plastic bags at Waitrose. Clearly, the poor man just wants to spend some time alone away from you.

Unless you have any reason to believe he is smuggling a third party into your bathroom, simply assume he is on the loo flicking through a year-old copy of *Grazia*.

Instead of being bugged by his absence, learn to appreciate it as 'you' time. Watch the TV programme you like, read, scratch your special places. Basically, enjoy the solitude.

Standing outside the bathroom door trying to hear water dripping is no way to spend your time. You have a boyfriend and can afford Crème de la Mer – hug your knees and give thanks to the Lord, you lucky thing.

Dear Graham,

Why don't British men ask women out on dates? I am a 29-year-old Californian living in London and have noticed that it takes an awful lot of effort to provoke a rush of blood to the loins of the average British male. Men on this side of the pond seem to prefer the company of other men. At parties, I find that only the women are friendly.

I have been here for nine months without being asked out on a single date, even though I've met a lot of people and work in a male-dominated environment (corporate finance). This is the first time in my adult life that I've been single for longer than three months, despite the fact that I'm blonde, athletic and, I am told, attractive. Friends tell me that British men don't formally date; instead they get drunk and reach for the nearest available woman.

Can you offer me some advice? How do I go about getting a boyfriend without going from first to last base in the blink of an eye?

Jennifer E, London/San Francisco

Dear Jennifer,

You are quite right. We don't date – we drink and take pot luck. British men never really advance emotionally beyond spin the bottle.

Because most of the men you meet are in a work situation, it is only natural that they don't ask you out on a date. If it doesn't work out, there you are, day in and day out, a memorial to their failure. No man's ego can bear that.

If it did go further, then having your partner working in the same office isn't very appealing either. Most men enjoy going to work to get away from their girlfriends and wives. Women at work are good for one-night stands and affairs. All you'll get out of an office romance are a few bunches of garage flowers and some awkward silences.

For relationships, look elsewhere. Go where the dates are. Join internet dating sites, place an ad in the personals. It may not be how you imagined meeting the love of your life, but you will at least find the dates you want, with men who know the rules.

Alternatively, join the boys. Drink as much as they do and pray to Bacchus that one morning you wake up with someone you love.

Ask Graham

Dear Graham,
My husband and I have separated, but we're still living together
because we cannot sell our house in Fulham. It's an
ignominious position, with both of us creeping about, trying not
to have yet another row.

I wonder if you can offer any advice on how to cope with this
awful situation? Neither of us can afford to move out until we
sell the house. We have a son, but he's away at boarding school,
so we have until the Easter holidays to sort something out.

I am the so-called 'guilty party', although I was never
unfaithful to my husband. The slow drip-drip of marital misery
(11 years) finally made me realise I'd be better off on my own.
Linda M, south-west London

Dear Linda,
What a hideous predicament. I really don't want to suggest ways of
making it easier for you to cope because only one thing needs to
happen – it has to stop. I know money is important, but maybe you
should knock just a couple of thousand off the price. Any profits lost
should be offset against the huge emotional cost of letting this drag on.

Because you ended the marriage, perhaps you are reluctant to
suggest such a radical move. But your ex-husband must be in hell too,
unless, of course, he thinks that as long as you have the house there is
the possibility of the two of you getting back together. Make sure he is
as keen to sell as you are.

Do you have any friends you could stay with for a maximum of
six months?

I think it is important for the mental health of both of you to get out
of this situation as soon as possible. Remember this will end. Your life
will get better and happiness will be yours once more. Good luck.

Your sports-mad Norwegian is perfectly happy in his pants, so leave him alone. Y-fronts? Why not!

Ask Graham

Dear Graham,
My Norwegian boyfriend wears Y-fronts, but I find boxers far sexier because they leave more to the imagination. My boyfriend refuses to change. I understand that Y-fronts are more comfortable for sport (he's very keen on cycling), but I'm worried they'll reduce his sperm count, which could be a problem if we decide to have children at a later stage. How do I reopen negotiations on this rather awkward subject without annoying him?

Maggie P, Paris

Dear Maggie,
I've only known you for a paragraph and you've already managed to annoy me. Y-fronts or boxers – it's hardly the referendum on the new EU constitution, is it? This poor Norwegian is perfectly happy in his pants, so just shut up and leave him alone.

Sperm count, Maggie? Are you seriously telling me that it would be a good idea to have children with a man you can't even agree on underwear with?

If this is truly a big issue for you, I suggest that your world has become somewhat small. Why don't you watch CNN for a few hours or spend an afternoon in the A&E department of a busy hospital and then go home and ask your Nordic pedal-pusher to drop his trousers. Do they really look that bad? Y-fronts? Why not, Maggie, why not?

Dear Graham,
I'm a single girl of 26 and don't have a problem getting dates, but because of nerves I find myself saying stupid things. Instead of laughing it off, I get more embarrassed and spend the rest of the evening apologising. How do I keep a cool head when talking to good-looking guys?

Melissa C, Kent

Dear Melissa,

You poor thing. With 30 hurtling towards you, the giggling and silly behaviour has to stop. If you have no problem getting dates and you describe them as 'good-looking guys', then I imagine you are no Ann Widdecombe in training. Until you become comfortable with a man, here's a top tip: say less!

The clever ones will find you an enigma, and the dim ones will think that you're interested in what they're saying. If something stupid does slip out, move on and never apologise. Chances are he was staring at your breasts and didn't hear a word you said. Stride sexily but silently towards a love-filled future.

Dear Graham,

I have been on nine dates with a Canadian merchant banker in his mid-forties whom I met at party. We come from very different worlds (I am a music therapist), but that hasn't been a problem. He has taken me twice to the opera and ballet, as well as to lovely dinners at Le Caprice. I find this man, who has never been married, very attractive, but he has made no attempt to kiss me. Is he a perfect gent or, God forbid, gay?

Laline P, west London

❝ If I'm to be completely honest, your bachelor with a penchant for the ballet, the opera and fine dining reeks of eau d'homo. ❞

Dear Laline,

If I'm to be completely honest, your bachelor with a penchant for the ballet, the opera and fine dining reeks of eau d'homo. You say he hasn't been married, but does he ever mention girlfriends? If he's trying to hide his gayness, would he take you to the ballet on a first date?

Trying to discover his dark secrets is a good game, but the reasons behind his lack of ardour don't matter. Get out now, because even if he turns out to be straight, and finally does sleep with you, he'll never be the man you want. Every woman wants to feel desired. Let's hope the next Canadian you meet is of the lumberjack variety.

Ask Graham

Dear Graham,

I'm absolutely dreading the office Christmas party.

Last year I got so drunk (on warm cava - ugh!) that I did unmentionable things with a fire extinguisher. Tales of my antics even reached our office in Dubai, where I was hoping to be posted. Very embarrassing.

My problem is that I don't handle alcohol terribly well. When I drink, I become rather wild and behave out of character. But refusing to drink is not tolerated by my colleagues. Only a visible pregnancy bump would let me off the hook and I haven't had a boyfriend for three years.

How can I keep a lid on things while not seeming to be a spoilsport?

Nicola W, Abergavenny

Dear Nicola,

The problem is drink, therefore the solution is don't go near it. Did you really need me to tell you that? I understand the peer pressure must be terrible.

I confess, if I'd seen the pictures from last year's bash, I'd probably be plying you with a bucket of cava as well.

The trick is not to make any announcement about not drinking. Make no fuss when people try to top up your glass and always be seen to be holding a drink. By all means, have a couple of sips so as not to arouse suspicion, but basically try not to drink all night and leave early.

If this makes you a spoilsport, so be it, because the sport in question is watching Nicola making a drunken spectacle of herself and then laughing at her when she shows up to work the next day with skin the colour of pea and ham soup, shaking like Kerry Katona on a tumble-dryer. Most decent folk will respect you for your restraint and the mob will simply turn its jeering attention to some new drunken fool.

By the way, given your particular weakness for booze, I suggest that a posting to Dubai will either be your salvation or we'll end up reading about you in the news section of the *Daily Telegraph*. Cheers!

Dear Graham,

My wife and I separated in January last year, having been together for 16 years. She and our three kids (12, 10 and 6) have dealt with the changes OK but I haven't.

I've had very few highlights considering I have made the effort to put myself out there. I've tried bars and clubs; internet dating; salsa dancing; gym and tennis membership and even dated a client briefly (I'm in financial services). The dancing was brilliant but most of the girls were either too young, or already dating.

My ex is very attractive and, although I realise that looks aren't everything, I haven't felt the same passion for the occasional girl I have dated since our separation.

What I really miss is the satisfaction of having a healthy physical relationship, as well as the day-to-day stuff like the chats, the hand holding, the hugs (my kids' hugs and kisses are great but not the same) and the company of being with someone I care for.

Loneliness is a horrible thing that messes with your head and my work as a financial adviser (dramatically affected by the credit crunch) means I spend a lot of time on my own, which only adds to the gloom. The pressure on my finances doesn't help my social life.

My usually optimistic attitude is being tested and I really would appreciate your view on what I should do next. I am 53, but I keep in good shape and am young in outlook.

'Jack' (no address supplied)

Dear Jack,

I'm afraid to say that there is no easy fix for what you are going through. Time is really the only thing that will help. After 16 years with one person, no amount of salsa classes or internet dating is going to replace what you had. Comparing new women in your life to your ex-wife is pointless because that is over.

Try to see that starting afresh with all the trial and error that entails can be an adventure not just a litany of failure. You haven't gone into detail about why the marriage ended but it sounds to me as if you aren't just lonely but really missing your ex-wife and your family life together. Remember why it ended – even if she walked out on you that

154

means she was profoundly unhappy and, no matter how you choose to recall things, a relationship can't be a good one if one person is miserable in it.

The trauma of your separation coupled with the global economic collapse is going to put a huge strain on you so try to stay strong.

Bad times – just like the good times – don't last forever. There will come a morning when you wake up next to someone you love and you will hold her and feel truly happy. I hope that time is soon.

Dear Graham,

I'm an ordinary, unassuming 30-year-old man with a penchant for large ladies. When I watched your television programme the other night and saw a lucky fellow being set up on a blind date with Dawn French, I was green with envy. The fact is that I like women with something to grab hold of.

Most of my female friends are model-thin and those who aren't wrap themselves in acres of black fabric, endlessly harp on about diets and, like vampires, only really come out at night. The result is that I'm permanently single because I don't fancy any of them. The thin ones are too thin and the fat ones are too damn miserable.

Any ideas?

Victor S, Coventry

Dear Victor,

If I'm correct, you are looking for happy fat women. I've never gone out of my way to try to find one myself, but I can't imagine it's that difficult. Getting a job in a Thorntons chocolates shop might expose you to some, or you could just hang around Madame Tussauds and wait for the Americans to show up.

The other thing would be to tell the miserable fat women you know how attractive you find their bodies and, trust me, that will put a smile on their chubby faces. If you are too shy for such an approach, then it strikes me that this kind of niche dating was what the internet was invented for. There must be some lardlover.com out there where you will be welcomed with open flabby arms.

Tie a cake to your face. Disguise yourself as an eclair… I'm on fire here – I don't think I've ever given better advice. You're welcome.

Ask Graham

Dear Graham,

I am a widow with three wonderful grandchildren who I don't see nearly enough of. My daughter is very close to her mother-in-law, who, like me, is a widow, but unlike me lives in a lovely, rambling house in Hampshire, with enormous grounds and lots of spare rooms.

Blessed as she is with plenty of money, she is able to have the children to stay with ease and can offer them wonderful treats.

Living in a small flat in Barons Court on a modest pension, I feel I can't compete. As a result I feel rather left out. Raising the matter with my daughter - who has a lot on her plate already - would be awkward and I have no wish to cause trouble or be a bore. She is clearly very happy with the status quo and I can quite see the attraction of having a place to take the children at weekends.

I don't want to get all bitter and twisted about this. Any words of wisdom would be gratefully received.

Eleanor S, west London

Dear Eleanor,

This is a very tricky problem and I think you are being wonderfully understanding. It is unfortunate that in a situation that involves so many people only one person is losing out and that's you. The obvious solution, though I'm not sure how practical it would be, is to befriend the mother-in-law. Then you could spend time with your grandchildren and have nice weekends in the country.

If you don't feel comfortable fishing for invitations, I think there is another approach you could take which wouldn't involve competing. Find an activity or invitation for one grandchild at a time.

It will be less economically draining for you and will tread on far fewer toes. And presumably the one-on-one quality time with each child will be even more valuable for both of you.

To be honest, I think you are giving your daughter a slightly easy ride. She ought to be aware of the problem and be addressing it rather than simply going with whatever makes her life easier. Maybe you would find it simpler to tell your son-in-law how you feel since there is less emotional baggage between you.

If all else fails just become the wild fun granny. Stock your fridge with Alcopops and get some certificate-18 DVDs and listen to your doorbell ring!

156

Dear Graham,

I'm a young mother who's just started work again and I'm loving it – skinny lattes, proper conversations with intelligent people, a sense of self-worth now I'm not a full-time housewife whose biggest excitement is looking for nits and pairing odd socks. My husband is very supportive of me going back to work and we've got a great au pair (from New Zealand, none of that class-war business you get with British ones). But the problem is our kids (six and five), who feel unloved and abandoned. Every morning there are terrible scenes when I leave for work.

Sometimes I think I'm going to die of guilt, or be punished in some terrible way for my selfishness. What should I do to restore peace in our house? Should I abandon all thoughts of having a career?

Sarah P, Bath

> ❝ All children are tiny conservatives – they hate change. ❞

Dear Sarah,

Well, you've come to the right place. I like to think of myself as a one-stop shop for all your childcare advice. Let's break down what is going on in your life. You have returned to work and you love it. That's a good thing. You have great childcare. Another positive. Your husband is supportive. More boxes ticked.

Your kids have a fit when you leave in the morning. Not pleasant but is it such a bad thing? Obviously, I can't imagine the guilt but all I would say is that it's very early days. Right now your kids don't like you leaving them behind, but that's simply because all children are tiny conservatives – they hate change. On the up side, surely one of the most valuable lessons you can teach your children is that they can't have it all their own way?

Imagine what sort of message you would be sending to your kids if you sacked the nanny, gave up work and sat with them all day. In the short term, it might assuage your guilt and their distress, but later down the line you will be bored and resentful and they will be smug control freaks. The choice is yours.

Please bear in my mind that all these words of wisdom come from a man who can't get his dogs to sit for a biscuit.

Dear Graham,

I suspect my wife is addicted to diets. She's never happier than when she's on one. While everyone else is feeling miserable and broke after the holidays, my wife is planning with secret joy her latest diet campaign in minute detail. It doesn't help, of course, that at this time of year all the papers and magazines are full of diet plans.

Egged on by Basha, our Polish cleaner, she's just embarked on something called the cabbage soup diet, a hideous regime that makes her bad-tempered, headachy and exhausted - and gives her evil brassica breath (we won't mention the other side effect). The fact of the matter is she never actually loses any weight at the end of these punitive diets. She just wastes an awful lot of time.

I like her just the way she is - curvy and solid. How can I get her to enjoy life and stop worrying about how she's going to look in a bikini? Our last beach holiday was in 1992. Next year we will be eligible for freedom passes.

It's ridiculous!

Freddy P, Northamptonshire

Dear Freddy,

You state very clearly that your wife is never happier than when she is on one of her fad diets – so apart from the odd bit of wind wafting past you and the Polish cleaner, where's the harm? I'm sure it's frustrating that your love isn't enough to reassure her and she needs the mirror to tell her that she looks beautiful but very few of us have a totally healthy body image.

Although she may not lose much weight when she is busy counting calories, imagine for a moment what epic proportions she might reach if she didn't do these diets every year. A freedom pass is of little use if you can't actually fit on a bus.

Perhaps you could make a deal where you set a time frame for putting an end to her dreams of salvation through starvation. Two more years and she can retire to graze peacefully until death and you don't have to listen to her wittering on about how she can't eat an egg until she has had a grapefruit first.

The problem with all the miracle diets and exercise regimes is that even if they work we are just a skinnier version of ourselves and who we really want to look like is the model on the cover of the video or the box of strawberry-flavoured powder. Watch a few episodes of *Extreme Makeover* to see the pain in the eyes of the participants when they see the mirror for the first time and realise that they are still the same person just with clean hair and whiter teeth.

Allow your wife to enjoy chasing after something she will never get because if she did ever achieve the perfect body it wouldn't make her happy. Greyhounds enjoy chasing that bit of rabbit fur on a roller skate – think how upset they would be if they ever caught it.

Dear Graham,
I'm planning to propose to my girlfriend over the New Year,
which we'll be spending with her parents in the Lake District.
Her mother is a dog-loving, salt-of-the-earth type who bakes
cakes and plants bulbs. Her father is ex-Army and rather
formal. What's the correct etiquette in these circumstances?
Should I ask for her father's permission first?

Ben F, Fife

Dear Ben,
I imagine that, if I met you at a party and the next day had to describe you to others, I'd say you were very sweet but a bit thick.

Your intentions towards your girlfriend are lovely. Congratulations and I hope that she accepts.

I feel it would be remiss of me not to point out that your girlfriend is more than likely to turn into a salt-of-the-earth, dog-loving, bulb-planting, cake-baker. But if that's OK with you, then so be it. As for asking the father for his permission, I have no idea what you should do.

But if I were in your situation, I'd propose first. If the answer is yes, then ask your new fiancée what she thinks you should do. Do fathers these days ever not give their permission? If he doesn't, then of course you have a whole new set of problems.

By the way, if all goes according to plan – and I think it will – then please don't invite me to the wedding. It's not that I wouldn't enjoy meeting you, but it's so hard to gift-wrap an Aga.

Dear Graham,
My widowed mother keeps begging me to go on holiday with
her. Her latest plan is a cruise around the Norwegian fjords.
She's had a really hard time since my father died and I
desperately want to do the right thing and be supportive, but I
go insane with boredom and irritation if I'm cooped up with
her for too long.

It's not that she isn't lovely - it's that typical mother/daughter
thing. We get really irritated with each other. While I'm always
happy to do lunches, or dinners, or cinema trips, I don't think I
could go on holiday with her without losing my rag and being
horrible.

I'm single, but I live a very full and hectic life. Adapting to
the geriatric pace of a cruise would be really hard. I can't
think of anything worse than being stuck on a boat, playing
canasta and talking to elderly couples from Ohio.

Any advice? I am 45. My mother is 83.

Gail L, Lincs

Dear Gail,

You can't think of anything worse than being stuck on a boat with your mother? Try sitting at your mother's funeral wishing you had taken her to see the Norwegian fjords.

Your mother is 83 and soon such trips will be beyond her so set sail sooner rather than later. I completely understand that you won't enjoy it and indeed it may be hell, but it's not about you. You have already lost your father so surely it makes sense to spend time with your mother.

Oddly, the pace of a cruise may help your relationship because you will have no distractions. You might just enjoy sitting around talking about your father, remembering childhood holidays or, if all else fails, laughing at badly dressed fat Americans.

We can't live our whole lives to please our parents but drifting around Scandinavia for a week doesn't seem like much to ask. It may inconvenience you but I doubt you'll regret giving your mother happy memories.

Dear Graham,

I'm an addict. No, it's not drink, drugs or (sadly) sex, but all those cheap, bodice-ripping novels that clog up the shelves of supermarkets and public libraries. Even though I have a perfectly good brain, I just can't read enough of the kind of books you cannot be seen with in public.

As with eating too many vanilla cupcakes or drinking one too many Cosmopolitans, I always feel a bit disillusioned and tawdry the next day, ashamed of myself for having such pathetic illusions and for being led astray by such nonsense. I know it should be a simple matter of marching towards the Classics section and picking up something by Dostoyevsky, but I always get ambushed by those marshmallowy covers.

How can I beat my addiction?

Tara A, Middlesex

Dear Tara,

So you're attracted to the wrong sort of books? There is no shame in that. We have all chosen to watch an episode of *Hollyoaks* over *The Sopranos*, but to do it constantly is, I suppose, a bit of a waste of time.

Why don't you upgrade to the top of your genre? Jackie Collins or Jilly Cooper will, I'm sure, satisfy your addiction. Then move on to Maeve Binchy. Next try lowering the sugar content with a few Barbara Vines and, before you know it, you'll soon be wading through all the titles from Richard and Judy's book club.

The other thing you could do is to put down the book with a picture of Fabio dressed as a pirate on the cover and leave the house. Maybe then you could run your hands through the coarse dark hair of a real man while your heart beats wildly and you feel the rain soaking through your thin cotton dress.

You may get arrested for attempted rape, but at least you won't have turned into a crazy old lady who smells of lavender.

Dear Graham,

Since we married two years ago my wife has stopped making any kind of effort. She has put on two stone, buys all her clothes from Per Una and often wears a hideous combination of fleece and old leggings that does her no favours. I can't remember the last time she wore heels and showed a bit of cleavage.

We don't have kids yet - we're only in our early thirties - so she doesn't have the excuse of children and sleepless nights. I'd like her to wear nice things but, whenever I drop hints, she goes into a major sulk.

Somehow standards have really slipped. She's a fantastic cook but now buys everything ready-made from Waitrose, even though she has a pretty undemanding job. The irony is that I had to really fight to woo her - there were two other guys circling like piranhas.

I do still fancy - and love - her, but I'd like her to be the woman I married, not this lazy supersize-me version of her former self.

Simon D, Henley

Dear Simon,

I feel that as an impressionable boy you may have watched too many episodes of *Dynasty*. Helmet-hair and inch-thick lipgloss may be what you want 24/7, but in the real world women tend not to wear full make-up and diaphanous gowns in order to sniff the milk to see if it's off.

I hope you realise that the power to change your situation lies with you, Simon. Book a table at a nice restaurant or organise a night out at a club and, hey presto – just like in the days of yore – the woman you married will scrub up nice. People only make an effort when they feel they have to and it sounds as if you have stopped providing your wife with any reason to shave her armpits, never mind clamber into 6in heels.

The problem probably stems from the start of the relationship – you had to work hard to win her and she was used to being wooed. Once you got together, I'm guessing you both breathed a large sigh of relief and stopped. It's up to you to restart the romance and make some moments special.

Why don't you surprise her with a romantic home-cooked meal? As clichéd as it sounds, buy her some expensive lingerie. The bottom line is that if you try so will she. Heartbreaking as it is, it's about time you realised that Joan Collins is the exception not the rule.

Dear Graham,
My IT consultant boyfriend Lars is addicted to stock car racing.
Every Saturday he races clapped-out old bangers in grim places
like Skegness, dressed in a grubby black leather jacket and filthy
Levis. At weekends, he's never around for parties, dinners or just
hanging out, because he's always either stuck on the motorway or
haring around on some godforsaken track. And when he's not
racing, he tinkers with his car.
    I don't want him to stop doing the things he loves, I'd just
like to see more of him.

Rose S, Kent

Dear Rose,
You are dating an IT consultant called Lars who prefers stock car racing to spending time with you and now you expect me to care when it's not working out? You don't have a boyfriend, just mysterious grease spots on the furniture. Grow a backbone and make a few demands.

Nobody wants to be a nagging harridan, but nor do you have to be a doormat. Ask him if he'd be willing to spend one weekend a month with you. I suspect that faced with even this very reasonable request he will say no and dump you. But then is dating Lars that different from not dating him?

Dab a little petrol behind your ears and try again. Maybe this time you could aim for Formula One.

Dear Graham,

I've just got back from a hen weekend at a seaside holiday camp with 20 girlfriends. It's not my thing at all, but I'm getting married in a month's time and it was booked as a joke by my best friend. We dressed up as policewomen on the Friday night, in Seventies outfits on the Saturday and in pyjamas on the Sunday. It was shrieky, boozy, tacky, funny, outrageous – and I absolutely loved it.

The bad news is I drank one too many cocktails on the last night and ended up kissing a man dressed as a chicken. Even worse, I slept with him, right under the noses of the girls sharing my chalet. It was very much a one-night stand – and not something I'm proud of – but my stuck-up sister-in-law (who we had to invite) heard all about it.

I'm worried that she'll say something to my fiancé or hold this trump card up her sleeve throughout my married life. Should I say something to her, or let sleeping dogs lie?

Rosie R, Kent

Dear Rosie,

When you watch movies, do you often find it difficult to know who is supposed to be the hero and who is the villain? Did you cheer for Glenn Close in *Fatal Attraction*? Were you quite fond of Anthony Hopkins' character in *The Silence of the Lambs*?

My point is that your sister-in-law is not the villain in this story. The person who comes out of it very badly is you. Thrilled as I am to learn that you enjoyed Butlins, I fear you took to it like a slutty duck to murky water. It's one thing to walk down the aisle with something borrowed and blue, but do you really want to be trailing some big dark secret?

Forget about talking to your sister-in-law. The only person you should talk to is your future husband. Normally, I would never advocate confessing an infidelity, but in this instance too many people know. Somehow, somewhere, sometime he is going to find out. If you really do love him, then you need to control that situation.

I hope you fully understand the severity of what you've done because the only useful advice I can give you is that, when you confess to your beloved, you should probably try to sound a little sorrier than you did in your letter.

Ask Graham

Dear Graham,

I went to a dinner party the other day and sat next to an amusing man who gave me a peck on the cheek and handed me his business card when he left at the end of the evening. What does that mean exactly? We are not in the same line of work, so it can't be a business proposition. But, if he fancied me, why didn't he just ask for my number, which I would have given willingly?

I'm now left in the maddening position of having to take the initiative (or not). It's left me feeling very confused. My friends, the hosts, think he's been out of the dating game so long he's forgotten how to approach women (he's divorced with two kids at prep school). But I'm inclined to be less generous. Is he simply lazy and a bit of a coward?

What do you think? Should I call him? And what on earth do I say?

Eliza C, London

Dear Eliza,

You have met a man you like and you have his number. That isn't so bad a situation. Calling him doesn't immediately turn you into one of those women who write to men on Death Row.

Not for a moment do I believe that giving you his card was lazy and, let's face it, in that sort of situation we're all a bit cowardly – you don't want to call him, do you? So, imagine for a moment how he felt. Also, he is a divorced father of two. He was probably trying to be discreet rather than be seen as playing the scene like some fake-tan Lothario with a baby-blue Mercedes waiting outside.

I don't think you're confused. You're just afraid because he has left the ball firmly in your court. The phone call can be as overt or as coy as you want to make it. You could say you're going to be in the area around his office one day next week and would he like to grab lunch? Or you want to get a gift for the person who hosted the dinner party and does he have any ideas? You are planning a charity bike ride to Slough – would he like to sponsor you? Whatever. The point is the ball will be back on his side of the net and then you'll get a clearer picture of where you stand.

A man likes you and is hoping against hope that you will call him. It's a good thing, so stop deliberating and start dialling.

Ask Graham

Dear Graham,

My husband retired recently and since then has become a total hypochondriac. The merest mention of the 'C' word sends him into paroxysms of anxiety. Rather embarrassingly, I recently received a call from a nurse at our local doctor's surgery asking if I could have a quiet word with my husband. Apparently, he keeps booking in for appointments and wasting GPs' valuable time.

He is absolutely convinced he's ill despite all appearances to the contrary - he's a very hale and hearty 66. Apart from the usual bouts of 'man flu' and one prostate problem in his forties, his experience of doctors and hospitals has been negligible.

He complains about all sorts of silly things - achy big toes, dry eyes, phantom rashes, waxy ears, blocked sinuses. He's now muttering about 'going private' - which we can't really afford - as he says the NHS doctors are clueless and far too busy, anyway, dealing with all those pregnant, unmarried mothers from sink estates.

Is there anything I could do to calm him down? Perhaps try to get him to channel his energy into some kind of new project? I don't believe for a minute that he's actually ill.

Juliet R, Derby

Dear Juliet,

Presuming that your husband is still alive by the time you read this, I think you already know the solution to your problem. Distract the old fool.

The trouble with the sort of minds that enjoy hypochondria is that, when you fill them with something else, they become equally boring and annoying about that. Get him interested in watching the birds in the garden and you'll find him driving to remote parts of Scotland to buy a special seed. A new-found love of collecting stamps will mean your living room is out of bounds as he covers the floor with rare first editions.

When men retire, they can't stop their heads needing that strange mix of preoccupation and anxiety. Being ill is merely your husband's hobby and the trouble is that no hobby will ever tick all the boxes. What he really needs is a pay-cheque. I'm sure that, if someone paid your husband to have man flu for eight hours a day, he'd come home at the end of it and feel fine.

Your husband needs another job or therapy. By the way, if he is dead or seriously ill, I guess we were both wrong and please ignore all of the above.

Dear Graham,

I rent the flat above mine to a Frenchman who is a high-flying management consultant. Up until now, he has been the perfect tenant: quiet as a mouse, rarely at home and punctual with his rental payments. The problem is that he recently acquired an Italian girlfriend, who appears to be living with him. My bedroom is below theirs and their strenuous night-time - and early-morning - sessions either wake me up or prevent me from sleeping in the first place.

It's all rather embarrassing. Is there a polite way of asking them to pipe down, without causing offence?

Percy W, London SW7

Dear Percy,

You want to talk to your tenant about the noise problem without causing embarrassment. He is French and his lover is Italian – the only person who will be in any way embarrassed is you. Don't just stand on his doorstep coughing and shuffling, talking in riddles. Be direct and try not to whine.

Let's hope they tone down their love-making, or at least do it at less anti-social times. If they don't, I'm afraid you will just have to learn to live with it.

So many landlords want to take their tenants' money but aren't prepared to accept that people can't live silently. Your Gallic Lothario didn't rent the flat from you so that you'd have extra cash. He wanted somewhere to live, play his music and provoke his Italian lovely to shriek louder than any diva at La Scala.

If you want a really quiet neighbour, why not rent your property out to an al-Qaeda sleeper cell?

Dear Graham,
I've been trying to find a boyfriend online for months and whenever I browse profiles my divorced father keeps popping up (predictably he's shaved 15 years off his actual age). I've no idea how long he's been at it but he called me the other day to say that he'd met someone (off the net) and was engaged to be married - that's right, not just dating but engaged!

My future stepmother is a Dublin-based widow with three university-age children. They're getting married this autumn and I can't help thinking that given the age gap - she's 20 years younger and infinitely more attractive - she must be after his money.

I'm 39, permanently broke and agonisingly single, and cannot believe that my father is beating me to the altar and quite possibly cutting me out of my inheritance. It is quite the most shattering news I've heard in a long time. Am I pleased for him? Absolutely not - I'm furious!

Tell me how I can beat him at his own game and get myself up the aisle before him.

Fran L, London

Dear Fran,

Do me a favour. Please get up and go outside. Walk until you find a sign with your street name on it and if it says neither Coronation Street nor Albert Square then I would suggest that your response to your father's upcoming nuptials is not very helpful or practical.

There is a great deal going on in your heart and head right now. But I think the only true emotion in your letter is when you tell me that you're furious. Of course you are angry – your daddy is moving on. It's not just his money that someone else will get – it's his love.

The emotional dynamics of what is happening in your life at the moment are hugely complicated, but please try to understand that your father is not living his life in an attempt to antagonise you. Just as you were surfing the web looking for happiness, so was he. He's found it. Dig deep and try to find some way to share his good fortune.

Trust me, Fran, there are lots of reasons to get married but doing it in order to score points against your father in some game he isn't even playing is not one of them. I hope you find your Prince Charming but, in the meantime, buy a new dress and feign delight.

And let's not be too quick to judge the Dublin widow – as far as she's concerned, your father is only five years older than her (assuming he's also lied about his age to her).

And while your dad might have some money, he also comes with a great deal of emotional baggage – and by that, of course, I mean you.

Dear Graham,

I think I may have fallen in love with my housemate. About a year ago, my spare room became free at the same time that she had to leave her flat, so she moved in. And that's where my troubles started. Now I can't stop thinking about her - to the extent that I had to break it off with the girl I was seeing.

I jump when she brushes past me and my voice goes up an octave when I try to have a normal conversation. The other day she came out of the bathroom wrapped in the skimpiest of towels and I was like a rabbit caught in headlights.

I long to tell her how I feel, but am afraid of what this will do to our friendship. Besides, she has a boyfriend (who I cannot stand). Should I risk everything and tell her I love her, or ask her to move out and banish myself forever to a monastery?

Tim W, Brighton

Dear Tim,

You seem to have worked yourself into a frenzy over very little. You love your flatmate. Great. We've all lived or worked with someone who was the innocent object of our adoration. If you do confess your feelings, you won't need to tell her to pack her bags. The front door will have slammed shut before you utter the third of those three little words. Whether you like her boyfriend or not, she does still have one. She is not available.

I feel you have left out some details. Has she done anything to encourage your feelings? Is there any flirting as you scrape the burned toast together? For some reason, I suspect not. It sounds to me as if this is all about wanting what you can't have.

Although moving to a monastery might be a marvellously romantic gesture, it isn't really the answer. If the woman you want doesn't love you, learn to love a woman who does want you. As a child I desperately wanted a chimp, but I learned to love my dog.

Ask Graham

Dear Graham,

One of our best friends changes girlfriends as often as he changes his Porsche 911, despite the fact that his age - late forties - makes him almost an embarrassment in our circle of friends, all of whom are happily married. We are all a bit fed up with the succession of Kates, Emmas and Julias he wheels out at every social occasion, only to discard them months later. Although he claims to be looking for a wife, he never commits to any of his (usually younger) girlfriends.

Soon he'll be 50 and we fear he won't be quite such an enticing prospect to women when that day dawns. There's something a little sad about an ageing management consultant hanging out in bars and nightclubs.

How can we help him get over his fear of commitment and settle down to marriage and parenthood, just like the rest of us?

Jim and Barbara S, Newbury

Soon, he'll be 50 and we fear he won't be quite such an enticing prospect to women.

Dear Jim and Barbara,

Maybe, just maybe, the reason your friend is terrified of settling down is because he doesn't want to turn into you. Did it ever cross either of your minds that, as he leaves your house with one of his walking sex toys, he wonders when his friends turned into such smug bores?

I know you are only trying to do what you think is best, but the point is that it's best for you. If he settles down like the rest of you, then it validates the choices you have made. Life isn't an exam where your friend may get marked down on his coursework. We all make choices and muddle through as best we can. He may say he wants a wife, but clearly he is still having too much fun.

If you still enjoy your friend's company, then try to accept his lifestyle. And if you find that impossible, then maybe you'll simply stop being such good friends. Again it's just everyone making choices, not judgements.

I'm thrilled you are both so happy, but you have to accept that not everyone wants to buy a hatchback car.

Dear Graham,

I've just started going out with a fellow musician who's unfortunately very chaotic and disorganised. We're going to Paris in a couple of weeks, but the shame is we're going to be travelling on separate trains. And it gets worse. I'll be arriving the day before him and he's catching the last train on the following day, so it looks like we're barely going to coincide at all.

I feel terribly glum about traipsing around the Musée d'Orsay on my own, like one of those sad, rainy characters in an Anita Brookner novel.

I'm hoping to see him tonight but - again - it could be a case of me waiting for him all evening (he loses his mobile all the time). Or him perhaps thinking he's meeting up with me tomorrow.

Any advice? I really like him. But going out with him sometimes feels worse than being single - at least when I'm unattached I can just schedule happy evenings alone with a box of Ferrero Rocher, or go to the movies solo (to see something he hates). How can I get him to be a bit more sorted?

Tara C, Herts

Dear Tara,

In the time it has taken me to read your letter, I have run out of patience with this man. He has obviously been indulged by so many people over the years that he has learned that this behaviour is acceptable.

It is your job to teach him that it is not.

Don't make a scene or raise your voice, but simply inform him that you aren't going to go to Paris. If he questions why, explain that you don't fancy hanging around the most romantic city on earth by yourself, so, until he can arrange a time when you can go together, you'd prefer to postpone the trip.

Similarly, if you can't be sure if he'll show up for a date, then always make another plan. Arrange to meet friends at the same time and place as you've arranged to meet him. If he does show up, he will be put out and probably claim you are exaggerating when you tell him why you double-booked yourself. People like this man always claim that it only happened once and they had a really good excuse. Again don't lose your temper; simply spell out the facts as you see them.

He may see the error of his ways and try to change, in which case you could start to indulge him a little. But what is more likely is that he will go into a major sulk from which he never emerges.

In the end, being late is all about power. He is testing you and pushing you further and further to see how much control he has over you. Once you push back, he may respect you more and everything can start to move forward, or he will run a mile.

Either way, you won't be spending hours sipping a drink you didn't want, staring at a clock that doesn't move and avoiding the sympathetic stares of strangers.

Don't be fooled – he isn't chaotic, disorganised or eccentric. He is simply selfish.

Dear Graham,
My husband and I are about to celebrate our first wedding anniversary.

We were friends for a long time before we started seeing each other and I have become retrospectively and irrationally jealous of his female friends, one of whom he was particularly interested in (she didn't fancy him but strung him along).

Whenever we go out, I become plagued by imaginings that he would rather be with her than with me, and that she is prettier and more fun. I become consumed by my own insecurity, especially after a couple of glasses of wine.

Please give me some straight talking and stop me ruining my relationship with my husband.

Eva M, north London

" Avoid being high maintenance. Men may enjoy working on things around the house, but their wife isn't one of them. "

Dear Eva,

Male eyes roam. Accept this now or be unhappy forever. This other woman may have been a focus for his attentions at one point in time but you are the one he proposed to.

When you said yes, you both drew a line under previous relationships. I fear he could become very irritated if you get clingy and paranoid every time you have a drink.

There is no shame in explaining – when sober – that you have certain insecurities. Perhaps suggest that he be a little more attentive when you are out.

After only one year of marriage it is natural that there are things you are both still discovering.

Be patient with yourself and your husband but, whatever you do, avoid being high maintenance. Men may enjoy working on things around the house, but their wife isn't one of them.

Dear Graham,

As a recovering alcoholic, I recently went on a weekend retreat in an old abbey in the West Country. The problem was that the retreat was overrun with Obsessive Eaters Anonymous, largely female. I made it quite clear that I'm with someone (my girlfriend is about to have twins) but one woman pursued me all weekend, flashing her gigantic bosom and planting her vast frame between me and the door.

Although I did manage to give her the slip on the last day and leap on to a train home, somehow she has got hold of my mobile number and keeps leaving flirtatious texts on it, suggesting we meet.

I'm not worried that my girlfriend will see them. I've told her about the woman and she just thinks it's funny. I just want to get rid of this woman politely without tipping her over the edge into a morbid state of obesity.

Any tips?

Nick H, Suffolk

Dear Nick,

Because I'm a nice person, I'm going to gloss over the 'somehow got hold of my mobile number' portion of your letter and move swiftly on to my advice. Ignore her. Any response from you, be it good bad or indifferent will simply feed her unhealthy appetite for you. Starve her and she'll move on.

The problem is that on some level you enjoyed her attention and are still flattered that this woman is obsessed with you. Shut it down. Change the number she mysteriously found if you must, but don't respond in any way. Should she find your home address and show up on the doorstep refuse to see her and don't react to her no matter how hysterical she may become.

I can only imagine how wildly attractive you are, Nick. But, trust me, your biggest fan will find other fish to fry. As for you, well, soon you'll have your hands full with two big actual babies.

Good luck!

Ask Graham

Dear Graham,

My fiancée and I have just bought a house together. But what should be an exciting and romantic adventure, where we lovingly position our cushions, is being ruined by our radically different tastes.

I'm what you might call 'traditional antique'. I like heavy, dark woods, velvet drapes, hunting pictures and pewter mugs. She prefers an edgy, minimalist look. Her old flat was full of stark white furniture and modern 'art' - the kind of thing my three-year-old nephew could knock up. She also has a collection of obscene carved figurines that we'll have to hide every time my parents visit. How can we marry our tastes, let alone each other?

Jamie C, Northumberland

Dear Jamie,

Let's get real – hunting pictures? Pewter mugs? Why don't you just move to Albert Square and live in the Queen Vic. No one wants to live in a house where the only thing you can serve at a dinner party is a hearty ploughman's platter or scampi in a basket. Why don't you get a garden shed and style it in sticky-carpet, full-ashtray chic?

On the plus side, you have agreed on a house to buy. That is an enormous decision and one that brings many couples crashing to the ground.

I suspect that you are both being unreasonable. Take a long hard look at the house and let it talk to you. Let it tell you how it wants to be decorated. If you can't hear anything, why not get a decorator involved so that you and your wife-to-be will be united in your hatred of its interior design? All I know is that if you are finding it this hard to decide how to decorate a few rooms, good luck with your wedding arrangements!

Dear Graham,
For the past six months, I've been going out with a guy who had
a messy divorce two years ago. I've discovered that, despite almost
moving in with me four months ago, he is still wining and
dining two other women. I don't make a habit of snooping but in
a weak, nosy moment had a look at the 'sent' box on his mobile,
where I found various larky messages with kisses attached.
   When I confronted him, he didn't deny he'd been taking
other girls out but said that they were 'just friends'.
   He promised to stop and said the reason he continued to
see other women was that he was frightened about closing off
all options.
   Unfortunately, I've discovered that he hasn't stopped seeing
them. What should I do? I don't think he's sleeping around, as
he's with me most nights, but I feel really insulted. I love him
and would hate to lose him, but I'm feeling increasingly
miserable. It's as if I'm not really good enough.
                                      Kimberley A, Roehampton

Dear Kimberley,
I fear this may be a case of right guy, wrong time. It's very likely that
he is telling you the truth when he says that he doesn't want to close
off his options.

After the pain of a divorce, I think it's understandable that he's
nervous of total commitment.

I realise this doesn't help you very much but at least he's being
honest with you rather than making up some story about an old friend
of his mother's being in town. Everyone wants to be loved completely
and without question, but right now the man you are with isn't
capable of that. I worry that the longer you stay in this relationship,
the more damaged you are going to become. It's not this man's fault
but you do deserve better.

It's all very well him telling you that he isn't sleeping with these
other women, but in a post-Bill Clinton world it is very hard to know
what constitutes cheating. In the end, the most reliable test is how his
behaviour makes you feel – and it is clearly making you very unhappy.

Perhaps if you leave him it will be the catalyst for him to realise how
much you do mean to him and you could start afresh with his head and
heart in a better place.

Of course, he may just be a two-timing scumbag blaming his divorce for his wandering eye, but either way I fear you need to get out.

Dear Graham,

I am in that post-fling limbo of wondering whether to end things or soldier on. The girl in question is a very beautiful 26-year-old redhead called Flora but I fear she might be mad. I recently made the mistake of agreeing to go to dinner at her godmother's. Flora behaved rather oddly throughout the evening, most of which she spent examining the pattern on the carpet, arguing that it was 'really quite interesting'.

She didn't have any of the food (gazpacho followed by fish pie – both barely edible) but instead bit into three apples, all of which she abandoned half-eaten. Noticing my startled expression, her crêpey-bosomed godmother leaned across the table and whispered: 'Don't worry about it, darling, she's been to art school.'

My question is this: is Flora a bonkers artist or is she excitingly creative? Is this normal behaviour for arty girls? (I work in a bank.)

Hans P, Swiss Cottage

Dear Hans,
You can't believe she's not a nutter? Trust me, the only option open to you now is to have as much sex as possible with the apple-munching loon and then get out of there as quickly as you can. In truth, it sounds as if she isn't really mad, just a pretentious loser, or perhaps a nice woman who is trying everything she can to make you dump her.

Her mental state isn't really the issue here, is it? Your name is Hans and you are a banker who lives in Swiss Cottage. She is a failed artist who enjoys staring at the carpet and having dates that include her godmother.

Even an ITV sitcom writer would think twice before trying to pitch this as a zany 'opposites attract' scenario. Accept that you are probably quite a dull man and date accordingly.

Dear Graham,

I'm suddenly back on the market after a horrible divorce and I'm finding it much tougher than I expected to find a new man. I've always been the kind of woman who turns heads. Other women might be cleverer or funnier, but I'm the one men usually go for. Even when I have unwashed hair and wear any old rubbish, men always fall over themselves to get my number. Now it's a very different story. No one seems to notice me any more and there's a raft of attractive, unattached women, many of them a good 10 years younger than me (I'm 46), who are intent on nailing a man of my vintage.

Perhaps it's a hard thing to sympathise with and I sound like a spoiled, self-regarding cow. But when you've once been beautiful, with the power that goes with it, it's terribly hard to accept that your allure is waning. If I'd been a plain Jane all along, I'm sure ageing wouldn't bother me much, but before I married, 15 years ago, I had the world at my feet. Throughout my marriage, other people's husbands were always flirting with me, so I had no idea I'd lost my old magic.

I'm finding it tough to accept and it's making me utterly miserable.

Jane P, West Midlands

Dear Jane,

I bet you are the sort of driver who runs out of petrol all the time because you forget to check the fuel gauge. How did you not see this coming? Rail against the gods as much as you like, curse men from the highest mountain you can find, but it is just the law of the sexist jungle. Put very bluntly, Jane, it is very hard to go to market with no eggs in your basket.

Obviously, it is possible for older women to still find partners, love and sex, but before you are able to, you will have to learn a new way of relating to men. A very pretty friend of mine was talking to a man at a party recently and told me after it was over that she thought he was gay. Since he clearly wasn't, this surprised me and I wanted to know why. 'He didn't flirt with me,' was her reply.

Don't think a conversation is going badly just because a man's eyes don't drift to your cleavage. As men become less immediately interested in you, you may have to be a bit more interested in them.

Ask Graham

Try to find things you have in common beyond the fact that you both think you're gorgeous.

But far more important than finding new ways of talking to men is finding new ways of having fun without men. If you don't discover a life where you enjoy being by yourself or hanging out with girlfriends, then I fear you'll spend your evenings crying over old photos of yourself in a bikini. Don't think of your new life as worse – it's simply different.

By the way, the days of not washing your hair are firmly over, but I'm guessing you knew that.

Dear Graham,

I am 52 and have been happily married for nearly 30 years. We don't have children but we do have two chocolate Labradors, which, I admit, are probably child substitutes. The dogs have always slept on our bed, but unfortunately they are not quite as fragrant as they used to be. My husband, who is not as doggy as me, now wants to ban them from the bedroom. Although I love my husband dearly, he is a terrible snorer, and I would rather it were he who decamped to the spare bedroom anyway. How can I achieve this without him thinking I have chosen the dogs over him?

Meredith W, Cumbria

Dear Meredith,

I think it's going to be quite difficult to prevent your husband thinking you have chosen the dogs over him, because that is precisely what you have done. You have coped with his snoring for 30 years, so I'm not sure why it should suddenly have become unbearable. If it really is, why don't you move into the spare room?

As for the dogs, here's an idea – wash them. Dog deodorisers are available in any decent pet shop, so get spraying. You say that they are child substitutes, but if your children stank I don't imagine you would be choosing them over your husband. The man is a saint and you need to get a grip of reality.

Dear Graham,

My partner and I are ambitious professionals in our mid-thirties who don't want children. We have 10 godchildren between us and lots of much-loved nephews and nieces, but we have no desire to become parents. For some reason this seems to upset and infuriate people. Our families and many of our friends (all married with children) have made it clear they don't approve.

It seems we are breaking a sacred code by choosing not to reproduce and are making others uncomfortable. Not a day passes that we don't find ourselves at the receiving end of a barbed remark about our 'lovely luxury holidays' or our 'endless trips to restaurants'. Although we are generous to all the children in our lives, sometimes to a ridiculous degree, our decision to opt out of parenthood is viewed as selfish and unpleasant.

I'd like some advice on how to handle the situation. We try to ignore the criticism, but I know that my partner gets rattled every time the subject comes up.

David G, Newcastle

Dear David,

Ah, the joys of being gay! The only voices of disapproval we hear are when we suggest that we would like to have children. What a pity you chose to combine your life of conspicuous consumerism with heterosexuality.

I imagine that your partner, as she's female, feels the barbs and digs more deeply than you do. Sadly, the only remedy to this situation that I can see is time.

Eventually, family members will give up hoping, as the ticking of the biological clock becomes fainter and fainter and then stops. As for your friends, you'll find yourselves growing ever more distant as their lives revolve around nothing more than loading and unloading buggies and nappy bags from SUVs, with a few trips to A&E to break up the monotony.

You have made a lifestyle choice, so get on with it and stop expecting other people to approve or accept it. When we walk, we shake our fists at car drivers; when we are behind the wheel, we scream at pedestrians. Life's complicated like that.

Have another holiday, but remember that no one will want to see the photos.

Ask Graham

Dear Graham,

I've started going out with a 35-year-old guy I met through a dating website. It's all going unexpectedly well. We've just got back from a week's skiing in Val d'Isère and we've already met each other's siblings and parents. But I recently went back on to the website and found he's put his membership on 'passive', whereas I've taken mine off completely. When I asked him why he was still on there, he said he'd paid for a whole year so he thought he might as well stay on in case things didn't work out.

Are men less romantic and more pragmatic than women? I'm upset that his profile is still on the website when he's not available any more. I don't know how to broach the subject again, but it's niggling away at me. It makes me feel as if I'm being put through some kind of exam and I feel resentful and unable to relax. Am I unreasonable to mind?

Imogen R, Hastings

Dear Imogen,

The short answer is yes, but that's not what they pay me for, so let me expand. A year is a long time and you don't tell me how long you have been dating him, but what would your new man gain from taking down his profile? It's not as if he is still actively looking, or spending any extra cash to stay on the website. Although it's easy to do, try not to confuse being unromantic with being lazy.

I'm far more curious about why you went back online. If I was your boyfriend, that's the bit that would really annoy me. He has, like any self-respecting man, been a big passive lump, while you have actively surfed the world of singles.

I wonder if you are being completely honest with yourself. Relax and don't go looking for problems where there aren't any. Work out when the year he paid for is up and then check the site once more. If he's still there, or his membership status has changed, then you have cause for concern. He took you skiing and agreed to meet your parents – that's as close to a dictionary definition of love as you are likely to get.

Dear Graham,
Why do women fall for bastards? I'm a decent, upstanding 31-year-old civil servant, with my own hair and teeth, no beer belly and reasonable hygiene and I've been single for four years. Supposedly, there are single girls all around, desperate to find steady boyfriends, but in my experience all they want is shallow, bed-hopping fund managers with red Ferraris and huge egos. All my university contemporaries who went into the City have girls hanging on their every word, even the really unattractive ones. I understand that money is a major aphrodisiac, but I don't understand why women like men who treat them badly.

I've read about a dating site called Toyboy Warehouse (www.toyboywarehouse.com) that's apparently full of eager, older women, but I'm not looking for some kind of Demi Moore/Ashton Kutcher scenario, just a nice, normal girl of my own age.

Where do I start?

Paul A, east London

❝ Sympathy sex and even pity sex are still sex. Perhaps after four years on your own, it's time to stop being so fussy. ❞

Dear Paul,
What is going on here? I thought I understood your plight – the old 'nice guys finish last' syndrome – but then you threw me a bit of a curveball with the website. If that's not what you want, why mention it? It's like a waiter coming to take your order and you saying that you don't want the smoked trout and then putting down the menu.

Is there a little bit of you that is so nonplussed by what women want that you'd quite like an older, perhaps slightly domineering, lady to tell you? If so, I completely understand. It sounds quite hot, so why not give it a go?

If you don't like it, you can just go back to being ignored by the girls as you wait for the lift. Trust me, whatever happens it won't be like Demi and Ashton. For starters, there are no Demis on the internet and, second, if you were Ashton, even with unreasonable hygiene, you would not be writing to me.

The only other thing I can advise is that if you aren't meeting girls in your current life then change it. Do all those clichéd things like joining clubs or societies – people constantly suggest them because they work. My other tip is to hang around with the girls who are dating the bastards because when they get dumped you can be there for them.

Sympathy sex and even pity sex are still sex. Perhaps after four years on your own, it's time to stop being so fussy.

Dear Graham,

My new boyfriend, Paul, is totally unadventurous when it comes to food. I have lost count of the number of times we have eaten chicken breasts and salmon steaks for supper. Whenever I suggest anything more exciting he's up in arms. His favourite thing is pancakes and when we go out he always has the dullest thing on the menu - soup of the day, or pasta with tomato sauce.

My last boyfriend hardly ate anything at all, apart from black coffee, a horrible thing called 'grits' and bagels. But I'm the kind of person who likes to cook when I'm in love. It's so depressing! Am I picking the wrong men?

Nicholas B, London

Dear Nicholas,

You have a boyfriend. That's right: you, the pretentious bore, have managed to find a boyfriend. Now imagine the two of you on the sofa watching a movie (I'm sensing subtitles – poor Paul!), eating bowls of dull pasta. Got that? Now picture the scene as you sit alone poking a plate of black cod with a chopstick. Which of these scenarios do you prefer?

As I have often remarked, no relationship is absolutely perfect and usually it is a stark choice between compromise or solitude. Reading between the lines, I feel that Paul is probably making huge compromises. It is highly unlikely that he went online and ticked the box next to 'dreary food snob'.

Relax, Nicholas. There is room in life for ketchup as well as truffle oil.

Dear Graham,

My wife has kept a diary since she was 15. It is very much a private affair and I assumed that after we got married (six months ago) she would abandon it. How wrong I was. I dropped a pair of cufflinks the other day and as I bent down to look for them under the bed I spotted a large A4-sized book wedged under the bedframe. On opening it, I discovered pages and pages of longhand (dating back nine months), with a recent, unfinished entry in which I glimpsed my name several times.

There was no time to take a proper look as my wife was calling my name from the bathroom next door. But now I know where her diary lives I'm consumed with curiosity. What does she write in it? What does she say about me? What are her views on our sex life and how do I compare to her previous lovers?

Would it be very shameful to take a quick look? My feeling is that it might even be good for both of us - so long as I don't tell her, of course.

Matthew W, Cheshire

Dear Matthew,

Yes, fire ahead! Read her diary – what could possibly go wrong? I mean, I've never heard a story about someone reading a diary and being upset about what was in it, have you?

Matthew, seriously, only read that diary if you are ready to deal with the end of your marriage. I completely understand the huge urge to stick your nose into her innermost thoughts, but try to resist. Tell her that you have inadvertently found where she hides her journal and she needs to find a better hiding place.

Frankly, the lack of imagination she has demonstrated by putting it under the bed suggests the contents must be fairly dull stuff. If she doesn't move it, then she clearly wants you to read it, so help yourself.

The trouble with diaries is that they don't come with an index where you can look up M for Me, so you must wade through pages of stuff about people at work and dreary literary passages where she imagines lives for the people she sees on the train. The bottom line is that you've married someone who writes a diary and, after the age of 14, that usually means they are that strangest of combinations – a boring fantasist.

I shut my eyes to visualise your wife and see Piers Morgan in lipstick. God help you.

Ask Graham

Dear Graham,

Married friends recently set me up with a really eligible lawyer. He's keen and keeps inviting me to expensive restaurants and to the opera.

My problem is that I don't fancy him. He doesn't excite me in any way. In fact, I find him a bit boring and predictable, even though I desperately want to fancy him (I'm 34 and have been single for five years).

Friends (married) tell me that chemistry doesn't matter. I should give it a go, even if I have to drink a bottle of Prosecco to kiss him. As the French say: 'L'appétit vient en mangeant.' But does it in matters of the heart?

Laura N, East Sussex

Dear Laura,

Perhaps the most depressing thing about your letter is that you aren't even willing to invest in champagne to consummate the relationship. Take this as a sign and move on. Being drunk might get you into bed with him once but, unless you want to live like Amy Winehouse, it's not a great basis for a relationship.

On top of that, consider for a moment how unfair you are being to this man. Doesn't he deserve to be with someone who adores him? Your friends may say chemistry doesn't matter, but I think you'll find your dream date disagrees.

You talk as if you are stranded on a desert island with this man and the future of mankind rests on the two of you getting together. He's a nice guy whom you don't fancy – keep walking, Laura. You may have been single for a while, but surely that is better than running out of excuses not to have sex and see a man slowly realise that you don't love him. Where's the fun in that?

Relationships may be all about compromise, but this is like chopping off a leg because you can only find one shoe. Unless this guy is an ex-Beatle, it's really not worth it.

Ask Graham

Dear Graham,

I need some no-nonsense practical advice. I am 32 and have a boyfriend who is generous, kind, loyal, bright and not bad looking either. In a nutshell, he's exactly the sort of person I know is good for me. My problem is that I'm a typical twisted female. I'm attracted to bad guys and have spent a long time trying to train myself off them. But having found myself a much more suitable boyfriend, with amazing qualities, I find it difficult to conjure up feelings of love.

Your advice would be greatly appreciated.

Camilla E, London

My problem is, I'm a typical twisted female attracted to bad guys.

Dear Camilla,

I admire your commitment to self-improvement. Like Fern with her gastric band, you have shed your old self. Goodbye to bad boys and all the emotional damage they can wreak on a young woman's heart. Wiping the tears from your eyes, you have sat up late at night listening to Norah Jones or perhaps a bit of Adele and made a list of the qualities you want in a man. So far, so self-improving.

The problems arise when you meet a new improved boyfriend. The part of your brain that drew up the list of desirable qualities is thrilled but, as you have now discovered, safe and sensible are the natural enemies of love and lust.

There is no practical advice for conjuring up love and so you must now decide how you want to move forward. You could decide to settle for this new Mr Right, but do you honestly believe that you won't get bored and break his heart when you run off with the man who checks the air pressure in your tyres?

The attraction of bad guys is that you might just possibly find one that will change for you, but no good guy has ever suddenly become exciting. Relationships aren't a science, so don't think about them so much. Remember that people search for a love potion, not a love formula.

Dear Graham,

How does one turn a friend into a lover? I have a large circle of single friends and one of them is so funny and nice that I've started to really fancy him. Sometimes the two of us meet for a drink or to see a film, but nothing has happened.

Just being myself doesn't seem to have lit any fireworks. Help.

Martha S, Stoke Newington, London

Dear Martha,

Sleeping with friends is often short-sighted. Although it might work out, the price for a night of passion will be your friendship, which will never be the same.

What sort of relationship could it possibly be when 'being yourself' isn't working? Are you planning to put on an act for the rest of your life? Sometimes there aren't meant to be fireworks, but that doesn't mean you can't enjoy the long slow glow of friendship for what it is. Slow down and enjoy what you've got, rather than worrying about what you are missing.

Ask Graham

Dear Graham,

I know this sounds petty but my husband refuses to take the bins out. In all our married life – two years – I have never been able to get him to perform this mundane but deadly task. It is always me who has to empty the clanking bin and lug out the full bag at midnight in my nightie.

With my parents, the deal was always that my father did the physical stuff (bins, logs, digging in the garden, packing the car), while my mother did everything else. I don't think they ever discussed it – they just agreed on things in a tacit, harmonious way. Of course, my mother got the raw deal, but I don't think she minded. At least my father did the bins, stoked the fires and knew how to wield a garden spade.

But I've married a clueless, selfish man who expects me to do everything.

It may sound crazy, but sometimes I think he can't possibly love me if he leaves me to do the rubbish every single time. Sometimes I almost wish we lived in one of those desperate, rat-infested areas where the dustmen only come by twice a month. At least I wouldn't resent my husband and we'd probably have sex more often.

Pippa L, west London

Dear Pippa,

Nobody wants to take the bins out. If I want to show someone I love them, I'll tell them so or buy them a gift – I won't lug great black plastic bellyfuls of slop out into the street. The fact is that for two years you have allowed this situation to exist. Why on earth would your husband want it to change? Even I would prefer to hear you whine a bit than to actually deal with the garbage and end up with mystery juice dripping down my legs.

There is only one thing you can do and that is to go on strike. Make it very clear that you don't mind sharing the task, but he must take the rubbish out next. Doubtless he will resist, but you must be firm. The only way you'll get what you want is by letting the bin bags pile up. The appearance of cockroaches snaking across your kitchen counters like passengers at a Terminal 5 check-in desk, or rats drinking from the tap, must not shift your resolve or else all is lost.

If it gets to the stage that the neighbours have called in the police

188

because they think there is a dead body in your flat, and he still won't budge, then I think it is safe to assume he doesn't love you and that walking down the aisle was about the most energetic thing he has ever done. At this point, it is safe for you to dump all your unwanted rubbish, including him.

Dear Graham,
I've just started going out with this drop-dead gorgeous girl, who's one of those Notting Hill trustafarians: hugely health-conscious, organic and green, even though Daddy's job involved demolishing the planet. She boycotts Tesco and eats only organic food, preferably covered in mud. And she's into yoga, of course. Nothing new there - plenty of girls have similar obsessions. But she's not quite the karmic goddess she seems. Sadly, her idea of a good time is to pile into the lavatories at weddings with a couple of other girls and snort a few lines of coke.
How can she be so hypocritical? How can a person be chemical-free on the one hand, yet pile their body full of drugs on the other?

Ewen L, London

Dear Ewen,
How many dates have you two been on? All you seem to like about her is that she is gorgeous. Everything else seems to irritate the hell out of you. Forget trying to make sense of her pretty head and leave her, because this relationship is going nowhere.

The ethical dilemmas you mention are interesting but, even if she reveals she is using 100 per cent natural fair-trade cocaine, you still aren't going to love her. If you stay with her simply because of her looks, then guess who's the bigger hypocrite?

Leave her to her white weddings, so you can get back to enjoying Tesco's Finest.

Dear Graham,

Ever since I can remember it's always been 'poor Camilla' in my super-high-achieving family. I flunked out of university halfway through my degree to become an artist, did a series of dead-end jobs in my twenties and most of my thirties and had so few boyfriends that people wondered if I was gay. When I was 19, I was prescribed anti-depressants and I've been on them pretty much continuously since then.

My sister in contrast has had a near-perfect life that almost replicates that of my parents - Oxbridge, a high-paying job, shiny friends, marriage (to someone equally successful), lovely kids, a beautiful house et cetera.

What is odd is that my life has suddenly turned around, while my sister's has nosedived. At 38, I'm engaged to a lovely man, I'm off the pills and my sculptures are suddenly in hot demand. Meanwhile, my sister is locked in a vicious divorce battle with her husband. She and her children have moved in with my parents, who are buckling under the strain of it all.

I've been trying to offer support but my family are finding it really hard to deal with the fact that I can't be at their beck and call - and now have a busy life of my own. You'd think they'd be pleased to see me happy, but it seems not. Everyone preferred me when I was depressed and lonely! How can I help out, while getting my family to accept that I no longer conform to their negative stereotype?

Camilla L, Aylesbury

Dear Camilla,

To be brutally honest, after all these years, your family will probably always think of you as 'poor Camilla'.

The important thing is that you don't. You must live your life for yourself, not your family. Everybody's circumstances change.

Hopefully, your sister will get back on her feet and everyone can have a slice of the lucky pie again. Your good fortune is not based on your sister's unhappiness. Don't get sucked into some weird masochistic competition with her. Enjoy your life in isolation, not relative to what your sister is going through.

It is only in fairytales that there is one sad princess and one happy princess. Real life is much more complicated.

The fact that the family feel able to ask you for help suggests that some of the 'poor Camilla' feelings are slightly in your head. If your parents are being too demanding, then just be firm. Ultimately, they will respect you for being clear and honest but do what you can because there may come a day when once more it is Camilla who is asking for help. I hope things improve for everyone very soon.

Dear Graham,

I've been with my French girlfriend, Juliette, for 22 months and, although I've always been a bit of a Lothario where women are concerned, I've never stuck around long enough to get to know any of them properly. Juliette is my first serious girlfriend (I am 29). She has a refreshing joie de vivre that is unlike most English girls, and that's part of the reason why I'm still hooked.

The problem is we have long periods of not getting on terribly well. Weeks can go by with her turning her back on me in bed. I have no idea if this is normal, or whether I'm with the wrong girl. She is keen to start a family, but I am not 100 per cent sure we are right for one another. Do other couples have similar ups and downs?

Jonathan S, London

Dear Jonathan,

Nearly 30 and so naive! There is an old Swiss proverb that says 'Marriage is a covered dish', which essentially means that no relationship is normal and that no one apart from the couple can guess why or why not the partnership works.

Fighting all the time sounds miserable to me, but it seems as if you thrive on it. Your French girlfriend's volatile spirit has kept you interested for nearly two years so perhaps it is worth considering whether the calm alternative is truly what you want. As for children – you haven't told me how old your girlfriend is, but if she isn't knocking at 40's door then you should see how things play out, because, however hard things are between you now, a screaming baby will only make things harder.

But from what you write it seems that the whiff of baby powder won't be happening too soon. I'm no expert on heterosexual sex but I'm pretty sure that turning her back on you in bed is not how babies are made.

Dear Graham,
I've just got engaged and my parents are not happy about it.
They say my fiancé and I are too young - I'm 21 and he is 22 -
and it's too soon for us to make that commitment, given that we
have only been going out since the summer. My fiancé and I
don't have any doubts at all and I feel my parents are being a
little hypocritical as they married young themselves.

I've always been old for my age and didn't go to college
because I was keen to start working and earn money as quickly as
possible. All through my teens, I did Saturday and holiday jobs,
and I've been working full-time in a legal chambers, running the
administrative side of things, since I was 19. My fiancé is equally
hard-working and responsible.

Why the fuss? I don't want to upset my parents but, when you
know it's right, why delay things?

Stephanie L, Berkshire

Dear Stephanie,

I'm glad you're happy. I'm thrilled you are in love. I'm impressed by your work ethic. Clearly, you are a mature woman in charge of her own destiny. The only thing that makes you seem like a kid is your hurry to get married.

Your parents love you and just want to protect you from pain. They know divorce is much more emotionally damaging than a simple break-up, especially if children are involved. The fact that they got married young doesn't make them hypocrites, it just means they know how hard it is.

Having said that, they may as well give you their blessing because clearly nothing is going to dissuade you from wanting to hear wedding bells and cut a cake with the man of your dreams. We all make choices and then have to live with them.

Life isn't an exam with right or wrong answers; everything we do turns out to be a bit of both. I really hope you have a special day and a wonderful life, but try to keep your girlish figure and then you can at least wear the dress again.

Dear Graham,

My husband lost his job this summer and we decided that it would make sense if I went back to work while he stayed at home to look after our baby. It has all gone surprisingly well - he's brilliant with her and she's really flourishing. The problem is that since he has become a house husband I don't find him as attractive as I used to. Some days it feels as if I'm living with another woman.

I know we have to find a way of making this work. My job makes more money - and his prospects of finding work in the current climate aren't good - but I'm finding the role reversal quite difficult. Often I yearn to be spending all day with my daughter and waving my husband off to work.

What would you do in my situation?

Fiona B, Kent

Dear Fiona,

How frustrating that the perfect solution to a tricky problem has caused an even trickier one. I imagine that looking at your husband washing your baby makes your heart glow with love, but hardly fills your loins with yearning. Still this is a problem that men must face all the time as their sex goddess becomes a milk-stained mummy.

In the short term, I think the most important thing is to stop your love life from disappearing altogether. Have sex even if you aren't in the mood. Think of it as the pilot light in your sexual boiler – you know how hard it is to relight once it goes out completely.

In the long term, work on ways of letting your husband assert his masculinity. It might sound ridiculous but watching him put up shelves or clear out the garage might just help you see him in an old light. If you are finding it difficult to improve your sex life by yourselves, then don't feel embarrassed about asking a sex counsellor for help.

As for not wanting to go to work some mornings, welcome to the world. No one looks forward to going to work every morning, that's why they pay you to show up.

Dear Graham,

My husband dropped down dead six months ago while teaching our five-year-old football in the back garden.

He was a high-flying City broker and we led a pretty extravagant life, living for each day, assuming he would go on earning for years to come.

Quite apart from the enormous hole it's left in my life - and my children's - it's been a colossal shock financially. My husband had no life insurance so I have had to downshift in a major way, moving out of our (rented) house and pulling the children out of their fee-paying schools.

My problem continues to be financial. I want to give the children a better life but I simply can't afford it. I haven't worked since I was 22 and, even if I did try to find some kind of job, I feel I'd be letting down the kids who really need me at home.

There is no family I can rely on. His parents are dead, my widowed mother is in a nursing home and, like me, my husband was an only child.

I know there are no simple answers but any advice would be welcome.

Delphine S, Guildford

Dear Delphine,

I know your husband died only six months ago but I'm afraid the answer is simple – you must get a job. I know it's not ideal but, as life has cruelly shown you, things rarely are. It's possible that you could do something from home which means you won't feel so guilty – perhaps offer childcare to friends who need it – but whatever happens, you need to start earning some money.

Things have reached crisis point after a few months and I fear they will just get worse the longer you avoid going back to work. Presumably you have already tapped into any social services or benefits you are entitled to. If not, do so immediately.

The other thing to do is to find women who are in the same situation as you. You can't be the only young widow in the country and I think finding out how other women cope will make you feel much better and, even more importantly, less alone. The future must seem insurmountable and exhausting right now but you have survived the worst and I'm sure you are tougher than you think.

Take comfort in the fact that life doesn't usually stay awful for long
– there will be bright spots in your future. Head towards them.

Dear Graham,
I launched myself on an old friend recently, partly out of
loneliness (we're the only singletons in our circle), partly
because I'd always vaguely fancied him. We spent the night
together and I woke up the next morning with a thumping
hangover, realising that I'd made the most awful mistake.
   We've been friends for ages, but I guess we never got together
before for a reason. It's hard to describe exactly, but I felt
almost incestuous the next day - as if I'd slept with my brother.
   What should I do? He keeps calling and leaving these sweet
messages. I feel awful about the whole thing.
                                         Rosamund I, Suffolk

Dear Rosamund,
You idiot! OK, we've got that out of the way. But now you must act
quickly. This is the sort of situation that, if you allow it to continue,
will turn bad faster than organic milk. I suggest a very posh lunch that
you are going to pay for.

Tell this guy exactly how you feel, right down to your line about
incest, and then sit back and pray. With luck, he will understand and
the two of you can stagger back towards the friendship you had. But
if he is so heartbroken that you lose him as a friend, at least you
haven't led him on.

Now the only thing that could go wrong is that you get drunk at the
lunch and sleep with him again because you feel guilty. Make sure you
have somewhere you have to be in the afternoon and don't agree to
meet him later that night to talk some more.

Good luck, and remember that sleeping with friends is lazy and
selfish: we don't cook our pets just because we're hungry and they're
sitting right by the oven.

Dear Graham,

I am godmother to my best friend's son. I am really fond of him, but I find that, since I was asked to be a godparent, my friendship with his mother has changed. These days I'm only ever invited over to 'bond' with my godson. What typically happens is that I am asked around for a so-called drink, but, while my friend tucks into a lovely bottle of sauvignon blanc downstairs, I'm stuck upstairs reading endless bedtime stories and beginning to feel like an unpaid nanny rather than a friend.

At the end of a busy day at work, what I want to do is sit down with a glass of wine and relax over some proper adult chat. I don't want to be reading stories about wolves and bears to a small, fractious child. But somehow the whole thing is presented to me like a favour (I'm childless and single).

How do I tell my friend that this is the last thing I feel like doing, without hurting her feelings? And am I just mean-spirited to mind?

Lara U, Bedfordshire

Dear Lara,

There are two approaches to this problem. The first is probably the more sensible. Start praising your friend to the skies. Marvel at her mothering abilities and declare that you just don't know how she does it. The next time you are due for a visit, ask if she minds if you come a bit late because of work. Obviously, you'll be very sorry not to spend time with your godchild.

The next time, cry off from the child care by explaining that you are too tired after work and again express your admiration for her amazing child-rearing skills. Slowly, like a baby with milk, you'll be weaned off child-care duty and have to do it only occasionally.

The alternative is morally suspect but much more fun. Every time you go upstairs to your godchild, pump him full of sugar. Smuggle in biscuits, sweets, cans of cola. The child won't sleep for weeks on end, you will be blamed and you'll never be asked again. I know this seems like the perfect solution, but do you really want an obese godchild?

Ask Graham

Dear Graham,
I've just met this rather nice man. It seems to be going well but
he just doesn't wash his hair. It smells funny and looks awful.
   Maybe a better person could put up with it, but I've got a
thing about dirty hair (only Kurt Cobain could get away with
it in my book) and it makes intimacy a bit of a struggle for me,
when he is otherwise so attractive.
   I think there may be an underlying issue: his hair is
thinning and I expect he worries that washing it makes it fall
out faster. How can I face this kindly?

                                              Lisa D, Hastings

Dear Lisa,
One of the really good and very bad things about living somewhere
like Hastings is that no matter how awful you look within minutes you
will see someone who looks a lot worse.

Under no circumstances must you raise this problem with your new
friend. You should engineer a situation where someone else will do it
for you.

Why not buy him some treatments at one of the many new men's
grooming places that have opened in London? Before he goes, call
them and explain the situation. These people are almost doctors. Ask
them to give him a range of shampoos and conditioners that promote
hair growth.

Obviously these don't work (check out my picture on the cover of
the book) but at least what he does have will be clean. If this is outside
your price range, then one night in the pub in front of others might
encourage him to shave his head for charity, thereby helping others as
well as him.

Think of me as you wake up next to someone who doesn't smell like
a wet dog.

Ask Graham

Dear Graham,

My wife is turning into a very dull woman. Is it shameful to say that? When I married her she was a hotshot lawyer with great legs and huge charisma. But now she's a woolly, dumpy mother of two, whose interests don't extend beyond the four walls of our house.

You're going to tell me she's exhausted from housework and child-rearing, and perhaps she is. But I'd be happy to employ armies of nannies and housekeepers so she could relax more and take care of herself generally. It's my wife who refuses all help.

If she suggested going back to work part-time, I'd be delighted. Not that we need the money; more that I'd like to see her revert to the bright, sparky person I married, and get back some of her old self-confidence. Although she's a good mother, it's no fun being married to her any more.

I'm not saying I don't love her, but I'm a hot-blooded, competitive male. I like women with chutzpah who challenge me. I don't want to come home every evening to a bedraggled wife whose only news is that the plumber has come.

Marcus E, Chichester

Dear Marcus,

Isn't it annoying when people change? It's such a shock. I remember the first time I saw Tom Selleck without a moustache. The trouble is you just don't see it coming. Who knew that getting married and having kids might transform a leggy hotshot lawyer into someone else?

Marcus, you need to realise that the woman you married is gone and unlike Tom's moustache is never coming back. The good news for you is that your wife is obviously very comfortable in her new role and the other bit of good news is that you're rich. Money may not solve every problem, but it is quite an effective solution to being poor.

Use that money to take your dumpy wife out of her comfort zone. Arrange childcare and whisk her off to Portofino, take her skiing in Whistler. In short, give her things to look good for. No one would dream of showing up at those locations without a new outfit or two.

Encourage her to meet people who may challenge her to do things outside of the home. Maybe you could ask her to help you with some

198

project? There is no reason for your wife to come up with ideas herself as she is obviously content working as a mother and homemaker.

As the children grow older, this new job may begin to bore her. Make sure she doesn't get bored with you.

Dear Graham,

I am a 27-year-old bachelor who needs your advice. Four years ago I lost a leg below the knee in an accident. Since then I have dated only within my circle of friends, who know about my situation. Now, however, I have met the most gorgeous girl and I am terrified of telling her in case she dumps me. Should I continue concealing it from her and enjoy it while I can? If I prolong it, I hope our love will have more time to grow even stronger. My false leg does not bother me, and we have been to bed several times without her realising. Help!

Tim L, Somerset

Dear Tim,

When I first read your letter, I wondered how it was possible to have sex with someone who has a false leg and not notice. Then it came to me in a blinding flash – it probably isn't. I believe really strongly that your gorgeous new girlfriend knows about your leg and just hasn't said anything. She's waiting for you to bring up what is, under any circumstances, a sensitive subject.

Think about it, Tim. Friends of friends are sure to have tipped her off long before you turned out the bedroom lights. Look around: you know who has a glass eye, who is trying to hide a withered hand, and certainly who has lost a leg. I'm not saying that it's obvious in any way, but everyone has some kind of grim fascination with the misfortune of others.

Test my theory. Over dinner, slip into conversation something about your accident or operation, and then casually confirm that she knows about your false limb. She will be thrilled that it's out in the open, and you can stop getting undressed in the dark.

She likes you – enjoy it.

Dear Graham,
My younger sister, who's only 15, has a crush on one of my
friends and it's really annoying. She hangs around us all the
time, saying ridiculous, inappropriate things, and staring at
him in this moony-eyed way. She's also started wearing really
horrible shouty make-up and these jangly ethnic bracelets that
drive me nuts.

He's far too nice to say anything but I can tell he's really
embarrassed. Luckily, I'm in my last year at school so she won't
be in my hair for much longer, but I'm wondering how I'm
going to get through the next few months. How can I get her to
leave me in peace when I have my mates around?

Ed L, Barnes

Dear Ed,
Your letter makes me so glad I have dogs instead of kids. Canine
children just sniff around each other and then either have a fight or try
a bit of half-hearted humping. I don't think I could bear shouty make-
up and ethnic bracelets.

Since you are leaving school this year, why not practise being an
adult? I'm sure you can remember a time when you found it hard to be
cool around girls you fancied and your sister is just in the same slightly
sweaty awkward boat.

Now what I'm about to suggest may make you scream and throw
the paper to the floor. What if your friend likes your sister? I know that
is the sort of thought that makes your breakfast want to say hello but
think about it. If he hates the attention, why does he keep coming to
your house?

Watch them more closely or perhaps ask your friend if your sister is
annoying him. The answer may surprise you. If you find out for sure
that your sister is barking up the wrong pimple-covered tree, then
maybe mention it to your mother who could perhaps break the bad
news to your sister better than you.

These situations never get easier. As you read this, someone in a
retirement home is trying to figure out if the man across the dining
room might be interested. Love may be a many splendoured thing, it
may be blind, but mostly it's not very bright.

Ask Graham

Dear Graham,

I've fallen madly in love with my flatmate. I've been cheering her up after she was dumped by her boyfriend a few weeks ago and now realise I have very strong feelings for her myself. I don't want to break the trust she has in me by telling her how I feel. But I'm not sure how long I can keep a lid on things.

Ever since her break-up she's been moping about the flat with her hair in a sort of Arab turban. When she gets back from work she goes straight into her pyjamas. Should I suggest taking her out to dinner one evening, or somehow get the message across when we're sitting down to our usual fish fingers in front of the TV?

Sean N, London

Dear Sean,

First things first. How long is your lease? If it is anything longer than three months, then keep your feelings to yourself. If you might be moving soon anyway, then what have you got to lose?

I'm not sure the fish finger route is the way to go so try your idea of going out together in order to cheer her up. To be honest, I'll be very surprised if you get anywhere because this woman is clearly not ready to move on. Wandering around the flat in a turban and pyjamas sounds like someone who is more in love with her heartbreak than she ever was with the man.

The other problem is you have now been placed in an area of her brain marked 'friends' and it will take more than a dinner and a back rub to refile you under 'l' for 'lover'. I'm sure it would be possible to choreograph some sort of drunken fumble but do you really want to feel like you have taken advantage of someone?

The fact is you have spent quite a bit of time with this girl and feel as if you've fallen for her. That tells me that you are probably a bit lonely – certainly for female company – and if your social life improved your crush might dwindle away. I fear the search for the love of your life may take you further afield than your own kitchen.

Dear Graham,

Our children are all over 18 and still living at home. It's making my wife and I frantic. In my day we couldn't wait to get away from our parents and have sex, smoke, conquer the world etc. Now all of these activities seem to take place under the parental roof. None of our children appears to want to leave home.

I fear we've been a bit over-indulgent so it's probably our fault not theirs, but we're getting fed up with the constant stream of teenagers and 20-somethings pouring in and out of our house at all hours.

Charming as they are, we feel as if we're running a crazy no-rules youth hostel. Whatever we cook is always gone in seconds. Wine bottles also vanish mysteriously. I now have to hide booze in the cupboard under the stairs.

Of course, we wouldn't throw our children out but what can we do to encourage them to leave of their own accord?

Michael L, London

> ❝ You and your wife have become such doormats you might as well lie face down in the hallway with 'Welcome' written on your backs. ❞

Dear Michael,

I would suggest that the reason you feel as if you are running a crazy no-rules youth hostel is because you are. Why on earth would any teenager want to leave this wonderful land of free food and laundry with the occasional drink thrown in for fun?

Of course, loving your children is unconditional but living with your kids should be full of conditions. You and your wife have become such doormats you might as well lie face down in the hallway with 'Welcome' written on your backs. Point out to your children that they aren't children any more. They are adults and must start paying their way. This could be in the form of rent or contributing to a household kitty.

Either way it will send them running to the pages of *Loot* faster than an investment banker clearing his desk. Add to this a list of chores and responsibilities and your nest will quickly empty. There will be tears and tantrums but be firm. You are doing your children no favours with the cotton-wool lifestyle you have given them. Fish gotta swim, birds gotta fly and kids gotta get a job. Enjoy the peace.

Dear Graham,

I'm a bachelor of 34 and, like most men, my requirements when it comes to women are pretty simple: food, kindness, warmth, television, alcohol and sex pretty much do it for me.

You'd think with such basic needs life would be a breeze, but I'm constantly amazed (and depressed) by the way women complicate everything. I'm always being drawn into arguments of their making, often when I'm feeling at my happiest and most relaxed.

Why are women so needlessly confrontational? Why must they unpick everything and go over stuff again and again? And why do they have to talk all the time about the smallest, most unimportant things? Yatter, yatter.

I'd like to know why women with degrees, good looks, good jobs (and breasts) do everything in their power to alienate their menfolk?

Can you shed any light on this?

Nick L, St Albans

Dear Nick,

Are you a time traveller? Have you journeyed from the Fifties? The idyllic lifestyle you describe where your every need is met by a little woman with no squeak nor demand disappeared in the Sixties, and here's a newsflash, Nick, it won't be coming back.

The problem here lies with you, not women. The list of your requirements may be very clear and concise but in any relationship the other party will have their own needs and desires.

Ignoring these is what leads to what you describe as 'yatter yatter'. If this all sounds like more trouble than it's worth, then, as Hamlet might have said, 'Get thee to a gay bar!'

Dear Graham,

My husband was diagnosed with colon cancer last year and is refusing to go ahead with the chemotherapy, or explore any other options that might improve his prospects.

I'm deeply frustrated by his defeatist attitude and his stubborn refusal of all medical help. He's always been fearful of doctors and hospitals, and simply won't discuss it with me. Is he in denial? Depressed? Too scared?

I've suggested we go away to Italy for a few days in the hope that some sunshine and gentle culture might draw us closer and help him open up. But he has no interest in going anywhere. It's terribly distressing, given his condition is treatable. Our two children (in their t hirties and working in London) are also finding the situation difficult.

We are in our mid-sixties and I feel that the double whammy of retirement and the cancer diagnosis have delivered such a blow that my husband is simply giving up on life. I would welcome your advice.

Elizabeth B, Surrey

Dear Elizabeth,

We all like to believe that, if we were given the news your husband received, we would fight the illness tooth and nail but the fact is no one can predict how they will react to a negative diagnosis. Perhaps your husband feels defeated already or maybe he's just sticking his head in the sand, but whatever he is doing it's unfair to the people who love him.

The good news is that he can't be the only cancer patient to have reacted in this way so there must be people out there who have faced this problem and overcome it. Once you have found them and discovered ways to move forward, everything will start to seem much brighter.

There are many cancer charities that could help. The Cancer Care Society and Cancer BACUP are just two I found on a very brief Google search. For now the only advice I can give you is to stay strong for your husband who is having to deal with something I don't think any of us can fully appreciate until we face it ourselves. Seek expert help and hopefully your husband and the people who love him will all turn a corner very soon.

Ask Graham

Whatever your husband is doing, it's unfair to the people who love him.

205

Ask Graham

Dear Graham,
Do you think that if there's something that makes you
fundamentally unattractive to the opposite sex your friends
would tell you? I only ask this because I haven't had a
relationship for 10 years (I am 34). Whenever I seek
enlightenment, girlfriends say things like 'don't be silly, you're
lovely' or 'men are idiots', or (the very annoying, usually from
my mother) 'it'll happen when you least expect it'.

I don't think I have any obvious defects - I don't have BO, or
a moustache. Nor do I sweat profusely. I'm not fat, although in
an ideal world I'd like to be a bit thinner. On a good day I'm
told I look a bit like Emma Thompson. Yet somehow I don't
attract men. Nobody ever asks me out. There are days when I
feel completely invisible. Where could I be going wrong? Do I
suffer from some awful defect that no one is prepared to point
out to me?

Jane T, Suffolk

> **❝ At least that hairy woman with thick ankles on**
> ***Britain's Got Talent* can carry a show tune, but**
> **it seems you don't bring very much to the**
> **party at all. ❞**

Dear Jane,

I haven't met you, so, of course I can't be sure, but I imagine there is
nothing wrong with you. Could your problem be that there isn't
anything particularly right about you either?

At least that hairy woman with thick ankles on *Britain's Got Talent*
can carry a show tune, but it seems you don't bring very much to the
party at all. It sounds like you just sit passively, waiting for someone
to notice you or find you attractive.

Trust me, even Angelina Jolie would be single if she didn't smile a
bit and engage with people.

You need to start enjoying spending time with yourself before
anyone else will want to. Sitting around with your girlfriends talking
about being single must have got a bit tired, even for you, after 10

years. Start living your life for you, and don't wait for other people. Is there a play or a movie you want to see? Just book a ticket and see what happens. Even if it's the worst night of your life, at least you'll have something to talk about. And that will help give you the appearance of someone who is interested in life and thus worth spending time with.

If the most positive self-image you can drum up is of a woman who isn't too fat or smelly or hairy, then surely you can see that a stranger isn't going to hang around digging for hidden assets.

Put your good side forward and over time you may grow to like yourself. Then, if some man likes you as well, it will simply be a bonus ball, not the jackpot.

Dear Graham,
My brother, who has always been popular with girls, was recently dumped by a girlfriend he'd been with for four years and was madly in love with. Since then, he has turned from a wonderful, sensitive guy into a serial philanderer.
He seems to be venting his rage on the female sex for the heartbreak he's suffered. His attitude to women has completely changed. He now talks about girls in entirely disparaging terms. To him they're just shag material. Every time I see him, there's a new girl dangling from his arm and they're always the same type: leggy blonde bombshells spookily similar to his ex.
I suspect that privately he's very miserable and may even be going through a breakdown. I want to help, but I don't want to make things worse. My boyfriend says blokes deal with things differently and my brother is just going through a 'phase'. What do you think I should do?

Naomi G, Merseyside

Dear Naomi,
Your interest in your brother's sex life strikes me as slightly creepy. He's hurting inside and if casual relationships are cheering him up so be it. The important thing to remember is that whatever his attitude to women, you will never – repeat, never – be the one he is going out with. Listen to your boyfriend because he's right. I know that's annoying, but in this very rare case it happens to be true.

Dear Graham,

I am a 44-year-old first-time mother. My daughter, now two, is a miracle child, loved to an almost embarrassing degree by everyone, especially my parents, who became grandparents for the first time when she was born.

I've always been exceptionally close to my mother and, although it's wonderful to see how much she adores Ella, it's also a little difficult.

So besotted is she that she has completely lost interest in me. My mother and my equally doting father barely acknowledge me or speak to me these days - I'm just a sort of conduit to their precious grandchild.

Of course, I'm very proud of Ella but I'm so sad that I seem to have lost the closeness I once had to my parents. I used to be able to talk about all sorts of things with my mother. Now all she wants to hear about is what her grandchild had for breakfast.

So despite my happy marriage (and motherhood) I sometimes feel as if I've been wiped off the radar.

Susie N, West Yorkshire

Dear Susie,

The simple truth is that, over time, the people around you will calm down about the miracle that is Ella and your relationships will return to normal. However, I suspect there is more going on here.

I've never had a baby but it seems odd to me that you aren't as wrapped up in the wonder of your daughter as everyone else seems to be. It's almost like you've got first-child syndrome – where your heart twists into a knot of jealousy as your parents walk through the door with your new little brother or sister.

I wonder if the relationship you describe as close with your parents was, in fact, them not allowing you to grow up. Being jealous of your own baby sounds like quite a serious issue to me and I wonder if you should seek some professional advice.

I may be wrong and it happens to everyone, but I think it would be wise to nip it in the bud before it sours your relationship with Ella forever.

As far as I'm aware, once you have a child, your life is never really about you ever again. You're still on the radar, Susie, you'll just never be in the middle of it again.

Ask Graham

Dear Graham,

My best friend is going out with a guy who works in my office. They met through me but it wasn't a set-up - we were all in the pub one night and the two of them got talking. They've been going out for a couple of months now and seem to be really in love and happy together.

Things have been a bit quiet lately at work and the other day I happened to glance at her boyfriend's computer screen on the way to the printer. Imagine my horror when I saw he had logged on to an internet dating site. And it clearly isn't a random one-off thing. Whenever I walk past, he seems to be at it - not just cruising but corresponding energetically.

I wouldn't dream of saying anything to his boss - I'm not that kind of person - but I'm wondering if I should say something to my friend. She's convinced she's met her dream man but wouldn't it be better if she knew the real truth now, rather than found out later?

Amy P, Cheshire

Dear Amy,

No! No! No! How many times must I explain this to people? You never pass on bad news about someone's partner because somehow it will invariably become your fault. 'Shoot the messenger' is an expression because that is what happens.

It's terrible to walk around with this knowledge but that is what you must do. The only way you can stray from this strict code is to tell another mutual friend. This will share the load and they may break the code of silence and be shot, but then at least your friend knows and your relationship should survive.

If there is talk of this couple living together or, even worse, getting married, then you may have to do something. Avoid your friend but approach the man at work and tell him that you know what has been going on. Hopefully, this will pressurise him into stopping or ending the relationship with your friend.

You may be wondering about how your friend will react when she finds out for herself and works out that you knew all along? Trust me that, upset as she may be, she will find it much easier to forgive your silence than your candour. Love isn't blind, it's just highly selective about what it wants to see.

Ask Graham

Dear Graham,

Last night, my 35-year-old boyfriend dropped a bomb. He'd been behaving oddly all week - he seemed stressed and very distracted. But I put his moodiness down to long hours getting his new business off the ground.

After three years with me, he told me he wanted to become a woman. At first I thought he was joking - but he wasn't. He is deadly earnest and has already researched things extensively on the internet and made contact with several doctors in London.

I am reeling from the shock of it all and feel as if my life has been shot to pieces. He says he still loves me, but I just can't accept he could do this to me. I almost wish he'd announced he was leaving me for another woman.

Emma-Louise J, Exmoor

My boyfriend of three years has told me he wants to become a woman.

Dear Emma-Louise,

I understand that you are shocked and hurt. You have every right to be, but at least your boyfriend has told you rather than carrying this secret for even longer.

Imagine how you'd feel if he hadn't had the guts to share this until after you'd got married and had kids? To be perfectly honest, you are getting out of this situation relatively lightly.

You just have to deal with a broken heart while his healing process will be a great deal more complicated.

I'm sure he's not lying when he says he loves you and he hasn't done this to hurt you.

Imagine how tortured he must have been for so many years to come to this conclusion. The man you have loved is deeply unhappy and he believes he knows the way to change that.

By all means encourage him to talk to people who can give him professional advice. Don't worry – these are not the sorts of operations that any doctor would rush into lightly.

Once you have got over the shock, you must explore your own feelings. Can you be friends with him and support him through this or do you need to protect yourself and your own emotional wellbeing by walking away? Time will answer these questions. There is an American film called *Normal*, which was made in 2003 and stars Jessica Lange and Tom Wilkinson. You can probably buy it on the internet.

In it the husband reveals to his wife after 25 years together that he is going to have a sex-change operation.

The wife turns to him and says, 'You could never be a woman. Only a man could be this selfish!'

Ask Graham

Dear Graham,
My husband was killed in a car crash just over a year ago leaving me a widow, with three small boys, at 33. Miraculously, money is not the main worry - my husband's parents have been very generous to us and the insurers have also stumped up. My worry is that my boys will grow up without a male role model of any kind. My husband was an only child - as am I - so the boys don't have any uncles and aunts and we live in a very remote part of the countryside. Other than school, my boys don't get a lot of opportunities for male bonding.

Please don't read this as a depressed letter. Of course, there's a chance I will one day meet a lovely man (who my boys love), but until such a miracle happens I wonder what I should be doing to make their childhood happier and more balanced.

Any advice would be so valued.

Tess L, Warwickshire

Dear Tess,
I like your attitude. A horrible thing has happened in your life and, rather than let it defeat you, you are looking for ways to move on. Well done. Childcare is not an area where I feel I'm an expert but my gut tells me that for the moment what these three little boys need is their mum.

Daddy has been ripped away, so 12 months down the line I imagine they just want to know that Mummy isn't going anywhere. Introducing random males into their lives may only serve to unsettle them. As they get older, male role models will surely come along, whether you meet someone or not. Teachers, sports coaches and (does this make me appear very old school and naive?) the cubs or the boy scouts.

I get the feeling that children are far more resilient than we give them credit for and, in much the same way as you are coping and getting on with your life without your husband, they will be managing without a dad. There is no denying that your children will grow up differently in a single-parent household but that doesn't have to mean worse.

I know that none of this is what you wanted for your kids but don't beat yourself up. These are three very lucky little boys.

Ask Graham

Dear Graham,

I'm in a dilemma. One of my closest girlfriends met a male friend of my husband at a party at my house the other day and is convinced there was 'a spark' between them, conveniently forgetting that she is married with twins.

Her husband is going away on business for two weeks and she's been badgering me for this man's number for days. What should I do? I don't want to do anything that makes me complicit - I'm very fond of my husband's friend. Nor can I tell her that a married mother of two who spends her days changing nappies and making carrot purée is much of a proposition for a handsome single guy.

Do I hand over the number and let her sad fantasy play itself out? Do I warn my husband's friend and turn it into a joke? Or am I standing in the way of true love (she claims to be unhappy in her marriage)?

Sarah L, Woking

Dear Sarah,

You are already too involved. If this woman really is one of your best friends, then you need to step away from this situation. I'm all for pursuing romance but if this woman goes after this guy it doesn't take Mystic Meg to tell you that it will end up messier than a Christmas Day episode of *EastEnders* and it will mysteriously have become your fault.

What your friend should be focusing on is her unhappy marriage. She needs to understand that relationships aren't like jobs – you don't line the next one up before you quit the one you've got.

I don't know what this woman looks like, but so long as she makes sure there is no visible baby sick on her shoulder then this guy might well welcome her advances. He is, after all, a man and they are rarely too proud or picky to pass on a sure thing.

To consider leaving her husband for this unsuspecting bachelor, however, would be like jumping out of the frying pan into the compost heap. As a friend, make sure you are there to help with the failing marriage, whether it's supporting her through a tough patch or helping her to walk away.

I don't think it is too harsh to explain all this to her when you refuse to hand over the phone number, but remember, if she ignores you and continues on this pointless quest, then she is an idiot and on her own head be it. Your hands are clean.

Ask Graham

Dear Graham,

After trying unsuccessfully to have children, my partner and I, who are in our early forties, adopted a baby girl from India a few years ago. We love her as if she were our own flesh and blood, but find our respective sets of parents a little detached. It pains me to watch my daughter, who started life in an orphanage, being overlooked by her grandparents. When I see her running around, all dark skin and skinny limbs against her plump blonde cousins, I worry that she's going to have to work harder to be accepted into the family.

I just want the very best for her. It's not about money - it's about love. And it just doesn't seem to flow with the sort of abundance that our parents show to their own kith and kin. I don't think it's consciously racist. It's more that they don't seem able to quite connect with a child who'll never look like them.

Laura P, Glos (names have been changed)

Dear Laura,

What you've done was never going to be easy. I completely understand your deep primitive yearning to have a child. I worry slightly that you never thought beyond the moment when someone would hand over the warm wriggling blanket that would be all yours. You've brought an Indian child to live with a white family in Britain – that will be complicated and it won't always go smoothly.

This will all have come as a shock to your parents, but give them time. Let them take their lead from your example. You need to anticipate the problems and try to protect your daughter as much as you can. I'm sure you could talk to other British couples who have adopted children of different races and learn from their experiences.

I know you mean well, but you shouldn't suggest that people ought to love your little girl because she was born into poverty and ended up in an orphanage. They should love her because she's your daughter and a part of the family. In the end, life in Britain will be harder for your daughter than her cousins, but your job is to love that girl and carry her proudly into the world assuming acceptance. You have chosen to make your daughter a minority – don't shy away from all the work that entails.

Ask Graham

Dear Graham,

I am being courted in an old-fashioned way by a widower in his late sixties. Having thought I would never find anyone (I am 57 and long divorced), I am amazed and grateful to have met him. And what a lovely man he is. He sends me flowers, writes me beautiful letters and is hugely considerate and kind.

There is only one major problem - after three months of full-on courtship we still haven't gone to bed with each other. Nor have we kissed - or not properly anyway.

He frequently compliments me on my appearance and takes an interest in what I wear. And he's very openly affectionate to me when we're out with friends. Despite all his declarations, there is no actual follow-through.

Is it up to me to initiate? I wonder how I should go about it? He's quite a cautious person and I would not wish to alarm him, or put him off in any way.

Edie M, Cumbria

Dear Edie,

Congratulations! So many women reading this will be wildly jealous of your good fortune and frankly mystified at your desire to take your relationship upstairs.

I'm afraid you may have to raise the subject yourself, since he is unwilling to do it. Perhaps it's not just the subject your widower has trouble raising. At his age, there may be all sorts of anxieties that you can help to quell.

You are both beyond grown up, so surely there is nothing that you can't talk about? Whatever the result of the conversation, I promise you that it will be a huge weight lifted from both your shoulders.

If he would like to have a full sex life but feels prevented from doing so in some way, then I'm sure there is a lot of help and advice available and you can find a way of making it work. If, however, he simply wants friendship and nothing more, then you must decide what you want to do. You are only 57 and, presumably, you have friends.

No relationship is perfect. We simply have to decide what compromises we are willing to make. Good luck.

Ask Graham

Dear Graham,
My younger sister is very flirtatious and competitive with men.
In any social situation where there's a man under 50 in the
room - married or single - she does this ridiculous hair
swishing, Bambi-eyed routine which almost always has a
hypnotic effect on them. She doesn't follow it up - in fact, she's
quite shy, really.

I've got a newish boyfriend, who I really like. He often makes
jokes about my sister and how much flesh she's showing. And I
laugh with him. But the problem is I can't help noticing that he
often ogles her too. I know he isn't intending to do anything -
and nor would she - but I mind that he stares. And I mind that
my younger sister plays up to it.

She wears these ridiculous Lolita outfits and pretends to be a
ditzy blonde whenever he's around even though she's starting
university in the autumn.

I don't want to make a massive fuss, but my sister's and
boyfriend's behaviour really bothers me. I've tried to bring the
matter up with my sister, but without success.

My mother's advice is just to ignore it but I can't. What would
you do in my shoes?

Laura O, Gerrards Cross

Dear Laura,

If I were in your shoes, I would be really irritated, but so long as you are dating a normal guy and your sister is a tramp in training this situation will continue.

Nobody is trying to hurt you here but men truly cannot help themselves. If a woman under 70 wears a low-cut top, a man will stare at her bosom.

You can almost hear the David Attenborough voiceover describing what is going on between your boyfriend and your sister. The good news is that you seem to think it won't ever go beyond stolen glances and a bit of hair flicking. Lucky you.

I'm not sure what sort of men you have dated before or if you were the only woman in a 100-mile radius (did you previously work on a space station or an Alaskan fishing village?), but I'm surprised you haven't encountered this behaviour.

Essentially, your mother is older and wiser than you. Take her advice. So long as it's only your boyfriend's eyes that are wandering, just grin and bear it.

The person I do worry for is your sister. If she really is at heart a shy little creature, then she is playing a very dangerous game. Sending out the sorts of messages she is could land her in all sorts of hot water. She is clearly just trying out her sexual wings but the sooner she gets a boyfriend of her own the better!

Dear Graham,
My husband died many years ago and, although I miss him enormously, I have got on with my life and enjoyed the attentions of a number of younger men à la Mrs Robinson. Up until now it has never been a problem, but my 21-year-old daughter has recently got a new boyfriend to whom I find myself enormously attracted. It appears he feels the same way, as he makes eyes at me over the breakfast table and suggestive comments when we are alone together. Half of me feels I should have an affair with him in order to expose his philandering nature. Please advise.
Mary G, Surrey

" A mother should be sympathetic, not pathetic. "

Dear Mary,
Your letter almost moved me to tears. What a beautiful selfless mother you are! To save your daughter from heartache, you would be willing to have sex with her gorgeous boyfriend?

Mary, are you really this self-deluded? Fine to have toy boys – I'm jealous – but at least leave the house to do your shopping.

Don't even try to tell her that her young man was making eyes at you. A mother should be sympathetic, not pathetic. Wait for her to tell you her fears and listen patiently. You are in your forties: time to grow up. Sleeping with 20-year-olds can seem like fun – and on a level it is – but do you really want to wake up with the same feelings of panic and fear that greet Demi Moore every morning?

Ask Graham

Dear Graham,

I proposed to my girlfriend six weeks ago and have started feeling like a condemned man. What really tortures me is the thought that she is the last woman I will ever sleep with. All the sunny weather only seems to make it worse. Wherever I look - parks, buses, trains - there are stunning girls wearing very little.

My wife-to-be is 35 and I'm only 29. I wonder if I'm about to make the biggest mistake of my life. All my male friends are still single and having a fantastic time, whereas I'm stuck with my future in-laws discussing flowers for the church and who we should put next to the vicar. Since we got engaged, we hardly even have sex any more. It's really weird.

Should I call it off?

Ben N, Richmond

> **Will your wild playboy mates give you a second thought as they walk down the aisle and you are left with nothing but a second-hand Porsche with a couple of mismatched earrings on the back seat?**

Dear Ben,

Decisions are never easy.

I panic when placing my order at Starbucks, so I can't imagine what it must be like deciding you have met the woman you want to spend the rest of your life with.

Try thinking back to what was going through your mind six weeks ago when the question popped out of your mouth. Were you drunk, or had you just had a particularly intense romantic encounter of the bedroom variety? If so, then maybe you should reconsider.

If, however, the proposal came out of a genuine and profound love for this woman, then try to look past the dreary in-laws and understandable nerves. No matter who you decide to marry, there will always be girls in summer dresses walking by.

You aren't a child, Ben. You must understand that no marriage can be based solely on sex and, if that really is still your number-one priority, then perhaps it is too soon to be thinking about marriage.

On the other hand, will your wild playboy mates give you a second thought as they walk down the aisle and you are left with nothing but a second-hand Porsche with a couple of mismatched earrings on the back seat?

Finally, and most importantly, you must voice all your fears and worries to one other person – your fiancée. Whether you are able to have that conversation or not will tell you more about this proposed marriage than I or anyone else ever could. Speak soon or forever hold your peace.

Dear Graham,

Have you any tips for surviving the misery of New Year? As usual, I'm going to a party where I won't know a soul, when what I'd like to be doing is hunkering down with a loved one, some expensive bubbly and a box of Ferrero Rocher. The worst part is being among strangers when Big Ben strikes the hour. Somehow this happens to me every year. Even though I have loads of friends, I always end up spending New Year with a bunch of people I don't know. Would it be disgraceful and pathetic to cry off and stay at home solo, allowing a bright new me to rise from the ashes on New Year's Day?

Ella F, Bath

Dear Ella,

New Year's Eve is a very overrated celebration. Hordes of sweaty faces looking at each other with slightly desperate eyes wondering: 'Is this fun? Is this the best fun I could be having right now?' Pressure to have fun to me equals no fun.

With or without a partner, Champagne and a box of chocolates sounds much better than standing around with some people you don't know and then having to re-mortgage your flat to pay for the mini-cab home. You don't need anyone's permission to enjoy yourself. You know what you want to do on New Year's Eve, so do it.

Ask Graham

Dear Graham,

I rent out the spare room of my two-bedroom flat to a girl I met at a party. Since she moved in two months ago, I haven't had the place to myself once. Apart from going to work, she never goes out.

She doesn't seem to have any friends and when I have friends over she's all over them. It's embarrassing and really invasive.

When I put the keys in the door, I always pray that she might be asleep. The slightest noise - my mobile going off, the plumbing rumbling, the kettle boiling - and she leaps out of bed and ambushes me.

It's all a bit much and I don't really know what to do.

I'm not in a relationship, so I don't have the escape route of a boyfriend's place. Although I'm trying to save money, I've now started going out nonstop as I can't face running into her. I feel as though I can't be in my own flat.

I'm actually slightly scared of her as she's rather intense - is that pathetic? We are both in our early thirties.

Louisa S, St Albans

Dear Louisa.

...or should I say, single white female? First things first – you want this woman gone! The only point of renting out a room is to enhance your life in some way – primarily financially.

The fact that this creepy creature is forcing you to go out all the time surely negates any monetary gain, so move on. Give a firm departure date and stick to it.

Lock your room securely and send any pets you may have to stay with your parents.

Don't let her try any sob stories about friends letting her down or strange wasting diseases. When you finally get her out, change the locks and have a good spring clean.

Hopefully, you will have learned a valuable lesson about vetting the people you rent out your room to. In an ideal world, there would be no lodgers, so never expect to enjoy having a stranger sleeping in your spare room.

But trust me, it can be better than this.

Ask Graham

Dear Graham,

I am madly in love with my new boyfriend but find it difficult to handle the fact that he is in constant contact with his ex. They split up a year ago, after five years together, but still seem to be in touch on an almost daily basis. He often pulls out of things with me because his ex makes demands on him.

When her car wouldn't start outside her flat, he was the person she called (he turned up within the hour with jump leads). Another time he went around to her flat in the middle of the night because a pigeon had got trapped in her bathroom.

I understand they're still close - but find it difficult that she makes such inroads on our time together. In all other respects we get on brilliantly, but every time we start getting really close his mobile starts ringing, or a text comes through from her. I'm not a jealous, possessive person, but I'm getting more and more upset by the situation. Any advice?

Freya L, Middlesex

Dear Freya,

You may not be a possessive person, but you're an idiot to put up with this treatment. Somebody, preferably your boyfriend, needs to explain to his ex that they are not together any more.

It's nice to stay friendly with people we were once very close to, but I don't think that includes fixing flat car batteries and freeing trapped pigeons. You don't have to be mean about it, but he needs to start putting you and your relationship first.

When we move house, we don't feel compelled to keep going back to mow the lawn. The grass that once needed us finds a way to cope.

Obviously, his ex enjoys the power she still has over your boyfriend and he must enjoy the feeling of being needed. Five years together is a long time and all sorts of co-dependent behaviour can develop. Time now to stop it.

If your boyfriend doesn't understand why the texts and calls annoy you, then I'm afraid you should probably move on because obviously he isn't going to.

Ask Graham

Dear Graham,

My American wife died 12 years ago, leaving me to bring up our daughter, who was just seven at the time.

She is now 19 and studying in the US and I have heard through friends that she is romantically involved with a man of 50.

He is a twice-divorced writer and no doubt cuts a very glamorous figure for a girl still in her teens. I'm told he also drinks heavily. In short, the man is every father's worst nightmare.

I despair at the thought of my beautiful daughter creeping out for assignations with her elderly lover, cutting herself off from all those nice Ivy League boys. But what really torments me is the breakdown of trust between us. Whenever we exchange news on Skype she denies everything.

What can I do to win back her trust and regain that closeness we've always had?

Jeffrey B, Oxfordshire

Dear Jeffrey,

You poor man. Everyone talks about the rites of passage of a young person entering adulthood but I'm afraid parents have their own rites of passage, which must be worst of all for the fathers of girls.

I often think of Catherine Zeta-Jones's father walking her down the aisle to give her away to a man older than himself. Surely that rocks the natural order of things, yet no one can deny that they seem happy and she has a brood of beautiful children she clearly adores.

This relationship obviously isn't what you'd wish for her, but your primary concern is the breakdown of communication. You know her better than anyone so you'll know if she's not telling you because she fears your displeasure, or is she playing a game where she wants you to freak out? Either way, I'm afraid it's all about waiting. Forcing her into the open will only provoke unwelcome reactions. Visiting her in America might help bring things to a head and you may feel less concerned if you see them together.

Whatever happens, I expect the closeness that's missing may return when her heart gets broken. Heavy-drinking divorced writers tend to quickly tire of 19-year-old students and, when he does, she'll need her father. Look out for signs that it's over so she doesn't have to suffer in silence.

It's clear you've done a great job of being a father so far but, as your daughter becomes an adult, that job changes. Sticking plasters and night lights were the easy part. Now you have to let go.

Dear Graham,
My wife and I have two wonderful sons. We divide our time
between a country house in Hampshire and a flat near Sloane
Square. I earn the money and my wife runs our two homes and
looks after the boys. A rather old-fashioned marriage, you
might say.
I would like us to have more children but my wife is
adamant that she doesn't want any more. She says that having
survived years of nappies and night-time feeds she wants her life
back, although she has no plans to go to work. She also argues
that as she's provided me with an 'heir and a spare' there is no
reason for us to keep going.
I'm one of five and have always wanted a big family. I long
for a daughter.

Rupert C, London SW1

Dear Rupert,
Real world to Rupert! Come in, Rupert! I'm no expert but apparently having children is really easy if all you do is have a fun time providing sperm and then show up to watch the resulting kiddies ride their ponies on a Saturday afternoon. Your wife, on the other hand, probably finds having children extremely taxing, especially when it sounds as if the only support she receives from her husband is financial.

My advice is to enjoy your boys and your lovely life instead of spoiling these precious years by yearning for phantom family members.

You are so lucky in so many ways. Look around at the lives other people are living – the couples that can't conceive, the people who can't afford to provide for their family.

Hug your boys, sir, and kiss your wife. Who knows, if you start really appreciating what you've got and treasuring your trio, an unexpected stork may come flying by.

Dear Graham,

My wife, who I love dearly, is privately wealthy. We have two children under five and she stopped working when our first child was born. We live a pretty normal middle-class life - nothing showy - and, as far as I know, she never dips into her money, although she has set up trust funds for the children. I'm from a principled, left-wing (and not moneyed) background. I've always sworn that I'd be the provider and I've done exactly that throughout our married life. But I was made redundant six months ago. Since then I've been paying the bills with my savings but the money is running out fast.

Finding a job in the current climate isn't easy. I would love not to go back into salaried work and do what I've always dreamed of - start my own business. But I would need to ask my wife to step in financially until I got things off the ground.

I feel wracked with guilt about going back on my promise to myself. And I'm not sure how my wife would react. We have a rather conservative marriage and I think she expects the man to be the breadwinner at all times.

Gavin H, Liverpool

Dear Gavin,

I don't care how conservative any marriage is because the 'for richer or poorer' bit seems very specific. The two of you are a family unit now and it seems crazy to be using up all your savings while somehow your wife's money is untouchable.

Presumably she has noticed that you aren't going to work any more, so where does she think the money to pay bills is coming from? It's very nice that your children have trust funds but they won't do them much good if they end up homeless.

It sounds as if the two of you have lived a rather charmed life so far and this is the first challenge your marriage has faced. Remember all the vows you both made and talk to her.

This is the woman you love.

This is the woman who is the mother of your children. Do you really think she is going to throw away your life together over money? Have you married Alexis Carrington from *Dynasty* or a pantomime villain? What you're going through isn't easy, but the great thing is that you don't have to do it alone.

Ask Graham

Dear Graham,

My (recovering alcoholic) brother, who's lonely and vulnerable, has taken up with a woman he met at an AA meeting, a chain-smoking mother of three, all of whose children have been taken away by social services.

I suspect that this awful woman joined his local group with the sole aim of hooking a rich man. The meetings she goes to are held in a smart London neighbourhood, miles from her home in Hackney.

Apparently, she has just announced that she is about to be evicted from her flat. And my brother, being soft-hearted, has agreed to let her stay with him 'temporarily'. I fear that, once she gets through his front door, he'll never get rid of her. My husband tells me not to get involved, but I worry that she might make my brother's life hell. I don't think for a minute that he's in love with her, or that she could make him happy.

He is 36. She claims to be in her mid-thirties but looks 10 years older.

What - if anything - can I do about it?

Karen D, London

Dear Karen,

You, I presume, are not an alcoholic or a member of AA, and so will never be able to understand the bond between two people battling the same illness. All you can do is be there to catch your brother should he fall once more.

Slight alarm bells ring for me because I'm fairly sure AA doesn't encourage relationships forming within the group. Perhaps you should talk to a support group for the friends and families of alcoholics who could give you more information and advice. Rushing to judge this woman does seem very harsh.

Obviously, she has made huge mistakes in the past, but she is trying to change and move on with her life and that should be applauded. I'm sure on paper your brother, as a recovering alcoholic, doesn't exactly look like a catch.

Whether the relationship will flourish once their problems are behind them, who can tell, but everyone deserves a second chance.

As for looking older than she says, well, she's an alcoholic. Work it out.

Dear Graham,

Do I have the rudest daughter-in-law in Britain? On our last visit to our son's house in Northamptonshire, we arrived with presents and bottles of wine only to find our daughter-in-law had arranged to go to a poetry reading on the one evening we were there. Our son was stuck late at work and, after the children had been put to bed by the nanny, my husband and I dined alone on a Chinese takeaway.

Perhaps I am a little difficult. Perhaps my standards are too high and out of sync with that of her rather more casual generation but it upsets me hugely that my daughter-in-law doesn't at least observe the basic formalities and pretend to like me.

She makes no effort at all and I always go home feeling hurt, upset and more than a little furious.

Any advice on how to build bridges?

Margaret B, Ipswich

Dear Margaret,

As night follows day and obscurity follows winning *Britain's Got Talent*, so a mother is destined to hate her daughter-in-law. Don't fight it, but rather relish the primeval inevitability of it all. She has stolen your baby and she is not good enough.

Now, consider for a moment how much this woman loathes you. After learning that your son was working late, she preferred to go to a poetry reading rather than be alone with you. A poetry reading? Gordon Brown hates Tony Blair less.

What both of you should realise is that your son is the prime cause of all these problems. If your standards are so high, then why not apply them to your baby? You are visiting for one night and he gets 'stuck' at work? No. He chose work over you.

He isn't some gullible fool who your daughter-in-law has ensnared. He is the adult you brought up and he has fallen in love with this woman and chosen to start a new life with her. If visiting them just upsets you, then stop. Clearly, your son and his wife won't care.

It's your expectations that are making you unhappy and probably alienating your daughter-in-law. Relax. This young couple are living their life their way. I sense you disapprove of the nanny, but you raised your boy yourself and look how he's treating you.

We all make our own beds to lie in – don't turn yours into a bed of nails.

Dear Graham,

I am newly engaged but daunted about those occasions when I meet my future in-laws.

My future spouse's father has recently made a fortune, which he has 'invested' in his cellar. Every weekend spent under his roof is a bacchanalian debauch. Lunch usually involves three bottles of Puligny-Montrachet, while dinner is preceded by martinis of knee-buckling strength. The bloody Marys served at breakfast on Sunday go some way to alleviating the inevitable hangover, but by Sunday lunch I'm ready to fall into the soup.

I'm a banker and need to maintain a clear head and manual dexterity when answering my BlackBerry 24/7. I don't want to lose blokish credibility by not keeping up (or suddenly developing an allergy). Any advice?

PS They don't have pot plants into which one can tip the odd glass.

Will Y, London

Dear Will,

I will answer your letter but I have to admit your problem seems very slight. Most men would settle for a room temperature can of Heineken, but you get delicious expensive wine.

I understand that you don't want a muddled head, but how often do you visit your in-laws? Even if it's once a month that's a mere 12 weekends a year. If that still seems more than you can cope with, then blame your busy work schedule – arrive late and leave early. Agree with your fiancée on an excuse for leaving early and then your blokish credentials won't be in doubt.

I hate to think of all that wine going unloved. Couldn't you learn to embrace the occasional lost weekend? I know I would always choose the grape over the BlackBerry.

Ask Graham

Dear Graham,

I've just got back from a disastrous summer holiday with my husband and children in Brittany. My husband was moody and sulky and spent the entire time buried in one-day-old British newspapers, fiddling with his BlackBerry and ignoring us. He often refused to join us for lunch and went to the local café on his own.

We've been together for a long time and it seems like we've been in a rut for as long as I can remember. Do we even love each other like we used to? I just don't know. We have sex rarely and when we talk it's almost always about the children.

I don't think he's having an affair, but I sometimes wonder if perhaps he's a bit depressed. His working life has been pretty insecure over the past few years. Perhaps that's affected his confidence/joie de vivre. Or maybe he's got bored with me – and with his responsibilities – and longs to be free of us? It's difficult to know what to do. I want to make my marriage work, not least for the sake of our children. I just don't know where to start, or how to get through to him.

Joanna S, Bristol

Dear Joanna,

Clearly something is wrong and you've done a great job of listing all the things that could be the problem, but ultimately the only person who can tell you what's going on in your husband's head is your husband, so ask him.

I understand that it won't be easy because he may tell you something that you don't want to hear, but that has to be better than drifting along in the dull chilly fog of your marriage. It can't be nice for children to see their father skulking off to cafés by himself when a holiday should be an opportunity to spend more time with them.

I always think in situations like this you should imagine the worst possible outcome – he wants to leave you, he has a brain tumour, he's murdered someone – and then talk yourself through how you would cope. No matter how awful the scenario, you can deal with it and survive.

Take strength from that and tackle your husband head on. He may just be in a general midlife malaise. Perhaps this isn't the life he imagined himself living. Marriages are bound to go through peaks and troughs and you've both got to decide if you want to wait for the next peak or if there's ever going to be another one.

You can't love each other in the way that you did because relationships have to change and grow in order to survive, but hopefully you will find a new way to love each other.

Of course, it may all be explained by your choice of holiday destination. Brittany? Just because there's a ferry doesn't mean you have to go there.

Dear Graham,
My boyfriend works insanely long hours. His job in advertising is pretty stressful and he refuses to go out on 'school nights' unless it's with colleagues or work contacts. When we're together, he either talks about work, or watches rubbish on TV, directing his frustrations at the box as if he's addressing a real person.

Is his job making him go a bit bonkers? Even on holiday he takes his BlackBerry to the beach. Most alarming of all, he wears Boden swimming trunks, just like David Cameron. How can I persuade him to get a life?

Maggie R, Bristol

Dear Maggie,
Your boyfriend works all the time and when you do see him he's really boring? His style icon is David Cameron and he talks to the television? You are going out with him because...? Surely being single is preferable to spending time with this work-obsessed yawn?

I'm particularly upset because I had just managed to clear my mind of that hideous image of David Cameron emerging from the waves like a giant wet veal sausage, and now it's back. Can we really trust a man to lead the country when he can't even grasp that waxing your chest is only sexy if you have a sexy body? If you don't, you just look like a giant baby.

Why not call your boyfriend's secretary and leave him a message. It's over. And so is Boden swimwear.

Move on, Maggie!

Dear Graham,

I'm a 40-something twice-divorced woman. My friends tell me I'm intelligent, lively, fun loving and not unattractive.

The trouble with living in Dorset is that, beautiful though it is, it's full of married couples and bored husbands, who long for a bit of extramarital excitement. Every time I get invited to dinner parties at least one of the married men hits on me. (There are rarely any single men at such evenings.)

Perhaps because I'm unattached they think I'm fair game. Maybe they view me as 'desperate' and expect me to be grateful. The men in question are usually pompous, arrogant and considerably overweight (I'm a self-confessed 'fattist'). Their wives are often smug, insecure and hostile - terrified that I might make off with their prize catches. As if! How should I rebuff their inept advances without causing offence? And where oh where might I find a like-minded guy? (Don't tell me to move to London - I hate the place.)

Melissa B, Dorset

Dear Melissa,

Fat pompous husbands are trying to cheat on their smug wives and you are worried about offending them by saying no? There is a time and a place for etiquette, and trust me this isn't one of them.

My main piece of advice would be to stop accepting invitations to these hideous dinner parties. As for meeting a like-minded man, well, that may not be so easy. Your letter seems strangely negative to me. The only things that come in for any praise are the Dorset scenery and yourself – nothing else seems to come up to the high standards of Melissa. It is all very well to have opinions and strong ones but don't expect other people to agree or like them. I imagine that the world according to Melissa is quite a hard one to live in.

You have two failed marriages in quite a short period of time and you are living alone in Dorset mixing with people you don't like. Something is wrong with this picture. I know I'm making assumptions based on a short letter but maybe you should try to judge less and open yourself up to new experiences.

Make your world bigger not smaller and maybe other people will want to share it.

Ask Graham

Dear Graham,
Could my husband be a secret alcoholic? He's been out of work
for four months and has taken to being rather liberal with the
drinks cabinet in the evenings and at weekends.

We've always been big social drinkers but this is different.

He now drinks heavily when we're on our own and finds any
excuse - good news, bad news, sunshine, rain - to pour himself
yet another nightcap.

When I get upset and ask him to stop, he usually does, but I'm
convinced he goes on drinking after I've gone to bed.

I've started being rather sneaky and putting pencil marks on
the whisky and gin bottles to see if the levels have gone down -
nine times out of 10 they have. When I confront him about it, he
denies it - in fact, he gets angry and defensive. I want to help,
but I'm intimidated by his furious denials.

We are both in our early fifties.

Angela P, Merseyside

Dear Angela,

I completely understand your worries but you must tread very carefully. A man in his early fifties who has lost his job has quite a bit to be depressed about so in one way it is no surprise that he is turning to drink as a crutch.

The difficulty is that, although it affects you deeply, this is his problem to solve, not yours.

Obviously, you could nag him to talk to someone, but if he doesn't want to go it will probably do no good at all.

Above all else, you don't want to turn him into a secret drinker.

It sounds very simplistic but perhaps you could arrange activities in the evening that require him to drive. Even if it's a trip to the cinema that's two hours sitting in the dark without a glass in his hand. And he might enjoy the feeling of being able to do without a sizeable tipple.

I clearly can't judge how serious your husband's drinking is or even if he has a problem but I guarantee that you will feel better if you speak to one of the many organisations that help the friends and families of people dealing with various forms of addiction and abuse. They will talk you through it step by step and help you to sort out what is really going on.

It is so easy to dive into a bottle and you've just got to help your husband get back out again as best you can.

Good luck!

Dear Graham,
My husband, who rarely does things by halves, has become a
devotee of Hatha yoga.

There's nothing wrong with that - I'm sure it's great for
fitness and lowering stress - it's just that Hatha yoga appears to
be practised entirely by women.

And not just any old women. The other day I decided to
surprise him by waiting at the doors of his school and found
myself staring open-mouthed as one beautiful girl after another
trooped out. It was like some ghastly nightmare. Nobody was
short, fat, plain or ugly.

When he came out he was chatting to this gorgeous blonde
American with perfect teeth and a pneumatic physique. Turns
out this Amazonian acrobat (from Texas) is his yoga teacher.

I feel so depressed - and jealous! How can he help but fancy
all these limber goddesses in their tight-fitting leggings and
tops? Does he compare them to his wife (three children, bingo
wings and a major muffin top)? The whole thing is making me
neurotic, not least because he's just announced he's planning to
do a three-hour 'Hatha workshop' this Saturday in Chiswick.

Hatty M, west London

❝Remember there comes a time when bingo wings actually look better on a woman than going down the Madonna route and ending up with arms that look like a gibbon crossed with an uncooked frog leg. ❞

Dear Hatty,

Forget the stress-reducing benefits of Hatha yoga and take a few Hatty deep breaths.

Imagine if you took up cooking classes with Gordon Ramsay. Do you really think he would be desperate to taste your food? I go to a gym full of gorgeous gay men but, trust me, just being there doesn't make me the object of their affection.

Similarly, the yoga lovelies aren't putting all that work into stretching and tightening so that they can pull some sweaty middle-aged man in an ill-fitting leotard. You may find him attractive, which is marvellous, but it's hard to believe that he's the one that Miss Texas has been waiting for all her life.

Your irritation is understandable but never let it show in front of your husband. Instead, tease him about his girlfriends at yoga.

Turn it into a family joke and an anecdote to share with friends. This way you don't seem threatened and there is every chance he'll stop going because he has been made to feel a bit foolish.

It might also be an idea if you tried to feel a bit more positive about your own appearance. emember there comes a time when bingo wings actually look better on a woman than going down the Madonna route and ending up with arms that look like a gibbon crossed with an uncooked frog leg.

My husband's yoga class is like some ghastly nightmare. No one is short, fat, plain or ugly.

Dear Graham,
Last Christmas almost killed my marriage and I'm desperately
worried that this year will be even worse. I've been married for
six years (two children under five) and my husband never
seems to want to be with his family.

He works very hard and I do understand that, with two small
children and an exhausted, emotional wife, home isn't
necessarily the most relaxing place to be. But he always seems to
prefer being out on the razzle with his male friends rather than
at home with us.

Last year, he barely lifted a finger on the day, even though I
was breastfeeding and at my wit's end. He didn't so much as
peel a Brussels sprout. When our respective parents arrived, he
put on a good show (we were 18 at lunch), but as soon as
everyone had gone he slumped in front of the television, refused
to speak to me and left me to clear everything up on my own.

We were really in love when we first met and I want our
marriage to work, but I feel so alone and miserable. It makes
me dreadfully sad that he takes so little interest in our
children. He has never even read a bedtime story to our four-
year-old. Every time I suggest it, he makes an excuse, or fails to
come home from work in time. We are both in our early thirties.
Rebecca G, East Sussex

Dear Rebecca,
A dog of a husband isn't just for Christmas, he's for life! The festive season may heighten matters but it sounds as if you're fairly unhappy for the rest of the 12 months as well. Your husband is the opposite of the gift that keeps on giving.

I have no doubt that you both loved each other and he truly believed that he wanted to get married. My concern is that perhaps as a man in his late twenties he wasn't quite ready for all the sacrifices and responsibilities that marriage entails. Are his male friends married? I doubt it since I find it hard to imagine many men finding wives as patient and understanding as you seem to be.

Nobody wants to become the naggy 'her indoors', but lines need to be drawn since this situation, for the sake of all concerned, cannot continue. It sounds as if he knows how he is letting you down since he bothers to put up a good front for his family and you've clearly asked him to become involved with the children. I'd suggest you get some professional mediation because being a great father and husband doesn't come naturally to everyone.

If this marriage fails, which it might, remember how unhappy you are now. Would things be that terrible without this man or would it be a huge weight lifted? You are clearly an incredibly strong woman – stay that way!

Dear Graham,

My sex life with my husband (of 17 years) has gone a bit quiet. The other day I overheard him telling one of his friends in the pub how much he fancied Jennifer Lopez in Maid in Manhattan. I had no idea he'd even seen it as he claims to hate romcoms.

His birthday is coming up and I'm wondering if I should book myself in for a St Tropez tan and dress up in a chambermaid's outfit. Would it inject a bit of va-va-voom into our marriage or would I be setting myself up for ridicule? I am a 48-year-old mother of five.

Fanny B, Gerrards Cross

Dear Fanny,

I'm choosing my words carefully here and really don't want to cause offence, but the point of a fantasy is that it should be fantastic.

If the chambermaid looks like J-Lo, that's sexy. If, however, the woman simply looks like a chambermaid, then a man will probably be more interested in what he can steal off her cart rather than writhing against her pale-blue nylon uniform.

You'll notice the producers of the movie didn't go with the title 'Maid in Gerrards Cross'. I think after 17 years anyone's sex life is allowed to calm down a little, especially if five children have been the result.

It's great that you want to show your husband a good time but trying to fulfil his fantasies may be a mistake. Far better to whisk him off to a place where you feel sexy – a spa or a posh lunch in a hotel where you could surprise him by announcing you've booked a room. It will also give him a chance to see what chambermaids really look like!

Don't be downhearted, Fanny. You have so much in your life to be grateful for and your husband is a very lucky man.

Dear Graham,

Five months ago, I had a one-night stand with an Irish/American banker I met at a party. What had been a wonderful, spontaneous night turned into something a bit sordid because I never heard from him again. I sent him a couple of light-hearted texts, but he didn't bother to reply.

Imagine my surprise when he emailed me out of the blue to ask if I fancied going to New York with him for a few days. His office would be putting us up in a swanky hotel. All I had to worry about was the flight.

My friends tell me I'd be mad to go, but everyone says New York is amazing, especially around Christmas. I've always wanted to go ice skating at the Rockefeller and see Central Park – and of course there's the shopping. Need I say more? I'm 33. My guess is he's about the same age. Should I stay or should I go?

Imogen P, west London

Dear Imogen,

Remember how sordid you felt after the one-night stand. Now imagine multiplying those feelings tenfold and it will give you some idea of your mental state when you return from New York. I'm in no position to judge you for having a fling but you are clearly not emotionally equipped to cope with such a cut and dried sexual contract. You want more.

Your description of your dream trip to the Big Apple reads like a montage from a fairly lame romantic comedy starring Reese Witherspoon. I guarantee that the way your date imagines the weekend going is from a very different sort of movie. If this man really likes you, then he needs to do some wooing at home before you pay for your own flight to NYC just to save him the trouble of trawling the bars or the expense of finding professional companionship.

Imogen – he didn't even pick up the phone to speak to you! What if he sent that email to several girls to see which one would bite? You deserve better treatment.

New York is one of the greatest cities on the planet but don't tarnish it forever with memories of being there with this man. If he is a nice person, he's not doing a very good job of showing it.

However, I get a sinking feeling that you have already made up your mind to go. As Julia Roberts once said – Mistake. Big mistake!

Ask Graham

Dear Graham,

I'm a 30-something mother of two with a husband who takes a very hard line when it comes to television. We don't have one in the house and he's adamant that our children should grow up without it. He is particularly incensed by the rise of reality television.

Ironically, my parents were bitterly opposed to telly so I never had one in my childhood, unlike my husband who had a wonderfully liberal upbringing. I grew up unfamiliar with words like 'Bagpuss' and 'Morph' and among my peer group I often felt like an outcast. My parents believed that evenings should be spent reading books and playing musical instruments.

I've tried to explain this to my husband but because his parents gave him unbridled access to television he just doesn't get it. He doesn't see that for all its iniquities it is often the glue that holds communities together. I don't want my children to be the odd kids at school. How can I get my husband to accept a television in the house?

Charlotte R, Berkshire

Dear Charlotte,

Your husband doesn't hate television or reality shows. He hates himself for not being able to stop watching it. Just because he is too weak-minded to pick and choose what to watch doesn't mean the rest of the family have to suffer. It is slightly ironic that you have ended up marrying your father, but that's another issue I suppose.

Presumably your husband doesn't hate computers and so we come to the modern marvel that is the BBC iPlayer (though, in fact, every channel now has an online on-demand service).

The other odd thing about your husband's rage is that times have changed and children watch far less television than they used to. Computer games and online stuff are rapidly sidelining it. Your husband can rail against the machine all he wants, he just happens to have chosen the wrong machine.

In the end, it's important to remember that television is a passive organ that simply churns out hours of programming. It doesn't care if those programmes are good, bad or *The Alan Titchmarsh Show*. That is the job of the parent. Tell your husband to grow up, face the real world and do his job.

Dear Graham,

I've started seeing the most wonderful man, who I met in the fifth-floor bar of Harvey Nicks (I spilled my Bellini on his blazer). He's not particularly handsome, but he's spontaneous and intelligent and fantastic company. And he's the first man I've ever gone out with who's solvent and generous - I'm not sure what he does exactly, but think he works in finance.

The problem is he's been divorced four times - yes, four! And he's only 39. I'm seven years younger than him and am a bit anxious about falling in love with someone with such a terrible track record. He's got three sets of children by four of the wives - he appears to be supporting them all - so his life is very complicated.

One of the ex-wives was his personal trainer, the other was his son's housemistress at school. I'm not being a snob, or anything, but I find that a bit odd. I can't work out if he's someone slightly desperate who can't bear to be on his own, or if he's an old-fashioned romantic who's been unlucky in love. I've agreed to go to Monte Carlo with him for a long weekend but I'm getting cold feet. What would you do in my place?

Isy L, Surrey

Dear Isy,

Your letter starts off so promisingly. You have met the most amazing man. By the end of the letter, the only thing that amazes me is that you didn't chuck a second glass of Bellini over him.

This man is a player of the worst kind and, if you decide to go to Monte Carlo with him, then frankly you deserve everything you get – which, let me clarify in case you aren't following, is a broken heart. Be clear in what you find attractive about this man – cash. That doesn't make you a bad person, but please be honest with yourself.

Are you seriously suggesting that old-fashioned romantics hang around the fifth-floor bar of Harvey Nichols, bumping into attractive women and flashing their platinum cards?

There is no doubt you could have a lot of fun, but don't delude yourself that you could have a future. Walking down the aisle to meet a man who is standing at the altar for the fifth time doesn't really equate with anyone's special day. Elizabeth Taylor has eaten less wedding cake than this man.

I'm positive I haven't told you a single thing you didn't already know. Now it is time to admit that all you should accept or expect from this man is a fling, not a ring.

Dear Graham,

I've done a terrible thing. Three days ago, when I was reversing my car out of the drive, I accidentally ran over my girlfriend's cat. I'm not fond of cats - in fact, I don't like them at all (she has three of them) - but I didn't do it deliberately.

Luckily, she was at work - she's a nurse and was on one of her early shifts - so I managed to clear up the mess and bury the remains in the back garden. I even said a sort of prayer under a tree, even though I'm not religious.

I can't bring myself to tell my girlfriend that her cat is dead, knowing how upset she'll be. She keeps ringing the Blue Cross and it breaks my heart to see her so upset.

What should I do? I'm in a right pickle.

Tim L, Tooting

Dear Tim,

What you should do is a crash course in a few science subjects at the Open University and then invent a time machine which you use to travel back to just before you killed your girlfriend's cat. But this time you'll look where you are going before reversing out of the drive.

Given that this is quite a tall order and you have already committed murder and then lied to your girlfriend, I don't think 'pickle' quite covers it, do you? Unlike the car, there is no reversing the choices you made and the price you pay for your brief act of cowardice is the guilt you must carry for the rest of your life.

It might be a kind gesture to dig the corpse up and leave it in some neighbouring street so that at least your girlfriend knows for sure that kitty is never coming home.

On the plus side, at least it was only a cat. If your letter was about a dog, I would have tracked down your girlfriend and told her myself what you did.

Dear Graham,

You know how couples who've been together for years have usually worked out some kind of dance routine? As soon as the music starts up, they'll hit the dance floor and blend in perfectly with a few nicely judged twirls and a bit of nifty footwork. Well, whenever my boyfriend and I dance together, it's horrible.

I'd rather be doing a bit of snaky salsa, but he doesn't feel comfortable with that at all. He only really comes to life when Eighties bands like Madness come on. What he likes is lots of grunting and jerky arm and leg movements. He gets really sweaty and hot. And if the dance floor's crowded he often crashes into people, particularly if he's had one too many.

I really envy other couples. Over the years things have become worse - not better. His latest trick is to dance in a semi-ironic way, pretending to be John Travolta and swinging his arms around. It's not funny, it's embarrassing, but I don't say anything because whenever the dreaded 'd-word' comes up we usually have a row and go home on non-speaks. Needless to say, he has refused to take up dance lessons. He is 42. I am 34.

Rachel P, High Wickham

" Try to keep things in perspective. Michael Flatley can dance but would you really want to go out with him? I rest my case. "

Dear Rachel,

My only advice is to turn on your television and glance at one of the 24-hour news channels. If you don't have a television, flick through any newspaper. Then do a little dance all by yourself, praising the heavens above that this is the biggest problem you have to worry about.

Your boyfriend can't dance. So what? Can he play the piano? Can he sing a haunting version of 'Wind Beneath My Wings'? If this is your only complaint about your partner, then you have come spectacularly close to finding the perfect one. Put down this book and kiss him and hug him. Having rows about his terrible dad-dancing is so foolish. Happiness is not easy to find so don't throw it away on the dance floor.

Try to keep things in perspective. Michael Flatley can dance but would you really want to go out with him? I rest my case.

Dear Graham,

I've started seeing a guy who has a real perspiration problem. Within half an hour of having a shower and putting on deodorant, he really starts to smell.

It's a real problem when we're going out for the evening, especially if he has had to rush around to get there on time. (It's also quite off-putting, travelling in the car or sharing a bed with him!) For some girls, the smell of manliness is quite a turn-on, but his strong body odour just makes me feel sick.

He has tried all sorts of products but I'm not sure how much more smell I can take. Am I being unfeeling and insensitive? And is there anything I can do to protect myself from the fumes?

Jenny M, Kent

Dear Jenny,

Even with swine flu gripping the nation, your boyfriend may suspect something if you show up sporting a bedazzled gas mask, and short of that I really don't know what's going to help. He stinks and can't help it. You feel sick and can't help it.

In fairness to you, it does sound as if this creature is sweatier and smellier than most men. Has he seen a doctor? It would be a pity to give up on the whole relationship just because a can of Right Guard let him down.

Even if there isn't medication, perhaps you could do some research into other cures. Would changing his diet help? Should he exercise more? There must be other avenues you can explore before you finally have to throw in the stinking towel.

It is a great start that he knows he has a problem but that doesn't really help you. We all have to put up with some unpleasant body odour – the waiter leaning across to clear a plate, the overcrowded lift, the person in front of you in a queue – but we don't normally have to sleep with these people. I know I'm always bleating on to people about compromise and that no relationship is perfect, but even I must admit a girl has the right not to expect a swarm of flies hovering above her in her wedding pictures. I wish you a fragrant future.

Dear Graham,

For our summer holiday in August, we're renting a gite near Avignon with friends who have children the same age as ours. It's the second year in a row we're doing this, and the problem is our friends, though better off than us, are a little tight.

Last year, we found ourselves lumbered with a £400 bill for damage to the swimming-pool sun-loungers caused by both sets of children. We paid it in full when the agency contacted us, fully expecting our friends to cough up their half share, but to our surprise never received their cheque, despite gentle reminders. The holiday itself, though a great success in other ways, was peppered with small incidents where somehow it was always one of us who got our wallets out.

Is there any advice you could give us to ensure there's a more equal share of costs? We don't wish to make too much of this, but are anxious to avoid a repeat of last year's scenario.

Helen and Hugo L, Glos

Dear Helen and Hugo,

Before I even start to address your tight friends, can we talk about your children? What sort of rabid monsters have you raised that can do £400 worth of damage to a set of sun-loungers? Did they eat them?

I can't help but feel that your reluctance to discipline your children is somehow connected to your inability to confront your friends about the money. When it comes to bad debts, gentle reminders are not a very effective route to take, just as a few feeble 'don't do that, darling's ended in poolside carnage.

I guarantee this holiday will not be a happy one if you arrive in Avignon with the anger and resentment of the missing £200 as part of your baggage. Be very clear with them. Say you were going through your travel details and realised that they had forgotten to pay their half of the bill and give them all your bank details.

If they don't want to pay, for some reason, then they will have to tell you why and you can address that issue. Or they cough up and you can all move on.

You could introduce a kitty system, but that might drive you mad as you see the other mother using it to buy lipstick or a souvenir straw donkey.

It might be simpler to suggest that you take it in turns to be responsible for dinner, whether that be buying the groceries and cooking or taking everyone out to a local restaurant. This way people can spend as much or as little as they want, but at least it is shared.

Feel free to send me a postcard to thank me for this advice, but I fear any mention of 'wish you were here' will not be reciprocated. Bon voyage!

Dear Graham,
My 35-year-old (female) partner is desperate to have a baby and is considering donor insemination with a friend. While I'm committed to my partner, I'm wondering what my role will be if she goes ahead. I'm not particularly maternal and it does worry me that I won't be biologically connected to the child – will I even love it? Should I encourage her to pursue her dreams of motherhood anyway? Or should I pull out while I can and look for another partner?

Sam B, Hastings

Dear Sam,

I'm assuming that you are a woman and a lesbian, although you don't actually specify. If I'm wrong and you are perhaps a man who lost his penis in a freak industrial accident, then forgive me, because this advice won't be very relevant.

All the questions you pose are valid, but perhaps you should be asking your partner instead of me. Having a child is a huge responsibility and, if you think you aren't going to be sticking around, then it probably is better to get out now before you leave a child with feelings of rejection and emotional scars.

If you decide you want to stay, then discuss what your role will be. As the live-in partner of the mother, I imagine you will be taking on a larger parenting responsibility than the sperm donor. Let's face it, agreeing to produce a sample isn't that big a commitment compared to the person hearing every cry and smelling every full nappy.

Parenthood isn't something you can prepare for. You either have a child or you don't, there is no in between. Just talk to your girlfriend because she should be talking to you about this, unless she is taking your silence as an implicit agreement. Speak now, or forever hold the piss-soaked nappies.

Dear Graham,

At the grand old age of 36, my girlfriend has developed a bit of a shoe fetish. She looks stunning in high heels, but she also makes me look like a midget, so on balance I'd rather she didn't wear them when we go out together.

Barefoot she is a willowy 5ft 11in, but once she dons her Louboutins she towers over me. At 5ft 6in I'm told I'm roughly the same height as Napoleon but that's not very cheering, is it? Whenever we go out I'm convinced blokes are eyeing her up and giving me funny pitying looks.

A mate of mine who finds the situation hilarious has suggested I follow Nicolas Sarkozy's lead and buy stacked heels, but I can't imagine anything worse. I've noticed that Carla Bruni tends to wear rather flat schoolmarm pumps when she's at official functions with her husband. My girlfriend, though, refuses point blank to humour me.

I'd like to settle down - and so would she, as her biological clock has gone into overdrive in the last few months. But what man wants to marry a woman who makes him look ridiculous?

Mark PJ, Vauxhall

Dear Mark,

Grow up! The only reason you might look ridiculous is because that's how you feel. When people see you with your Amazonian girlfriend, they are simply wondering if you are very rich, powerful, well endowed or a combination of all three.

Those looks that men give you aren't ones of pity but rather of envy. They want your self-confidence even if you don't seem to possess any. You are 5ft 6in, which doesn't exactly qualify you to be the mayor of Munchkin land, but equally the chances of you falling in love with someone shorter than you aren't high.

You love this girl and presumably you'd like your children to get out of the shallow end of the gene pool, so hurry up and marry her before she realises how much sky there is going to be in your wedding photographs. Perhaps you could have the ceremony on a mountain top where the slope might flatter the happy couple.

This is one of those situations where nothing is going to change, so you either need to accept it or move on. Remember most of your married life will be spent lying or sitting down. Oh and stacked heels are only acceptable at a Seventies fancy-dress party or if you are a nurse in a psychiatric hospital. Reach for the stars, Mark.

I'm told I'm the same height as Napoleon but that's not very cheering, is it?

Ask Graham

Dear Graham,

I gave up work six months ago to focus on my children and find that, now I'm no longer a working mother, I'm shunned by other working women. And it's not just the women - it's the men, too. At dinners, I'm treated as if my views are rather pathetic and out of date. Just because I spend the best part of my day at home, people assume I don't have opinions worth listening to.

I've worked as a corporate lawyer for the best part of 15 years - I'm now 36 - so find it very galling to be dismissed routinely by friends. As a former high flyer, I don't really fit into the non-working-mothers brigade either. I love my kids, but I'm never going to be baking cupcakes or stitching smock dresses late into the night. It just doesn't interest me.

I realise I'm in a very privileged position as a woman who doesn't have to go to work (my husband earns enough to pay for everything), but I feel socially isolated. And it feels as if my self-confidence is being chipped away by my peer group. Any advice would be very welcome.

Lorna S, east London

Dear Lorna,

You have made a choice and like every choice it comes with consequences. I'm afraid it comes back to the age-old debate about women wanting to have it all. The point is, nobody has it all. No man. No woman. If you go out to work, you earn money and a sense of self-worth, but you live with guilt about the amount of time spent away from your children. Equally, you have chosen to focus your life totally around your children – many people would be jealous – but spending your days with little people who can't read or even use cutlery is bound to distance you from people who are spending all their time at the coalface of adulthood. I know this is a tough pill to swallow, but a part-time job might help, or even some volunteer work.

It's amazing how defined we are by our occupation. Perhaps you are right in thinking that we shouldn't be, but for the moment that is the way of the world. 'What do you do?' will always be in the top three questions we ask a stranger and their answer will set the course for how that relationship develops.

It's interesting that you don't want to fit into the role of traditional homemaker when that is precisely the one you have chosen. You don't say how old your children are, but perhaps as they get older you will find life at home with them more rewarding. I do hope so. Otherwise, I really think you may need to rethink your original decision.

Dear Graham,
My southern Italian girlfriend is from the Julia Roberts school of hair removal. In other words, she waits until her armpits are sprouting small Amazonian rainforests before she gets out her razor. When things get really out of hand, it can feel as if I'm sharing my bed with another bloke. Is there a tactful way of asking her to depilate without offending her?
Giles P, London

PS She also has a bit of a moustache.

ff No one wants to wake up feeling as if they're sharing their bed with an extra from *Gorillas in the Mist.* 55

Dear Giles,
Part of me wants to slap you for being so shallow, and yet I have to admit that I might feel the same way if I were in your position. No one wants to wake up feeling as if they're sharing their bed with an extra from *Gorillas in the Mist.*

Since it's present-giving time why not get your perfumed yeti a lovely day at some luxury spa, while ensuring that hair removal is part of the package?

Then, when your very own Sophia Loren comes home, make a huge fuss of her and bleat on about how much you love her smooth armpits and how much you enjoy kissing her without getting a beard rash. Hopefully, this will solve the problem. No matter what happens, the good news is that judging from your reaction to her jungle pits you're definitely not gay. The bad news is that she might be.

Ask Graham

Dear Graham,

My wife and I are at loggerheads over our son, who at 29 is showing every sign of being a classic 'boomerang kid'. My view is that we should take a tough line and give him a deadline for moving out (and financial assistance should he require it) but my wife refuses to back me up on this.

Our son is much loved by us all, but has a very relaxed work ethic (short-lived spurts of freelance journalism). At home he is waited on hand and foot by my wife. A big house, free laundry and hot dinners on tap seem to have locked him into a state of eternal studentdom. I hasten to add that he has plenty of friends and is not in any way a social misfit - just rather unusually Mediterranean in his living arrangements.

I worry that if this situation continues we will be holding him back in life. By giving him free bed and board, are we stripping him of any ambition and drive? He is our youngest and I suspect my wife, who gave up work when our first child was born, is finding it hard to let go.

Any advice?

Christopher B, north London

The little darling is, in reality, a hulking man of almost 30.

Dear Christopher,

It is time to fly in the face of tradition and make a concerted effort to throw the baby out with the bath water. I think everything you say makes sense but now your wife must see the damage she is potentially doing your son.

Surely charging him a little rent wouldn't be the end of the world? The little darling being pampered is, in reality, a hulking man of almost 30. Does he have any love interest in his life? I can't imagine any partner would find his infantile lifestyle attractive.

Perhaps you could convince your wife that if he leaves home then it could lead to grandchildren, otherwise known as real children. I fear in the short term you will be very unpopular with your wife and son but take solace from the fact that they will thank you eventually.

It's nearly Christmas and it's time for a wise man to let the baby know that there is no room at the inn.

Dear Graham,

My widowed father-in-law is finding it increasingly hard to live on his own and, without consulting me, my (Greek Cypriot) husband has told him he can come and live with us from Christmas onwards.

The strange thing is my husband doesn't get on with his father, even though they are remarkably similar. They are both strong, stubborn characters and tend to lock horns whenever they get together.

My husband's suggestion that his father moves in with us is more out of guilt, I'd say, than real affection. I'm very fond of my father-in-law, as are our children (all under 10), but I'm dismayed at the prospect of him moving in with us. It's a massive responsibility to take on the care of an elderly person in a household that's already full to bursting.

As a stay-at-home mum I'm grimly aware that the majority of the care will land on me. And what worries me most is that it could threaten my marriage. My husband isn't an easy man - and having his father on top of us 24/7 could make him even more moody and difficult.

Any advice?

Eliza A, Herts

Dear Eliza,

Act fast! I fear it is too late to prevent your father-in-law coming to live with you, but it is not too late to read your profoundly stupid husband the riot act.

Make it very clear to him how unhappy you are about the arrangement and the lack of consultation. Draw up a very straight-forward agreement. For instance, you will agree to the widower moving in for six months.

If, after that time, you or he can't bear it, then your husband must find an alternative solution.

Make sure you have some serious threats to back up this contract – will withholding sex be enough or must you threaten to leave him? You decide.

The irony is that it sounds like you and your children will quite like having Granddad around while your husband will be driven to distraction. If I were you, I would just sit back and enjoy watching these two men wind each other up.

Since it sounds as if your relationship with your father-in-law is a good one, I think your only hope might be to talk to him and point out all the pitfalls of this move. Make it crystal clear that you are only concerned about his wellbeing and be very careful to never make it sound like you are retracting your husband's invitation.

There's no fool like an old fool apart from the young fool who invites the old fool to move in

" There's no fool like an old fool apart from the young fool who invites the old fool to move in. "